PRAISE FOR *THE GOSPEL ACCORDING TO PAUL*

"Twenty years ago, Dr. John MacArthur sounded an alarm warning that nothing less than the loss of the gospel was at hand. In *The Gospel According to Jesus*, MacArthur prophetically called the church to the affirmation of the gospel as preached by Christ. Now, facing a new crisis in evangelical Christianity, MacArthur sets the record straight again with *The Gospel According to Paul*. This is the right book by the right author for the right time. I urge every evangelical Christian to read this book."

—R. Albert Mohler, Jr., president of the Southern Baptist Theological Seminary

"In this present hour of spiritual darkness, the gospel of Jesus Christ is under attack on every side. John MacArthur, having exegeted and exposited all thirteen epistles by the apostle Paul in his own pulpit with depth and precision, is the right man to document and defend the saving message of Jesus Christ. This theologically rich book, *The Gospel According to Paul*, is desperately needed and carefully delivered to the church today. Here is a work that needs to be read by every person, Christian or not."

—Steven J. Lawson, OnePassion Ministries, Dallas, Texas

"In the wake of alarmist voices that we have fundamentally misunderstood Paul, the church desperately needs fresh material on the apostle and his understanding of the gospel. I can think of no one better to provide this material than John MacArthur. Edifying, rich fare indeed on crucial gospel topics that should be known by every Christian. I am thrilled that yet again, Dr. MacArthur has given us a timely and much-needed book."

—Derek W. H. Thomas, senior minister, First Presbyterian Church, Columbia, South Carolina; Robert String Professor of Systematic and Pastoral Theology; RTS Atlanta Fellow of Ligonier Ministries

"We don't need a new perspective on Paul; we need a biblical perspective. Dr. John MacArthur, as always, delivers."

—Todd Friel, radio host

"Nothing is more important than our understanding of the gospel. It must be rightly understood and clearly communicated. John MacArthur has made this his life's passion. Having helped a generation steer clear of a variety of heretical assaults on the gospel, he now provides a clear and vibrant expression of the doctrine of salvation by insightfully unpacking the inspired words of the apostle Paul. *The Gospel According to Paul* is a welcomed and needed articulation of the timeless truths bound up in the gospel of grace. These insights into the life and teaching of the apostle Paul are sure to enrich your faith and strengthen your grasp on this principal doctrine of the New Testament."

—Dr. Mike Fabarez, pastor of Compass Bible Church, Aliso Viejo, California; host of Focal Point Radio

THE GOSPEL ACCORDING TO PAUL

THE GOSPEL ACCORDING TO PAUL

EMBRACING THE GOOD NEWS AT THE HEART OF PAUL'S TEACHINGS

JOHN MACARTHUR

An Imprint of Thomas Nelson

Published in Nashville, Tennessee, by Nelson Books, an imprint of Thomas Nelson. Nelson Books and Thomas Nelson are registered trademarks of HarperCollins Christian Publishing, Inc.

Edited by Phillip R. Johnson.

Thomas Nelson titles may be purchased in bulk for educational, business, fund-raising, or sales promotional use. For information, please e-mail SpecialMarkets@ThomasNelson.com.

Wherever italics are used in Scripture quotations, they have been added for emphasis.

ISBN 978–1400203512 (eBook)
ISBN 9780718092870 (IE)
ISBN 9780718096243 (TP)

Library of Congress Cataloging-in-Publication Data

Names: MacArthur, John, 1939-author.
Title: The Gospel according to Paul: embracing the good news at the heart of Paul's teachings / John MacArthur.
Description: Nashville, Tennessee: Nelson Books, 2017. | Includes bibliographical references and index.
Identifiers: LCCN 2016036969 | ISBN 9781400203499
Subjects: LCSH: Bible. Epistles of Paul—Theology. | Paul, the Apostle, Saint.
Classification: LCC BS2651 .M23 2017 | DDC 227/.06—dc23 LC record available at https://lccn.loc.gov/2016036969

Printed in the United States of America

18 19 20 21 22 LSC 10 9 8 7 6 5 4 3 2 1

I am blessed to have the unwavering support of a steadfast crew of volunteers who devote their time and labor every week to the ministry of Grace to You. They work without receiving any earthly wages (and little recognition). But the Lord whom they serve keeps a record of their faithfulness and I know He will reward them abundantly (Colossians 3:23–24). Meanwhile, these dear friends bring unflagging energy and enthusiasm to our ministry, and they are a source of perpetual encouragement and profound joy to me personally. Their obvious love for me and the ministry we share is matched by their remarkable productivity. To them—including many former members of the team who have already gone to glory—I dedicate this book.

CONTENTS

INTRODUCTION

If I preach the gospel, I have nothing to boast of, for necessity is laid upon me; yes, woe is me if I do not preach the gospel! . . . I have been entrusted with a stewardship.

—1 CORINTHIANS 9:16–17

Paul was unique among the apostles. Unlike the rest of them, he never spent time with Christ during our Lord's earthly ministry. In fact, he would not have been a good fit in the circle of the twelve disciples. They were mostly common, provincial Galileans, lacking any spiritual credentials or academic clout. The best known and most influential of the Twelve included fishermen (Peter, Andrew, James, and John); a tax collector (Matthew); and a former Zealot (Simon)—a mix of working men and outcasts.

By contrast, Paul (or more precisely Saul of Tarsus, as he was known in those days) was a well-respected, well-educated, and well-read rabbi, born into a family of Pharisees and thoroughly trained in the Pharisees' ultra-orthodox traditions. He was amazingly cosmopolitan—a Roman citizen, a seasoned traveler, a distinguished legal scholar who was born in Tarsus, educated in Jerusalem at the feet of Gamaliel (Acts 22:3), and full of zeal—a Hebrew of the Hebrews. "If anyone else thinks he has reason for confidence in the flesh," he wrote, "I have more" (Phil. 3:4 ESV). His curriculum vitae always outshone everyone else's. Saul of Tarsus would never lose in any contest of intellectual or academic achievements. In that regard, he stands in sharp contrast to all the other apostles.

Saul's mentor, Gamaliel, was by all accounts the most prestigious and influential rabbi in early first-century Jerusalem. Gamaliel was a grandson of the legendary Hillel the Elder—one of the most learned and quotable rabbis ever. Acts 5:34 tells us Gamaliel was "held in respect by all the people." He clearly had tremendous influence among the Sanhedrin (vv. 34–40). That council, consisting of seventy-one elite priests and scholars, was Judaism's highest ruling court of religious affairs. As a group, the Sanhedrin of Paul's and Jesus' time was notoriously corrupt and often motivated by sheer political expediency. But Gamaliel stands out, even in the New Testament narrative, as a learned, peaceful, cautious, and basically honorable man. The Mishnah, a record of Hebrew oral tradition written in the early third century, refers to him as "Gamaliel the Elder" and quotes him numerous times. Here's how the Mishnah commemorates him: "When Rabban Gamaliel the Elder died, the glory of the Law ceased and purity and abstinence died."[1] In all the world, there was no more highly venerated Hebrew scholar—and Saul of Tarsus was trained at his feet. So the apostle's academic credentials were impressive by any measure.

Before his famous encounter with the risen Jesus on the Damascus Road, Saul of Tarsus despised any challenge to the Pharisees' traditions. When we first meet him in Scripture, he is "a young man" (Acts 7:58) so thoroughly averse to Christ and so hostile to the faith of Jesus' followers that he presides over the stoning of the first Christian martyr, Stephen. Giving his testimony years later, Paul confessed:

> Many of the saints I shut up in prison, having received authority from the chief priests; and when they were put to death, I cast my vote against them. And I punished them often in every synagogue and compelled them to blaspheme; and being exceedingly enraged against them, I persecuted them even to foreign cities. (Acts 26:10–11)

The fact that he had a vote in such matters suggests that he was either a member of the Sanhedrin or part of a tribunal appointed by them to judge religious dissidents. Rarely were young men appointed to such positions.

But Paul was clearly a precocious scholar who stood out in his generation as a zealous activist, a ready worker, a gifted administrator, and a tough enforcer. (He was probably a skilled politician as well.)

Yet after his dramatic conversion on the road to Damascus, Paul was a completely different kind of man. He spurned every pretense of superiority. He abominated the notion that human wisdom might add anything of value to the preaching of the gospel. He emphatically opposed any suggestion that eloquence and erudition could enhance the native power of the gospel. He therefore took great pains *not* to put any stress on his own intellectual and academic achievements, lest he unwittingly undermine the simplicity of the evangelistic message. To the church at Corinth, he wrote,

> I, brethren, when I came to you, did not come with excellence of speech or of wisdom declaring to you the testimony of God. For I determined not to know anything among you except Jesus Christ and Him crucified. I was with you in weakness, in fear, and in much trembling. And my speech and my preaching were not with persuasive words of human wisdom, but in demonstration of the Spirit and of power, that your faith should not be in the wisdom of men but in the power of God. (1 Cor. 2:1–5)

In Philippians 3:5–6, in order to refute the claims of some false teachers, it became necessary for Paul to list some of his most impressive religious and academic achievements. "But," he quickly added, "what things were gain to me, these I have counted loss for Christ. Yet indeed I also count all things loss for the excellence of the knowledge of Christ Jesus my Lord, for whom I have suffered the loss of all things, and *count them as rubbish* [literally, 'dung'], that I may gain Christ" (vv. 7–8).

Still, Paul's towering intellect is obvious in the way he worked and what he wrote. He could with equal alacrity rattle off lines in Greek from ancient Mediterranean poets or quote from memory any number of passages from the Hebrew scriptures. He spoke with bold confidence to the most elite philosophers in Athens. He also stood fearlessly in royal courts where his life was on the line. No one intimidated him. On the contrary, his driving ambition was to stand in the throne room of the Roman capitol, give his testimony in Caesar's presence, and thereby preach the gospel to the world's most powerful ruler in the hub of the largest, most far-reaching empire the world had ever seen.

APPOINTED FOR THE DEFENSE OF THE GOSPEL

Of all the apostles, Paul was the one most intent on guarding the purity, accuracy, and clarity of the evangelistic message. Christ uniquely commissioned him for that purpose—"the defense and confirmation of the gospel" (Phil. 1:7 ESV). He embraced that role as a personal assignment from on high. He wrote, "I am appointed for the defense of the gospel" (v. 17). This was so deeply ingrained in Paul's consciousness that when he spoke of the gospel, he often referred to it as "*my* gospel" (Rom. 2:16; 16:25; 2 Tim. 2:8).

Of course Paul was in no way taking credit for the gospel or declaring private ownership of it. Never would it occur to him to question the divine origin of the gospel. Just as frequently, he referred to it as "the gospel of God" (Rom. 1:1; 15:16; 2 Cor. 11:7; 1 Thess. 2:2, 8–9) or "the glorious gospel of the blessed God" (1 Tim. 1:11). More often still, he called it "the gospel of Christ" (Rom. 1:16; 15:19; 1 Cor. 9:12, 18; 2 Cor. 9:13; 10:14; Gal. 1:7; Phil. 1:27; 1 Thess. 3:2) or "the gospel of the glory of Christ" (2 Cor. 4:4). Sometimes it was "the gospel of peace" (Eph. 6:15) or "the gospel of your salvation" (Eph. 1:13).

These were not disparate gospels, but Paul's assorted titles for the one true gospel. The suggestion that there is more than one gospel would have been met with fierce opposition by the apostle Paul. He sternly instructed the Galatian churches, "Even if we, or an angel from heaven, preach any other gospel to you than what we have preached to you, let him be accursed" (Gal. 1:8). And to make his point as emphatic as possible, he repeated the curse again in the very next sentence: "As we have said before, so now I say again, if anyone preaches any other gospel to you than what you have received, let him be accursed" (v. 9).

A SURVEY OF PAUL'S EPISTLES

Virtually every one of Paul's New Testament epistles defends and clarifies some crucial point of doctrine germane to the gospel message. The book of Romans is a carefully ordered discussion of the doctrines that constitute the very heart of gospel truth. It is laid out in a careful, logical, ordered outline. Starting with the doctrine of universal sin and human depravity, Paul moves systematically through the whole catalogue of gospel truth, dealing with justification, sanctification, eternal security, election, reprobation, the grafting of Gentiles into the people of God, and the ultimate restoration of Israel. Romans is Paul's most ordered and comprehensive exposition of gospel doctrines.

In 1 Corinthians he defends the gospel against various corruptions that were being smuggled in under either the guise of human wisdom or a cloak of carnal chaos. In 2 Corinthians he answers attacks that had come against the gospel from false teachers who evidently self-identified as "super-apostles" (11:5; 12:11 ESV). These heretics seemed to understand that in order to subvert the true gospel they needed to discredit the apostle Paul, so they focused their attack on him in particular. Paul was forced therefore to answer those attacks. But he was really defending the authority and purity of the gospel, not merely his own reputation (2 Cor. 11:1–4).

Paul's epistle to the Galatians is a wall-to-wall argument against false teachers (commonly known as the Judaizers) who insisted that Gentile converts must adhere to Old Testament ceremonial law in order to be saved. In particular, they taught that Gentile men could not become Christians unless they were first circumcised. Their doctrine was an implicit denial that faith is the sole instrument of justification. That error was so subtle that even Peter and Barnabas seemed prepared to go along with it (Gal. 2:11–13). So Paul wrote the Galatian epistle to demonstrate why the Judaizers' doctrine was a fatal corruption of the Christian message—a completely "different gospel" (Gal. 1:6). That is why Galatians begins with that famous double curse against "any other gospel" (vv. 8–9).

Ephesians is a simple rehearsal of gospel principles, with an emphasis on the essential truth that lies at the heart of the message: salvation is entirely God's work. It is not something any sinner can amplify or embellish with human merit. Much less can a fallen person achieve redemption for himself. "By grace you have been saved through faith, and that not of yourselves; it is the gift of God, not of works, lest anyone should boast. For we are His workmanship, created in Christ Jesus for good works, which God prepared beforehand that we should walk in them" (Eph. 2:8–10).

Although the theme of Philippians is joy, and the epistle is mostly filled with practical counsel and exhortations, chapter 3 includes a sharp warning about "dogs," "evil workers," and mutilators of the flesh (v. 2). These were clearly the very same type of gospel-corrupters Paul refuted so thoroughly in his epistle to the Galatians. He goes on in Philippians 3 to give a personal testimony that ingeniously summarizes the very heart of the gospel message.

There were some in the early church who tried to corrupt the gospel with high-flown human philosophy, ascetic forms of self-denial, manmade traditions, and other standard religious contrivances. Paul's epistle to the Colossians addresses all such deliberate attempts to make the gospel seem complex or ostentatious. Of all the apostles, the Holy Spirit chose Paul, the profound scholar, to defend the gospel's simplicity against any hint of academic elitism or philosophical gentrification.

Paul begins 1 Thessalonians with a powerful commendation for the church in Thessalonica because of the way they had eagerly embraced the gospel from the very start. He writes, "Our gospel did not come to you in word only, but also in power, and in the Holy Spirit and in much assurance" (v. 5). The closing two verses of that opening chapter (vv. 9–10) contain this crisp summary of gospel truth: "You turned to God from idols to serve the living and true God, and to wait for His Son from heaven, whom He raised from the dead, even Jesus who delivers us from the wrath to come." Paul goes on in 1 and 2 Thessalonians to instruct and encourage that church to continue their patient waiting for Christ's return while living in a way that honors the far-reaching implications of the gospel.

The epistles to Timothy and Titus are full of urgings for those two young pastors to carry on Paul's legacy by carefully safeguarding the truth of the gospel. In 1 Timothy 6:20, for example, when Paul writes, "O Timothy! Guard what was committed to your trust," it should be clear that he is talking about the gospel. He had previously described "the glorious gospel of the blessed God" as that "which was committed to my trust" (1:11). To Titus, Paul writes one of his trademark summaries of the gospel message. This is simple, profound, and amazingly comprehensive:

> The grace of God that brings salvation has appeared to all men, teaching us that, denying ungodliness and worldly lusts, we should live soberly, righteously, and godly in the present age, looking for the blessed hope and glorious appearing of our great God and Savior Jesus Christ, who gave Himself for us, that He might redeem us from every lawless deed and purify for Himself His own special people, zealous for good works. (Titus 2:11–14)

Then he adds this exhortation: "Speak these things, exhort, and rebuke with all authority. Let no one despise you" (v. 15).

Paul's shortest epistle, the letter to Philemon, is an intensely personal, practical note written to help reconcile a runaway slave (Onesimus) with his master (Philemon). But even here, Paul manages to paint a crystal-clear picture of gospel truth while exemplifying the spirit of Christ through his own actions. He includes this plea, which perfectly epitomizes what Christ did for His people: "Receive him as you would me. But if he has wronged you or owes anything, put that on my account" (Philem. vv. 17–18). Thus Paul illustrates in a very real and practical way the principles of imputation and vicarious atonement.

NOTHING BUT THE GOSPEL

Gospel truth permeates everything Paul ever wrote. The gospel was at the center of his thoughts at all times. That was deliberate. He wrote, "Necessity is laid upon me; yes, woe is me if I do not preach the gospel!" (1 Cor. 9:16).

"I determined not to know anything among you except Jesus Christ and Him crucified" (1 Cor. 2:2). "God forbid that I should boast except in the cross of our Lord Jesus Christ, by whom the world has been crucified to me, and I to the world" (Gal. 6:14). "As much as is in me, I am ready to preach the gospel" (Rom. 1:15).

All the apostles had important roles to play in the founding and spread of the early church. John was the only one who lived to old age. The rest became martyrs, starting with James, whom Herod "killed . . . with the sword" (Acts 12:2). Some of them took the gospel to the far reaches of the known world. Early church history records, for example, that Thomas went as far as the east coast of the Indian subcontinent. Legend has it that Nathaniel (also called Bartholomew) took the gospel to Armenia and was martyred there. Although Scripture does not record the final whereabouts for each of the apostles, we know for sure that they very quickly spread the gospel far and wide throughout the known world. In Acts 17:6, the angry mob who seized Paul and Silas in Thessalonica referred to them as "these who have turned the world upside down."

No one did more than Paul to spread the gospel across the face of the Roman Empire. Luke carefully chronicled Paul's three missionary journeys in the book of Acts. Beginning in Acts 13 through the end of that book, Paul becomes the central figure. And Luke's record of Paul's ministry is breathtaking. Paul's influence was profound wherever he set foot. He preached the gospel, planted churches, and left new believers in his wake no matter where he went—from the land of Israel, throughout Asia Minor, across Greece, through Malta, Sicily, and finally to Rome. And while doing all that, Paul wrote more New Testament epistles than any other author. In an age long before modern conveniences made travel and communication relatively easy, Paul's accomplishments were extraordinary.

More important, no one did more than Paul to define, delimit, and defend the gospel. The other apostles clearly gained an appreciation for Paul's devotion to the gospel. Their belief that he was appointed by Christ to be an apostle "untimely born" (1 Cor. 15:8 ESV) was rooted in the fact that he had learned from the risen Christ the very same truths that they themselves, during their Lord's earthly ministry, had been trained and commissioned to proclaim (Gal. 2:2, 6–9). Paul learned nothing about the gospel from the other disciples that he had not already heard from Christ by special revelation (Gal. 1:11–12; 2:6).

PAUL UNDER SIEGE

It's no wonder Paul felt such a significant weight of responsibility to preach and defend the gospel. Wherever he went, agents of opposition to the gospel followed close behind, attacking the message he proclaimed. The powers of darkness seemed keenly aware of Paul's strategic role, and they focused their relentless attacks against the churches where his influence was especially strong. Therefore Paul was constantly engaged in "the defense and confirmation of the gospel" (Phil. 1:7). So much controversy surrounded Paul and his ministry that almost no one wanted to be identified with him. In the final epistle he wrote before giving his life for the gospel, he described how his arraignment in Rome had gone: "At my first defense no one stood with me, but all forsook me" (2 Tim. 4:16). In the opening chapter of that letter, he told Timothy, "All those in Asia have turned away from me" (1:15). And his closing words included this doleful plea: "Be diligent to come to me quickly; for Demas has forsaken me, having loved this present world, and has departed for Thessalonica—Crescens for Galatia, Titus for Dalmatia. Only Luke is with me. Get Mark and bring him with you, for he is useful to me for ministry" (4:9–11).

Had Paul not been a man of such profound faith, he might have died feeling alone and abandoned. As it is, he most likely did not fully realize how far his shadow would extend over the church and how deeply his influence would be felt by generation after generation of believers. But he did not die discouraged. He knew the truth of the gospel would ultimately triumph. He understood that the gates of hell would never prevail against the church Christ was building. He remained confident that God's purposes would assuredly be fulfilled—and that God's plan was indeed already being fulfilled, even in Paul's own impending martyrdom. He wrote, "I am already being poured out as a drink offering, and the time of my departure is at hand. I have fought the good fight, I have finished the race, I have kept the faith. Finally, there is laid up for me the crown of righteousness, which the Lord, the righteous Judge, will give to me on that Day, and not to me only but also to all who have loved His appearing" (2 Tim. 4:6–8).

THE GOOD FIGHT

I have the utmost esteem for Paul and his passionate devotion to the gospel. Other than Christ Himself, Paul is the one example whom I most desire to follow as a model for evangelistic and pastoral ministry. Writing under the Holy Spirit's direction, Paul himself said, "I urge you, imitate me" (1 Cor. 4:16)—and then more specifically, "Imitate me, just as I also imitate Christ" (11:1). That command has been ringing in my head ever since I began to train for ministry as a college student.

Of course, anyone who sincerely aspires to imitate Paul as he imitated Christ will find it impossible to steer clear of all controversy. I have written a number of books on the gospel over the years, and virtually all of them (of necessity) have been somewhat polemical. I have pointed out and opposed various attempts to modify the gospel, abbreviate it, tone it down, alter its focus, or even replace it with a completely different message. Two of my best-known books on the gospel are in-depth critiques of the preposterous notion that repentance, self-denial, the cost of discipleship, and the lordship of Christ are all truths unnecessary for salvation and thus best left out of our gospel proclamation.[2]

Paul clearly had a more full-orbed understanding of the gospel. The Thessalonian epistles alone would stand quite well as Paul's answer to those who think the lordship of Christ has no place in the gospel message. In 2 Thessalonians 2:13–14, for example, he writes, "God from the beginning chose you for salvation through sanctification by the Spirit and belief in the truth, to which He called you by our gospel, for the obtaining of the glory of our Lord Jesus Christ." Thus he nicely summarizes—and wholeheartedly affirms—the view that certain critics often deride as "lordship salvation."

Nevertheless, from the middle of the twentieth century until the early 1990s, a severely truncated version of the gospel was more or less dominant among evangelicals. Its supporting argument was that repentance and submission to the lordship of Christ are human works, and since we know that salvation is "by grace . . . through faith . . . not of works" (Eph. 2:8–9), we should bend over backward not to make the lordship of Christ an issue when we proclaim the gospel. Several leading evangelical writers aggressively promoted that opinion, and they pinned the nickname "lordship salvation" on the view they opposed.*

My books *The Gospel According to Jesus* and *The Gospel According to the Apostles* addressed every argument I had ever heard or read against lordship salvation. *The Gospel According to Jesus* included a verse-by-verse study of practically every evangelistic encounter Jesus Himself ever had. It also examined several of His key parables and His teaching on repentance, faith, atonement, and other gospel themes. It demonstrated conclusively that the gospel message Jesus proclaimed was precisely the message that was being dismissed as "lordship salvation." The book generated a surprising amount of response, both positive and negative. Many of the critics were merely dismissive. Others tried to employ logical and theological arguments to bolster the case for a toned-down gospel. No one made any serious attempt to examine the gospel accounts themselves and make a biblical case showing that Jesus Himself preached the kind of gospel they were arguing for. How could they? Jesus' preaching speaks quite well for itself. That was my point in the first place.

The Gospel According to the Apostles likewise took key passages from the New Testament (including some from the Pauline epistles) and sought

* The term seems to have been popularized, if not coined, by A. Ray Stanford in his *Handbook of Personal Evangelism* (Miami: Florida Bible College, 1975), chapter 7. The idea that it corrupts the gospel to preach about repentance from sin or to call for surrender to the lordship of Christ was aggressively promoted by Charles Ryrie in *Balancing the Christian Life* (Chicago: Moody, 1969) and Zane Hodges in *The Gospel Under Seige* (Dallas: Redencion Viva, 1981)—as well as several other popular books and tracts of that era.

to make an exegetical case proving that in apostolic gospel preaching, the lordship of Christ was always kept front and center. In fact, the gospel message preached by Paul and the other apostles quite simply contradicted all the twentieth-century rules against lordship salvation. *The Gospel According to the Apostles* was organized systematically, each chapter dealing with some major point of *soteriology*, or the doctrine of salvation. Individual chapters dealt with topics such as faith, grace, repentance, justification, sanctification, assurance, and eternal security.

This time the response from critics was more muted. In fact, only a handful of the most tenacious critics of lordship salvation responded negatively to *The Gospel According to the Apostles*—and those few critiques seemed almost halfhearted. Within a decade and a half, only a fairly small faction within evangelicalism were still campaigning to strip any mention of Christ's lordship from the gospel message. The tide had obviously turned. No-lordship doctrine simply could not withstand scrutiny under the clear light of a careful, thorough, biblical examination of what the gospel is and how it should be preached.

Sadly, though, even before the lordship controversy faded, a different kind of threat arose within the evangelical movement in the form of pragmatism. By the early 1990s several seeker-sensitive megachurches were aggressively advocating a philosophy of ministry that was almost devoid of any concern about sound doctrine and very thin on biblical content. The result was a shift away from anything that could legitimately be called preaching. The Bible was purposely relegated to a footnote or an afterthought. Speakers focused instead on themes like success in life and business, relationship advice, and whatever topics were trending in popular culture. The gospel was often omitted altogether from these motivational-style talks. Mere attendance figures were generally deemed the main measure of success and influence. I wrote about that issue as well in a book titled *Ashamed of the Gospel*.[3]

When the seeker-sensitive movement became common and familiar enough, the triteness and frivolity it nurtured became distasteful to many young people who had grown up with it. The backlash gave rise to the

Emergent movement, a mostly liberal and highly postmodernized repudiation of virtually everything historically deemed distinctive to evangelical Christianity. Leading voices in that movement aggressively promoted unorthodox teachings, attacked the doctrine of the atonement, denigrated the authority of Scripture, and endeavored to redesign and redefine the gospel. Perhaps most ominously, Emergents seemed to despise the concept of substitutionary atonement and all other truths related to God's wrath against sin. This (as we'll see in our study of Paul's teaching on the gospel) was like tearing the very heart out of the gospel message.

I've dealt with those and various other assaults on the gospel in several other books in the intervening years, including *Hard to Believe*, *Reckless Faith*, *The Love of God*, *The Freedom and Power of Forgiveness*, *Charismatic Chaos*, and *Strange Fire*. I wrote two books, *The Truth War* and *The Jesus You Can't Ignore*, to answer elements of Emergent confusion.

Reflecting on all those controversies, what is most surprising is that in every case, the threat I was writing about had originated within the evangelical movement. When I was in seminary, I had prepared my mind and heart to answer assaults from the world against the authority of Scripture and the truth of the gospel. I did not anticipate that so much of my time and energy would be spent trying to defend the gospel against attacks from inside the visible church—including assaults on gospel truth from respected leaders in the evangelical movement.

I've been invigorated and encouraged, and not the least bit disheartened, to see what inevitably happens when the people of God "contend earnestly for the faith" (Jude v. 3). The Lord always vindicates His truth. I suppose there has never been a single moment in the history of the church when the gospel has been free from assaults and controversies. And it is uncanny how old heresies get resurrected and the same threats to the gospel resurface again and again, threatening to lead astray each new generation. Satan is a relentless foe.

But "we are not ignorant of his devices" (2 Cor. 2:11). There are indeed times when "we are hard-pressed on every side, yet not crushed; we are perplexed, but not in despair; persecuted, but not forsaken; struck down, but not destroyed" (4:8–9). We know that all the combined forces of hell could never defeat God. Though they may rage against the truth and perhaps steer multitudes into skepticism and unbelief, they will never totally squelch the truth of God's Word. Therefore, to take a stand with the truth is to be triumphant—even when it seems the whole world is against us. Christ proved that fact conclusively when He rose from the dead. Satan, despite his persistence, is an already defeated foe.

The enduring power of truth is evident in the ebb and flow of contemporary evangelical trends. At the beginning of the new millennium, evangelical pundits were solemnly assuring young evangelicals that the Emergent movement's freewheeling abandonment of historic evangelical principles would revolutionize and revitalize our churches. But the Emergent community began to disintegrate before 2005, and thankfully, by the end of the decade the movement was all but defunct.

TRUTH TRIUMPHANT

Meanwhile, the truth is by no means being vanquished. Some of the most encouraging growth in the church today is happening among those who take the Word of God seriously. They understand the importance of guarding the gospel, and they love sound doctrine. Over the past decade, for example, we have witnessed the birth and expansion of Together for the Gospel, a broad-based conservative coalition of young believers who are committed to proclaiming a much more robust view of the gospel than any of the large evangelical movements that flourished from 1960 to 1990.[4] There is currently a resurgence of Reformation values among conservative evangelical churches. That has given rise to a corresponding emphasis on biblical preaching, a newfound interest in church history, and many young people who have repudiated the rank superficiality that their parents tolerated in the name of seeker-sensitivity.

Of course, none of the old aberrations are completely gone. The Emergent movement may be dead as a movement, but a lot of their wrong ideas and false doctrines still linger. Some influential voices in the evangelical movement today still teach that obedience to Christ is an optional and unnecessary adjunct to "accepting Him" as Savior. Some still would deny that the gospel calls sinners to repentance or instructs them to follow Christ. There are even a few new flavors of "hyper-grace" and antinomianism. (*Antinomianism* is the belief that Christians are not bound by any moral law, or the notion that behavior and belief are unrelated.) Those and similar opinions still pose a serious potential threat within the broad evangelical movement. But the biblical arguments given in *The Gospel According to Jesus* and *The Gospel According to the Apostles* still stand as decisive answers to all such errors.

Therefore, in this volume, my main purpose is not polemical. I'm not going to be quoting many opinions in order to refute them or otherwise loading these pages with footnotes and documentation. My aim is simply to examine some vital biblical texts as straightforwardly as possible, taking a careful, thorough, honest look at the gospel as Paul proclaimed it—not in a dry or merely academic analysis, but in a way that will ignite our hearts with the truth of Jesus Christ crucified, buried, risen, and ascended. No truth in all the universe is more uplifting than the good news that we have a living Savior who removes the great burden of guilt and cancels the power of sin for those who truly believe in Him.

I've chosen a handful of passages from Paul's epistles that are narrowly focused on the gospel, and we will devote a chapter or two to each one. There are, of course, recurring themes throughout—the doctrines of universal human depravity, divine grace, the call to faith and repentance, the nature of atonement, and so on. I have tried to avoid unnecessary repetition, but in order to do full justice to the various texts, it is essential to revisit some of Paul's keynote ideas more than once. Paul himself was relentlessly and unapologetically repetitive. He told the Philippians, "For me to write the same things to you is not tedious, but for you it is safe" (Phil. 3:1). Or to paraphrase: *It's no trouble to restate what I have already said; in fact, it's good for you to hear it again.* That is true especially when the topics being reviewed and rehashed are vital points of gospel truth.

My design in this book is to explain the most important gospel texts from Paul's epistles as clearly and as thoroughly as possible. I hope to underscore (as Paul did) the eternal importance of gospel doctrine and the absolute necessity of getting it right. My aim is to write in a way that any believer—whether a seasoned theologian or a new Christian—will benefit from the study. A brief glossary is included at the book's end to explain terms that might not be familiar to lay readers. These are mostly technical terms that will already be familiar to anyone who has studied theology, but I have tried to give the simplest possible definitions for the benefit of lay readers. Each term is also defined the first time it appears in the body of the text, but if you lose track of a word's meaning or have a hard time remembering the definitions of unfamiliar theological words, the glossary is there to help.

I have also included four appendixes. The first is the most important. It deals with the nature of Christ's atoning work. This is an issue that comes up repeatedly in Paul's writings—and it is also a doctrine currently under assault on a number of fronts. The appendix deals with controversies about the atonement more thoroughly and in a more polemical fashion than you will find in the main body of the book. But because a right view of the atonement is essential to understanding the gospel according to Paul, I wanted to be sure this book included a solid defense of penal substitution and easy-to-grasp explanations of the major opposing theories about the atonement.

Appendix 2 is a transcript of one of my sermons, edited for reading. It is a gospel message with a distinctively Pauline motif. (I have preached variations on this theme in venues all over the world for the past forty years.) It is essentially an explanation of the biblical term *propitiation*—a word and a concept that is vital to Paul's teaching on why Christ died. I include it here because several people have pressed me for an example of how I try to preach the gospel without backing away from hard truths or dumbing down the message.

Appendix 3 is a brief article explaining the truth to which Pauline soteriology ultimately points: the ultimate purpose for everything that exists and everything that happens is for the glory of God.

The final appendix is drawn from the sermons of Charles Spurgeon, especially highlighting Spurgeon's remarks about why Paul repeatedly referred to the gospel as "my gospel." I have included it because his words so perfectly summarize the theme of this book.

I trust you will find this study both profitable and profoundly fascinating. Paul was nothing if not passionate about the gospel. I find his passion contagious. I hope you will too.

One

THINGS OF FIRST IMPORTANCE

It was necessary for the Christ to suffer and to rise from the dead the third day, and that repentance and remission of sins should be preached in His name to all nations, beginning at Jerusalem.

—Luke 24:46–47

The apostle Paul had an extraordinary gift for bringing the gospel message to light in just a few clear, well-chosen words. His epistles are filled with brilliant, one-verse summaries of the gospel. Each of these key texts is different from the others. Each has a distinctive emphasis that highlights some essential aspect of the good news. Any one of them is capable of standing alone as a powerful declaration of gospel truth. Or put them all together, and you have the framework for a full-orbed understanding of the biblical doctrine of salvation.

That's the approach I will be taking in this book. Using some of the principal evangelistic texts from Paul's New Testament epistles, we will survey the gospel as Paul proclaimed it. We'll consider several important questions, including: *What is the gospel? What are the essential elements of the message? How can we be certain we have it right? How should Christians be proclaiming the good news to the world?*

NO OTHER GOSPEL

Paul himself might have begun a study of this subject by stating categorically that *there is only one true gospel.* Anyone who suggests that Paul introduced an altered or embellished version of the apostolic message would have to contradict every point Paul ever made about the singularity of the true gospel. Although he expounded the gospel far more thoroughly and painstakingly than any other New Testament writer, nothing Paul ever preached or wrote was in any way a departure from what Christ or His apostles had been teaching from the start. Paul's gospel was exactly the same message Christ proclaimed and commissioned the Twelve to take into all the world. There is only one gospel, and it is the same for Jews and Gentiles alike.

It was the false teachers, not Paul, who claimed that God had appointed them to polish or rewrite the gospel. Paul flatly repudiated the notion that the message Christ sent His disciples to preach was subject to revision (2 Cor. 11). Far from portraying himself as some kind of super-apostle sent to set the others straight, Paul wrote, "I am the least of the apostles, who am not worthy to be called an apostle, because I persecuted the church of God" (1 Cor. 15:9).

Indeed, one major factor that set Paul apart from the others was the abundance of divine grace that had transformed him from what he once was (a fierce persecutor of the church) to the man we know from Scripture (an apostle of Christ to the Gentiles). The vast scope of the mercy shown to Paul never ceased to amaze him. His response, therefore, was to labor all the more diligently for the spread of the gospel and the honor of Christ in order to make the most of his calling. He wrote, "By the grace of God I am what I am, and His grace toward me was not in vain; but I labored more abundantly than they all, yet not I, but the grace of God which was with me. Therefore, whether it was *I* [Paul] or *they* [the rest of the apostles], *so we preach* and so you believed" (1 Cor. 15:10–11). Notice he expressly stated that all the apostles preached the same gospel.

There is nevertheless a small but vocal faction in the visible church today who deny that Paul's gospel was the same message Peter proclaimed at Pentecost. Calling themselves "Pauline dispensationalists," they teach that there are at least three distinct gospel messages given in the New Testament, each narrowly applicable to a different dispensation or a specific ethnic group. They say Jesus' "gospel of the kingdom" (Matt. 9:35; 24:14) was a call to discipleship, together with the announcement and offer of an earthly kingdom; when it was rejected by the majority of those who heard it, the offer was withdrawn and the "gospel of the kingdom" was set aside.

Next, they say, Peter's "gospel for the circumcised" (Gal. 2:7) pertained only to the Jewish nation. It was a call to repentance (Acts 2:38; 3:19) and a summons to surrender to the lordship of Christ (2:36). This was the message preached by the apostles as long as the church was predominantly Jewish.

But with the introduction of Gentiles into the church in Acts 10, they claim Paul introduced a brand-new "gospel for the uncircumcised" (Gal. 2:7, 9). They say this Pauline message superseded those two earlier gospels. They teach it is a distinctive message that cannot be harmonized and must not be confused with the gospel according to Jesus or the gospel according to Peter. Furthermore, they insist, Paul's gospel is the only gospel that has any immediate relevance for the present dispensation. In effect, major portions of the New Testament—including all the major sermons and discourses of Jesus—are relegated to a place of diminished significance.

Most who hold these views also insist that it is wrong to speak of the lordship of Christ in connection with the gospel. Our Lord's own teaching on the cost of discipleship and Peter's call to repentance at Pentecost are both set aside as irrelevant to the present dispensation. Every theme that hints of Christ's authority is deemed an artificial addition to the gospel message—because any reminder that Christ deserves our obedience supposedly corrupts grace with the implication of works.

Such a system defies Jesus' Great Commission: "Make disciples of all the nations . . . teaching them to observe *all things that I have commanded you*" (Matt. 28:19–20).

Paul himself would have been a fierce opponent of "Pauline dispensationalism." He vigorously denounced the notion of multiple gospels. He took pains to defend his apostolic status by documenting his perfect agreement with the rest of the apostles. He said he learned the gospel directly from Christ Himself, just as the others had. He stressed the truth that authentic Christianity has only "one Lord, one faith, one baptism" (Eph. 4:5).

Because Paul was not a member of the original core apostolic company, and since his ministry rarely intersected directly with theirs, his complete agreement with them may not have been immediately obvious to all. Furthermore, on one occasion, Paul had publicly disagreed with Peter (Gal. 2:11–21). That disagreement was not about any point of doctrine; it had to do with Peter's potentially divisive behavior toward some Gentile brethren when Peter was in the presence of some legalistic false teachers.

But a careful look at the biblical record reveals that Paul never set himself or his message against the preaching of the other apostles. Even the expression "my gospel" (Rom. 2:16; 16:25; 2 Tim. 2:8) wasn't a claim of exclusive ownership or ascendancy over the others. The expression simply indicates Paul's deeply personal devotion to the message Christ had graciously commissioned him to proclaim. The apostles were all in full agreement when it came to the content of the gospel, and Paul was prepared to prove it. He does so in Galatians 1–2.

AN ABBREVIATED BIOGRAPHY OF PAUL

In the process of documenting the proof of his agreement with the others, Paul, who normally avoided talking about himself or his "visions and revelations of the Lord" (2 Cor. 12:1), gives us a rare bit of personal biography. He was the last of the apostles to be converted and formally commissioned—"one born out of due time" (1 Cor. 15:8). Humanly speaking, he was probably the least likely person in the universe to find agreement and acceptance from the other apostles. Well known and feared throughout the early church as "Saul of Tarsus," he comes onto the pages of Scripture as the most feared and ruthless persecutor of Christians, passionately "breathing threats and murder against the disciples of the Lord"

(Acts 9:1). Then Christ stopped him in his tracks one day on the road to Damascus, instantly transforming his heart and dramatically changing the whole course of his life (vv. 3–19). In Philippians 3, Paul himself describes how his conversion radically reshaped his whole worldview and religion. (We'll look at that passage in this book's epilogue.)

Given the reputation Paul had earned as a brutal inquisitor, it would obviously have been awkward for him to go immediately to Jerusalem to try to meet with the leading apostles. So instead, shortly after his conversion, he went to the desert to spend some time in solitude. In Galatians 1:17 he says, "I went to Arabia." That is undoubtedly a reference to the wilderness of Nabatean Arabia, a mostly desolate region covering the Sinai Peninsula (an area known today as the Negev). He returned from there to Damascus and entered public ministry before he ever consulted with (or even personally met) any of the original Twelve.

In the first decade and a half of Paul's ministry, it seems the only one of the Twelve he met with was Peter. That occurred when Paul finally went back to Jerusalem, this time as a Christian. By then, Paul had been a believer at least three years. He stayed with Peter for just over two weeks (Gal. 1:18). He was perhaps still trying to remain incognito during that visit, because the only other major church leader Paul met was "James, the Lord's brother" (v. 19).

The point Paul was so keen to make when he recorded those details was that he did not learn what he knew of the gospel from the other apostles; he got it directly from Christ by special revelation. "I make known to you, brethren, that the gospel which was preached by me is not according to man. For I neither received it from man, nor was I taught it, but it came through the revelation of Jesus Christ" (Gal. 1:11–12).

Fourteen years after that first meeting with Peter, Paul returned to Jerusalem again (Gal. 2:1). This was probably the same visit described in Acts 15. False teachers had spread abroad from Jerusalem, "certain men [who] came down from Judea and taught the brethren, 'Unless you are circumcised according to the custom of Moses, you cannot be saved'" (Acts 15:1). Because their teaching confused and divided the mostly Gentile churches Paul had planted, it became urgently necessary for the apostles to convene in order to answer the false teachers—and to announce clearly and publicly the apostles' full agreement regarding the one true gospel. That's what the first church council, described in Acts 15, was all about.

During this visit, one of the first items on Paul's agenda was to meet privately with the leading apostles in order to verify among themselves that they were all on the same page about the content of the gospel. This was evidently Paul's first face-to-face meeting with the apostle John (Gal. 2:9).

Far from needing to settle any disagreement about the gospel or adjust their preaching to some dispensational shift, the apostles all found themselves in complete agreement. Paul describes the scene in a way that makes clear his utter indifference to personal prestige, ecclesiastical titles, or other badges of human stature. Equally significant is the fact that he makes no claim of superiority for himself. He doesn't flash his academic credentials. He doesn't cite the extraordinary "visions and revelations of the Lord" that had given him such a thorough understanding of the gospel message (2 Cor. 12:1). There is no attempt to intimidate the others with either sophistication or sanctimony. He writes:

> From those who seemed to be something—whatever they were, it makes no difference to me; God shows personal favoritism to no man—for those who seemed to be something added nothing to me. But on the contrary, when they saw that the gospel for the uncircumcised had been committed to me, as the gospel for the circumcised was to Peter (for He who worked effectively in Peter for the apostleship to the circumcised also worked effectively in me toward the Gentiles), and when James, Cephas, and John, who seemed to be pillars, perceived the grace that had been given to me, they gave me and Barnabas the right hand of fellowship, that we should go to the Gentiles and they to the circumcised. They desired only that we should remember the poor, the very thing which I also was eager to do. (Gal. 2:6–10)

When Paul says the church leaders in Jerusalem "added nothing to me," he means that they gave him no new insights regarding gospel truth.

They did not attempt in any way to revise what he was preaching or nuance it differently. They saw at once that Paul had been taught by the same Master who had trained them.

This would not have been the case if Paul had been preaching a different message. As Paul makes clear in that first chapter of Galatians, he himself would not have tolerated it for a moment if he had discovered the other apostles (or an angel from heaven, for that matter) were preaching a gospel that differed from the truth he had learned from Christ. Likewise, Peter, James, and John would not have received Paul so readily if they thought he was preaching anything other than what they had learned from Christ.

Thus when Paul speaks of "the gospel for the uncircumcised" and "the gospel for the circumcised" in verse 7 of the above-quoted passage, it is quite clear from the context that he is speaking of two different *audiences*, not two distinct *gospels*. In other words, what differentiated Paul's ministry from Peter's was only the ethnicity of the people on whom they focused their respective ministries—not the content of what they preached.

Paul then goes on to recount the reason he and Peter had their famous disagreement. It was not a disagreement about the substance of the gospel message. The problem, rather, was that Peter was "not straightforward about the truth of the gospel" (Gal. 2:14). He was being hypocritical, unintentionally denying by his conduct what he had proclaimed with his own voice.

Paul's point in recording this incident is not to embarrass or belittle Peter, but to defend the integrity of the gospel. The soundness of the gospel is infinitely more important than the dignity and prestige of even the most eminent apostles—including Paul himself. The importance of getting the gospel right supersedes even the honor of the highest angel. This is consistently Paul's position: "Even if we, or an angel from heaven, preach any other gospel to you than what we have preached to you, let him be accursed" (Gal. 1:8).

Peter implicitly conceded that he deserved Paul's admonition. In his second epistle, he referred to Paul as "our beloved brother." He acknowledged "the wisdom given to [Paul]." Indeed, he cited Paul's writings as

"Scriptures." And he admonished his readers to pay careful heed to Paul's writings and take care how they handle the "things hard to understand" in Paul's writings, lest they twist God's Word to their own destruction (2 Peter 3:15–16).

MATTERS OF FIRST IMPORTANCE

Paul himself might have said the surest way to twist Scripture to one's own destruction is by altering the gospel—or even by passively tolerating those who preach a modified gospel. He strictly cautioned readers to beware "if [someone] preaches another Jesus whom we have not preached, or if you receive a different spirit which you have not received, or a different gospel which you have not accepted" (2 Cor. 11:4). He said alternative gospels are rooted in the same brand of deception the serpent used to deceive Eve (v. 3).

So this theme reverberates throughout Paul's inspired epistles: *there is only one gospel.*

That fact will become even clearer as we examine the principal gospel texts in Paul's epistles. The truths he contends for are all rooted in the teaching of Christ, and they are all echoed in the preaching of the early church. Every page of the New Testament is in perfect agreement. From Jesus' Sermon on the Mount to the book of Revelation, the message is consistent. It acknowledges the hopelessness of human depravity, but it points to Christ as the only remedy for that dilemma. Starting with the historical facts of His death and resurrection, it proclaims salvation by divine grace (rather than by the sinner's own works); the full and free forgiveness of sins; the provision of justification by faith; the principle of imputed righteousness; and the eternally secure standing of the believer before God. Those truths all constitute the very heart of the gospel. They are matters "of first importance" (1 Cor. 15:3 NASB), and it was Paul's unique role to highlight and explain all those facets of gospel truth with the utmost clarity and precision.

"THE GOSPEL WHICH I PREACHED TO YOU"

For anyone familiar with Paul's writings, one of the first texts that will come to mind as a succinct summary of the gospel is 1 Corinthians 15:1–5. Paul himself identifies this passage as a digest of essential gospel truths:

> Moreover, brethren, I declare to you the gospel which I preached to you, which also you received and in which you stand, by which also you are saved, if you hold fast that word which I preached to you—unless you believed in vain. For I delivered to you first of all that which I also received: that Christ died for our sins according to the Scriptures, and that He was buried, and that He rose again the third day according to the Scriptures, and that He was seen.

Verse 3 would be better translated, "I conveyed to you the principal matters." That's the true sense of what he is telling them. Both the English Standard Version and the New American Standard Bible say, "I delivered to you as of first importance what I also received." What Paul clearly has in mind here are the elements of gospel truth that come first in order of importance. He goes on to give an abbreviated outline of historical facts in chronological order. He names four events that constitute the key climactic events of the whole gospel narrative: the crucifixion, burial, resurrection, and subsequent appearances of the risen Christ.

This is significant for several reasons. First, it is a reminder that the gospel is grounded in actual history. The Christian faith is not a theory or a speculation. It is not mystical, as if based on someone's dream or imagination. It is not an abstract philosophy or an idealistic worldview. Much less is it merely a list of sterile doctrines that have been relegated to a formal statement of faith. The gospel of Jesus Christ is divinely revealed truth established in the meticulous historical fulfillment of several Old Testament prophecies, documented by mountains of irrefutable evidence, confirmed by a series of public events that no mere mortal could possibly have engineered, and corroborated by an abundance of eyewitness testimony.

On the other hand, by listing facts of history as matters of primary importance, Paul is by no means dismissing or even minimizing the doctrinal content of the gospel message. Nor is he suggesting that the Christian faith rests on bare historical facts and eyewitness testimony alone. Twice in this short passage Paul reminds us that these events happened "according to the Scriptures." That, of course, is the true ground and foundation of saving faith. "Faith comes by hearing, and hearing by the word of God" (Rom. 10:17). It's not "faith" merely to believe that these events occurred. True saving faith will also embrace the biblical *meaning* of sin, atonement, divine grace, and other elements of gospel truth—the doctrines that explain why the historical facts are so significant.

Indeed, loaded into the simple statement "Christ died for our sins according to the Scriptures" is everything Scripture teaches about the penalty of sin, the principle of substitutionary atonement, and the sinless perfection that qualified Christ to be "the Lamb of God who takes away the sin of the world" (John 1:29). In other words, what Paul says here in very few words has significant ramifications for *hamartiology* (the doctrine of sin), *soteriology* (the doctrine of salvation), and *Christology* (the doctrines of the person and work of Christ). So his short list of historical facts in 1 Corinthians 15:3–8 is laden with far-reaching doctrinal implications.

THE PROBLEM IN CORINTH

Context is crucial. Paul wrote this chapter to deal with a doctrinal error, not a dispute about the facts of history. The Corinthians already believed in Christ's death and resurrection. What they questioned was the future bodily resurrection of believers who die. So Paul was writing to defend that point of doctrine. He did so by outlining the gospel message with a list of historical events that no one in the Corinthian assembly of believers ever would have questioned. "So we preach and *so you believed*," he said in 1 Corinthians 15:11.

His review of commonly believed gospel facts in verses 1–5 was therefore merely a prelude to the central point of the chapter. Paul states his main point plainly in verses 16–17: "If the dead do not rise, then Christ is not risen. And if Christ is not risen, your faith is futile; you are still in your sins!" Conversely, if Christ was raised from the dead, then there's no reason to be skeptical about the future bodily resurrection of the saints. "If Christ is preached that He has been raised from the dead, how do some among you say that there is no resurrection of the dead?" (v. 12). The whole of chapter 15 is an exposition of that simple argument.

What concerns us here, however, is the brief gospel outline Paul gives in verses 3–5. He cites four events from history to construct a firm skeletal framework for the weighty doctrinal substance and spiritual significance of the gospel message. As I've mentioned, by naming these four historical facts rather than stressing the doctrine, Paul is not suggesting that the gospel's doctrinal content is irrelevant or inconsequential. Paul would never indulge in that kind of reductionism. (The whole book of Galatians proves how strongly he believed in doctrinal soundness, especially in the matter of gospel preaching.) Here he is merely summarizing and outlining—not truncating—the message. By repeatedly using the phrase "according to the Scriptures," he makes it clear that a right understanding of and true belief in these four events necessarily entails a proper view of the gospel's doctrinal implications.

Furthermore, none of this would have been new to the Corinthians. Paul founded that church and pastored it for more than eighteen months before his ministry took him elsewhere (Acts 18:11, 18). The Corinthians had received sufficient teaching from Paul, so they already knew quite well the crucial doctrinal implications of the statement "Christ died for our sins according to the Scriptures." That, of course, is the first point of the outline Paul constructs.

ATONEMENT

Paul wants to highlight not merely the historical fact that Christ died. He is much more specific: "Christ died *for our sins*." It is the language of atonement. Paul's statement echoes precisely what the apostle John wrote in 1 John 2:2: "[Jesus] Himself is the propitiation for our sins." That word *propitiation* speaks of an appeasement. Specifically, it signifies the satisfaction of divine justice. Or to say the same thing differently, a "propitiation" is a sacrifice or offering that placates the wrath of God against sinners.

Many people find such a concept repellent. It certainly challenges the popular notion of a grandfatherly god who is always benign and lenient toward sin. It's a doctrine that tends to rankle anyone who has imbibed too much modernist or liberal religion (which would include, perhaps, a wide majority of professing Christians in the world today). In recent years a handful of well-known writers and teachers on the evangelical fringe have emphatically rejected the biblical claim that the death of God's own Son on the cross was a propitiation—labeling the idea "cosmic child abuse." Liberal theology simply cannot tolerate the biblical teaching that God "sent His Son to be the propitiation for our sins" (1 John 4:10). Indeed, this is practically the whole crux of liberal religion: it stresses the love of God to the exclusion of His righteousness and His wrath against sin. Liberals therefore typically take the position that Christ's death on the cross was nothing more than a noble act of exemplary martyrdom.

But Paul's point in 1 Corinthians 15:3 is not that Christ died *because of* our sins. Paul isn't suggesting that Christ's death had some vague, mystical, ethereal connection to human fallenness—as if He died merely because wicked people in a mindless frenzy made Him a martyr. The point is that Jesus voluntarily "died for our sins *in accordance with the Scriptures*" (ESV). He is the fulfillment of everything the Old Testament sacrificial system illustrated. He is the answer to the conundrum of how a truly righteous God can forgive the unrighteousness of ungodly sinners. A right understanding of Christ's death—its true significance and full meaning—can be clearly seen only in that light.

"The wages of sin is death," and "without shedding of blood there is no remission" (Rom. 6:23; Heb. 9:22). This principle was clearly established and vividly illustrated in the daily spectacle of Old Testament sacrifices. In Leviticus 17:11 the Lord told the Israelites, "The life of the flesh is in the blood, and I have given it to you upon the altar to make atonement for your souls; for it is the blood that makes atonement for the soul."

So animal sacrifices graphically illustrated several vital truths: the exceeding sinfulness of sin, the inflexibility of judgment under the law, the incomprehensibly high cost of atonement, and both the justice and the mercy of God.

And the blood was no incidental feature. The sacrifices resulted in an inundation of blood, an intentionally shocking, appalling reminder of the wages of sin. It was impossible to miss the point. Hebrews 9:18–22 points out that virtually everything in the temple was sprinkled with blood—including the people who came to offer sacrifices. The blood thus served as a necessary emblem of sanctification, showing the high cost of atonement and cleansing for anything and anyone defiled by sin.

But it was clear that animal blood had no real or lasting atoning value. "It is not possible that the blood of bulls and goats could take away sins" (Heb. 10:4). Blood sacrifices were offered daily (Ex. 29:38–42). Countless Passover lambs were also slaughtered annually each spring. Bulls and goats were sacrificed on Yom Kippur, the Day of Atonement, each fall. Work in the temple was never finished. Levites, musicians, and guards were on duty "day and night" (1 Chron. 9:33). And priests in the Old Testament literally never got to sit down on the job. There were no chairs among the furnishings of the temple. "Every priest *stands* ministering daily and offering repeatedly the same sacrifices, which can never take away sins" (Heb. 10:11).

To anyone who considered the priesthood and sacrificial system carefully, it was clear that all the sacrifices and ceremony did not provide a full and complete atonement for sin. They were symbolic. How, after all, could mere animal blood placate the divine justice that demands the death of a sinner? There was a reason animals needed to be slaughtered repeatedly, daily—endlessly. It underscored the truth that the blood of a common animal is no real substitute for a guilty human life.

So Old Testament saints were left with a perplexing mystery: If animal sacrifices provided no true and final atonement, what else could possibly make God propitious to sinners? After all, God Himself said, "I will not justify the wicked," and anyone who does justify the wicked is an abomination to Him (Ex. 23:7; Prov. 17:15). So how could God ever justify the ungodly without compromising His own righteousness?

The answer is that Christ willingly died in place of those whom He saves. He is their Substitute—and unlike all those animal sacrifices, He is the perfect propitiation. Finally, here was a sufficient sacrifice. In Peter's words, "Christ . . . suffered once for sins, the just for the unjust, that He might bring us to God" (1 Peter 3:18). Paul agreed: "[God] made Him who knew no sin to be sin for us, that we might become the righteousness of God in Him" (2 Cor. 5:21).

We'll examine that text from 2 Corinthians 5 thoroughly in an upcoming chapter, but the point here (affirmed by Peter as well as Paul) is that Christ took the place of sinners on the cross. He died as their proxy. He absorbed the wrath of God against sin in their stead. He took the punishment we all deserve. All of that is essential to Paul's meaning when he says, "Christ died for our sins according to the Scriptures." This is the principle of *penal substitution*, and it is vital to a right understanding of the gospel. Christ bore the penalty of our sins. That's how "Christ died for our sins."

BURIAL

You may be surprised to see the burial of Christ in such a short list of gospel essentials. The ancient Apostles' Creed includes it as well. That familiar creed, one of the earliest, most enduring, and most important extrabiblical statements of faith, includes a formal confession that Christ "was crucified, died, and was buried."

But the burial of Christ is a point you won't necessarily find in more recent evangelical attempts to summarize the essential truths of the gospel. That's mainly because this is not a point that even the most determined skeptics would typically challenge directly. Even the very earliest enemies of Christianity would not have tried to argue that the body of Christ was never placed in the grave. It's a simple fact of history affirmed by all who were involved in the interment. That includes Jewish leaders, Roman officials, soldiers, disciples of Christ, and the two Marys who helped prepare the body for burial.

So why does Paul list it here? Very simply, it furnishes undeniable proof that Christ was truly dead. The cross was no pretense. Jesus was not still alive and quietly spirited off to some secret location and nursed back to health. The story of Christ's crucifixion is not a cunningly devised fable or a mere story with an instructive moral. Christ really died, and all who witnessed His death (friends and foes alike) affirmed that fact. No eyewitness to the crucifixion ever suggested that He survived the ordeal.

The soldiers who nailed Jesus to the cross were under the direct command of Pontius Pilate. They had legal possession of Christ's body as long as He hung on the cross. These were professional executioners. Overseeing crucifixions was part of their official business. They had every skill necessary to determine with ruthless accuracy whether their victims were absolutely dead. They would not have allowed the body to be removed from the cross or handed over for burial if there had been any question whatsoever about whether they had finished the job they were assigned to do.

Mark 15:34–37 says it was about "the ninth hour" (three o'clock in the afternoon) when Jesus "cried out with a loud voice, and breathed His last." Matthew 27:50 says in that very moment, "Jesus . . . yielded up His spirit." John 19:30 says, "He said, 'It is finished!' And bowing His head, He gave up His spirit."

Sometime later in the afternoon, Pilate ordered that the day's executions be hastened so "that the bodies should not remain on the cross on the Sabbath" (John 19:31). (The method used to speed up crucifixion was gruesome: they broke the victim's legs, making it impossible for the condemned criminal to push his own body up, relieving compression on the diaphragm in order to breathe. Breaking the legs therefore caused the victim to die quickly by suffocation.) But when the soldiers approached the body of Jesus, they "saw that He was already dead" (v. 33), which suggests that by then He had been dead long enough for the signs of death to be visible. This would include hypostasis (the settling of blood, giving portions of the skin the appearance of massive bruising, and making the rest of the skin a lifeless, pale color), rigor mortis (which begins within three hours after death), and opacity and discoloration in the eyes.

Matthew 27:57 says evening had already come when Joseph of Arimathea approached Pilate to ask for the body. By the time Jesus was removed from the cross, His corpse would already have been cold and very stiff. There was no question in anyone's mind whether He was dead.

Matthew gives the most complete description of Jesus' burial:

> When Joseph had taken the body, he wrapped it in a clean linen cloth, and laid it in his new tomb which he had hewn out of the rock; and he rolled a large stone against the door of the tomb, and departed. And Mary Magdalene was there, and the other Mary, sitting opposite the tomb.
>
> On the next day, which followed the Day of Preparation, the chief priests and Pharisees gathered together to Pilate, saying, "Sir, we remember, while He was still alive, how that deceiver said, 'After three days I will rise.' Therefore command that the tomb be made secure until the third day, lest His disciples come by night and steal Him away, and say to the people, 'He has risen from the dead.' So the last deception will be worse than the first."
>
> Pilate said to them, "You have a guard; go your way, make it as secure as you know how." So they went and made the tomb secure, sealing the stone and setting the guard. (Matt. 27:59–66)

The "seal" would have been an official marker with Pilate's own emblem, similar to the wax seal used to close and identify a formal legal document. Such a seal was not to be broken except by the authority of the ruler or administrative body who ordered the seal. The "guard" was a detachment of Roman soldiers answerable to Pilate. These were elite special forces, not army rejects. They were not the type to shirk their duty or sleep on the job. That could cost them their lives.

But they were susceptible to bribery, if the price was right. And when the tomb was found empty on the morning of the resurrection, the guards and Jewish officials were all desperate to cover up what had happened:

> When they had assembled with the elders and consulted together, they gave a large sum of money to the soldiers, saying, "Tell them, 'His disciples came at night and stole Him away while we slept.' And if this comes to the governor's ears, we will appease him and make you secure." So they took the money and did as they were instructed. (Matt. 28:12–15)

If there had been the remotest possibility that they might convince the public that Jesus never really died, the priests and soldiers certainly would have used that story instead of telling one that put their own livelihood in jeopardy.

So the burial of Jesus is a vital part of the gospel narrative, mainly because it serves as another reminder that the gospel is rooted in history, not mythology, the human imagination, or allegory. The good news is not a legend subject to interpretation. It's not an elastic worldview that can be reconciled with Corinthian philosophy, academic skepticism, or postmodern preferences. The sacrifice Christ rendered for sins was a real event, seen by countless eyewitnesses, verified by Roman officials, and sealed by Pilate himself with the burial of our Lord's body.

RESURRECTION

Of course, Christ's burial was by no means the end of the story. The pinnacle of all these events, and the glorious truth that makes the gospel of Jesus Christ such good news is "that He rose again the third day according to the Scriptures" (1 Cor. 15:4). In the words of the angel at the empty tomb: "He is risen, as He said" (Matt. 28:6).

Remember the context of our passage. Paul's primary concern in 1 Corinthians 15 is the doctrine of bodily resurrection. This is by far the longest chapter in the New Testament epistles. (And 1 Corinthians is the longest of all the epistles.) Its importance is proportional to its length. Of all the truths Christians affirm, none is more essential to our faith than a belief in literal, bodily resurrection. That starts, of course, with the literal resurrection of Christ's physical body, and (as Paul argues meticulously in this long chapter) it extends to the literal resurrection of our own bodies. Without that article of faith, Paul says, everything else about Christianity dissolves into irrelevance: "If Christ is not risen, your faith is futile; you are still in your sins! Then also those who have fallen asleep in Christ have perished. If in this life only we have hope in Christ, we are of all men the most pitiable" (vv. 17–19).

What follows immediately is a triumphant confession: "But now Christ *is* risen from the dead" (v. 20). The resurrection is God's seal of approval on the atoning work of Christ. On the cross, just before He bowed His head and yielded up His spirit, Jesus said, "It is finished!" In the resurrection, God the Father added His amen. In Romans 1:4, Paul wrote that Christ was "declared to be the Son of God with power according to the Spirit of holiness, *by the resurrection from the dead.*" Paul likewise told the intellectuals of Athens, "[God] has appointed a day on which He will judge the world in righteousness by the Man whom He has ordained. He has given assurance of this to all by raising Him from the dead" (Acts 17:31). In other words, the resurrection of Christ is the ultimate proof of the truth of the gospel.

Christ's resurrection is the central point around which all biblical truth revolves. It represents the culmination and triumph of every righteous expectation that preceded it, starting with Job 19:25–27 ("I know that my Redeemer lives, and He shall stand at last on the earth; and after my skin is destroyed, this I know, that in my flesh I shall see God, whom I shall see for myself, and my eyes shall behold, and not another"). It is the basis for the apostles' unshakable faith and the pivotal point in the message they proclaimed. It is the living guarantee of every divine promise from the beginning to the end of Scripture. Every other miracle described in Scripture—including creation—pales in significance by comparison.

Although all four gospels bear witness that Christ had repeatedly foretold His own resurrection (Matt. 20:19; Mark 8:31; Luke 9:22; John 2:19–21; 10:18), the disciples were not predisposed to believe it. They were clearly surprised—even inclined to skepticism—when they found the empty grave. Thomas was emphatic: "Unless I see in His hands the print of the nails, and put my finger into the print of the nails, and put my hand into His side, I will not believe" (John 20:25). But after His multiple appearances, often in the presence of multiple eyewitnesses, they were so firmly convinced of the truth of the resurrection that no argument, no threat, no form of torture could silence them. All of them ultimately gave their lives rather than deny the resurrection. After all, they had seen Him, touched Him, eaten with Him, and fellowshipped with Him after the resurrection. That explains the amazing boldness and determination with which they carried the gospel to the nations. "We cannot but speak the things which we have seen and heard" (Acts 4:20).

PROOF

That eyewitness testimony is the fourth and final point of history Paul cites in his outline of gospel facts in 1 Corinthians 15. He underscores the fact that it was not just the inner circle of apostles who saw the risen Christ. There were literally hundreds of eyewitnesses to the resurrection—"over five hundred brethren at once, of whom the greater part remain to the present, but some have fallen asleep" (v. 6).

It's as if he is saying, "Don't take my word for it. Go ask these people." They were, after all, easy to find, because they had fanned out over the Roman Empire and into all the known parts of the world beyond, proclaiming the message of Christ. In the words of those who despised them, these witnesses to the resurrection had basically "turned the world upside down" (Acts 17:6).

The resurrection is nothing like the pseudo-miracles performed by religious charlatans on television nowadays. Ask a televangelist to subject his miracle claims to any kind of careful scrutiny and he will balk or make excuses. The so-called miracles featured today in charismatic meetings are either totally invisible (back pains relieved or migraines cured) or common parlor tricks, like the lengthening of a leg or causing people to fall over as if "slain in the spirit." They don't stand up to any kind of scrutiny. From time to time some charlatan will claim to have raised someone from the dead in an obscure meeting in an undeveloped country. But don't expect to see such miracles on television; don't bother looking for credible eyewitnesses; and don't ask to subject the claim to any kind of careful investigation. Today's miracle workers are promoting gullibility, not authentic faith. Ask them for evidence and your desire to get the facts will automatically be derided as sinful, cynical unbelief.

Paul invited scrutiny. So certain was he of the truth that he urged people to investigate the evidence. And to make the point, he stressed the abundance of eyewitnesses and their willingness to testify.

Indeed, they were more than willing to testify. The majority gave their lives rather than deny the resurrection. As we discussed, eleven of the twelve original apostles were killed (most of them by horrific tortures) and not one ever recanted his testimony. The only one who lived to old age was the apostle John. Even he was hounded, threatened, tortured, and finally exiled to a penal colony on a small island because he refused to deny the resurrection.

Take just the first of the specific examples Paul cites as a witness: Peter. Throughout 1 Corinthians (and in Galatians 2:9) Paul calls him Cephas. That is the Aramaic equivalent of *Peter* (which is derived from the Greek word for *rock*). His given name was Simon, but when Simon first met Jesus, the Lord nicknamed him "Rock," using the Aramaic version, "Cephas" (John 1:42). That's how Paul normally refers to him.

Consider the resurrection from Peter's point of view. It must have seemed amazing (and no doubt somewhat embarrassing) to Peter that Christ appeared to him first of all. When Jesus' life was on the line, Peter had denied Him angrily, with an oath. Peter was totally broken. He might have seemed the least likely of all the apostles to assert himself as a preacher of the resurrection because he was so ashamed. He was a coward, and a sniveling one at that. He was weeping bitterly the last time he saw Jesus.

And even after the resurrection, Peter had so little confidence that when Jesus told him to go to Galilee and wait for Him to come, Peter made plans to return to the fishing trade because he felt himself so inadequate as an apostle and preacher. He was more keenly aware than anyone that he had proven himself unfaithful many times. He looked like a disaster. Peter wasn't a likely candidate to be the one who would go out at Pentecost and start bombastically preaching the resurrection.

But Jesus came to him, elicited from him a threefold declaration of his love for Christ, and commissioned him to preach. At Pentecost, Peter was a totally different person. The fact that he could give such bold testimony about the risen Christ is a clear indication that he did, in fact, see the risen Christ. Peter was not about to invent a phony story about Christ's resurrection, nor would he be prepared to give his life for a lie he had fabricated. Peter—the same person who once cowered when challenged by a servant girl and denied that he even knew Christ—would ultimately be crucified upside down rather than deny the truth of the resurrection. The only thing that could explain such a radical transformation is the resurrection of Christ.

As we're going to see in subsequent chapters, Paul doesn't necessarily mention the resurrection of Christ explicitly every time he summarizes the gospel. Sometimes his emphasis is on the principle of substitution. Sometimes he stresses the righteousness that is imputed to believers. Sometimes he puts the focus on the price that was paid for our forgiveness. All these elements are essential aspects of the gospel according to Paul.

But we're not to lose sight of the fact that the gospel is grounded in historic events; and above all, *the resurrection is the seal and the linchpin of gospel truth.* Elsewhere Paul says that Christ "was delivered up because of our offenses, and was raised because of our justification" (Rom. 4:25). Christ was "declared to be the Son of God with power according to the Spirit of holiness, by the resurrection from the dead" (Rom. 1:4). Again, the resurrection was God's seal of approval on the propitiation Christ offered. Without the resurrection, there would be no gospel.

Every element in Paul's outline is equally significant. It is an ingenious summary of the critical historical events in the gospel story. But as we have said from the start, Paul himself would be the first to emphasize that there are many other indispensable gospel truths—chiefly doctrines—such as sin, justification, vicarious atonement, grace, faith, security, and others. Paul explains those doctrines and stresses their importance throughout his epistles, as we will observe. But here his design is to give the most simple, pithy account of gospel history possible—one that comprehends and implicitly affirms all the vital doctrines as well. Each point he lists is indeed a matter of primary importance: "Christ died for our sins according to the Scriptures . . . He was buried . . . He rose again the third day according to the Scriptures, and . . . He was seen."

That is the whole gospel. The rest is explanation.

TWO

FIRST, THE BAD NEWS

The Scripture has confined all under sin, that the promise by faith in Jesus Christ might be given to those who believe.

—GALATIANS 3:22

The word *gospel* is the Middle English version of an Old English term, *godspel*, meaning "glad tidings," or "good news." The Greek equivalent, *evangelion*, likewise means "good message." The term evokes the idea of a welcome pronouncement or a happy declaration. So it is ironic that quite often the gospel is not gladly received by those who hear it. It is likewise ironic that when Paul begins his most thorough systematic presentation of the gospel message, he starts with a statement that is decidedly *bad* news: "The wrath of God is revealed from heaven against all ungodliness and unrighteousness of men" (Rom. 1:18). Paul then goes on for the equivalent of two full chapters, making the argument that the whole human race is fallen and wicked and hopelessly in bondage to sin. "As it is written: 'There is none righteous, no, not one'" (Rom. 3:10). Furthermore, "the wages of sin is death" (6:23).

Obviously there's a close connection between the two ironies. So many people spurn the good news because they can't get past the starting point, which requires us to confess our sin. Sinners left to themselves are neither willing nor able to extricate themselves from the bondage of sin.[1] Therefore instead, they "suppress the truth in unrighteousness" (Rom. 1:18). They are objects of God's wrath—because "knowing the righteous judgment of God, that those who practice such things are deserving of death, [they] not only do the same but also approve of those who practice them" (v. 32).

People love their sin. Respectable sinners are especially prone to defend their genteel approach to sinning. Gross sinners are often more likely to confess their sin and turn to the Lord for redemption. Jesus was remarking on that phenomenon when He said, "Those who are well have no need of a physician, but those who are sick. I did not come to call the righteous, but sinners, to repentance" (Mark 2:17).

That aspect of Jesus' teaching differs sharply from the conventional wisdom of all this world's religious elite. Virtually all the major world religions teach that humanity is fundamentally good—or at the very least that there is in each person some spark of divinity, giving us the ability to redeem ourselves. We must nurture our native goodness, they say. That is the way to gain heaven, achieve Nirvana, reach a higher level of consciousness in the next reincarnation, or whatever.

Of course, various religions have vastly differing notions of what constitutes "good." To some, righteousness is achieved by quieting the mind or extinguishing the flames of human desire. To others, righteousness means waging jihad against the infidels. But what all manmade religions and all the doctrines of demons teach in common is that the rewards of righteousness are within reach, and you can achieve redemption for yourself by following the tenets of whatever religion you have chosen. They promise merit in exchange for good deeds, religious rituals, and human willpower.

That's because all false religions are *systems of human achievement.* Many are harsh and rigorous with standards that are barely (if at all) attainable. Others feature such a minimal standard of righteousness that only the very grossest of sins are deemed worthy of any reproof. In one way or another, most false religions "call evil good, and good evil; [they] put darkness for light, and light for darkness . . . bitter for sweet, and sweet for bitter!" (Isa. 5:20). They teach people to be "wise in their own eyes, and prudent in their own sight!" (v. 21). At the end of the day, all of them are works-based religions. The focus is on something the creature is supposed to do for God—or worse, for oneself. (Indeed, the most thoroughly evil religious systems are those that literally aim at the deification of the individual—thus echoing the false promise the serpent made to Eve in Genesis 3:4–5: "You will not surely die. . . . You will be like God.")

By contrast, the gospel of Jesus Christ is *a message of divine accomplishment.* It is an announcement that Christ has already triumphed over sin and death on behalf of hopeless sinners who lay hold of His redemption by faith alone. This is grace-based religion. The focus is on what God has already done for sinners.

But to appreciate how such a message is good news, a person must know himself to be a wretched sinner, incapable of making an adequate atonement, and therefore powerless to earn any righteous merit of his own—much less obtain redemption for himself. The sinner must feel the weight of his guilt and know that God is a righteous Judge who will not sanction sin. Indeed, he or she must be prepared to confess that perfect justice demands the condemnation of guilty souls.

That means a clear message about the reality of sin and the hopeless state of fallen humanity is a necessary starting point for the gospel's good news. That's why the gospel according to Paul begins with a guilty verdict that applies to all humanity: "All have sinned and fall short of the glory of God" (Rom. 3:23). People apart from Christ are "condemned already" (John 3:18). Any person "who does not believe the Son shall not see life, but the wrath of God abides on him" (v. 36). Or, as Paul says in the preamble to his brilliant gospel summary in Ephesians 2:8–10, unredeemed people are "dead in trespasses and sins," walking "according to the course of this world, according to the prince of the power of the air, the spirit who now works in the sons of disobedience," conducting themselves in the lusts of their flesh, "fulfilling the desires of the flesh and of the mind." They are "by nature children of wrath," dead in trespasses (Eph. 2:1–3).

We'll look more closely at Ephesians 2 in an upcoming chapter, but as we noted in the opening paragraph of this chapter, Paul also makes that truth the starting point for an extended exposition of gospel doctrines in his epistle to the Romans. His commentary on human depravity runs from Romans 1:18–3:23. He returns to the subject of sin in his discussion of sanctification in Romans 6–7. All told, Paul devotes more space to the doctrine of sin in Romans than he does to any other single aspect of gospel doctrine.

THE UNIVERSAL GUILTY VERDICT

In Romans 3:9–18, Paul gives the following summary of that long opening discourse in which he says all of humanity—every tribe, tongue, and nation—stands guilty before God:

> What then? Are we [Jews] better than they [the Gentiles]? Not at all. For we have previously charged both Jews and Greeks that they are all under sin.
>
> As it is written:
>
> *"There is none righteous, no, not one;*
> *there is none who understands;*
> *there is none who seeks after God.*
> *They have all turned aside;*
> *they have together become unprofitable;*
> *there is none who does good, no, not one."*
> *"Their throat is an open tomb;*
> *with their tongues they have practiced deceit";*
> *"the poison of asps is under their lips";*
> *"whose mouth is full of cursing and bitterness."*
> *"Their feet are swift to shed blood;*
> *destruction and misery are in their ways;*
> *And the way of peace they have not known."*
> *"There is no fear of God before their eyes."*

Although virtually all people like to think of themselves as basically good, the testimony of God's Word is precisely the opposite. Scripture states unequivocally that the entire human race is evil. In the vernacular of our times, humanity is bad to the bone—corrupt to the core. To put it in familiar theological terms, we are totally depraved.

We are naturally, intuitively, painfully aware of our guilt too. A ubiquitous sense of shame goes with being a fallen creature. It's what made Adam and Eve try to mask their nakedness with leaves. That's a perfect metaphor for the futile ways people try to paper over the shame of their wickedness. They don't want to face it. They try to eliminate that sense of guilt by adopting a more convenient kind of morality, or by silencing their crying conscience.

The culture all around us is loaded with encouragements and incentives for people to indulge their favorite sins, ignore their own culpability, deny their guilt, and silence their conscience.* In fact, a strong sense of guilt is popularly regarded as a mental-health defect. Seeing oneself fundamentally as a victim is much easier, and certainly more gratifying, than facing the reality of sin. WebMD.com, the premier online source offering simple medical advice to lay people, features an article titled "Learning to Forgive Yourself" that includes this quote from a clinical trainer at a rehab center: "People do things—intended or not—that hurt others. You may not intend to harm, but the other person is no less hurt." Now, you might think the article would go on to encourage the offender to seek forgiveness from the person whom he or she offended, even if the offense was unintentional. Not so. The very next sentence says, "That's when you need to stop at some point and forgive yourself."[2]

That's very bad advice. That attitude toward guilt has created a society full of people convinced they are purely victims, not malefactors. They won't hear of their own culpability, much less confess it; and therefore they cannot hear the good news of the gospel, much less believe it.

Admittedly, we don't like the dishonor that our sin inevitably brings us.

---

* I wrote an entire book on this breakdown in the moral underpinnings of Western culture. See John MacArthur, *The Vanishing Conscience* (Dallas: Word, 1994).

Naturally, we want to be free from the weight of our guilt. But suppressing guilt and denying our sinfulness is not the answer to our sin problem. That is Paul's point in Romans 1:18, before his discussion of sin really gets started: to "suppress the truth in unrighteousness" is to incur the wrath of God.

Living under the frown of God's wrath, under the reality of His condemnation, and under threat of eternal judgment is frightfully worse than facing our guilt. However miserable life in this world may seem because of guilt and shame, life in the next world will be infinitely more miserable for those who have to face God's endless judgment.

Those are inevitable fruits of sin: misery in this life and eternal, unimaginable misery in the life to come. People try to squelch their earthly despondency by artificial means such as frivolous diversions, the pursuit of pleasure, alcohol, drugs, or ultimately even suicide. But if those who give themselves over to such things manage to retain any semblance of sanity, the guilt will persist anyway, because, according to Romans 2:15, the basics of God's moral law have been inscribed on our hearts by God Himself. Romans 2:15 also says the human conscience bears witness to that law. So whether the thoughts of our minds accuse or excuse us, the conscience bears witness to our guilt. No matter how hard we try to suppress, muffle, or shout down the voice of conscience, in the end, Paul says, "God will judge the secrets of men by Jesus Christ, according to my gospel" (v. 16).

It is a universal dilemma. The whole world is guilty before God (Rom. 3:19). And Paul is meticulous in making that point. Jews and Gentiles alike have a law written on their hearts. The Israelites coming out of Egypt under Moses' leadership received the law in more explicit fashion, inscribed by the finger of God on tablets of stone. Still more detailed laws and prophecies were recorded on papyrus scrolls. And today the entire Word of God is easily available to practically anyone on paper or in electronic form. No one gets to claim ignorance. And no one gets to claim innocence.

But worse than that, no one has the ability to break free from this sinful condition. Sin is a bitter bondage, and people under the power of sin are absolutely helpless to rid themselves of guilt in this life or escape horrible judgment in the life to come. This is not a problem only for derelicts, mass murderers, evil dictators, and other especially foul types of sinners. In our natural fallen state, we "are *all* under sin" (Rom. 3:9). And "by the deeds of the law *no* flesh will be justified in His sight" (v. 20). That's Paul's point, and no one gets an exemption.

This, then, is the clear, bottom-line, starting-point truth in the gospel according to Paul: "*All* have sinned and fall short of the glory of God" (v. 23). No one escapes that verdict. We have no capacity to break free of our sin or eliminate its guilt. Left to ourselves, we would be eternally damned. And that's what we deserve.

PROOF FROM THE OLD TESTAMENT

Paul could have made this argument many ways. Indeed, in the course of his epistle to the Romans, he returns to this point and sometimes brings up additional arguments that prove the sinfulness of all humanity. For example, in Romans 5:14, he points out that "death reigned from Adam to Moses" even before there was a written law defining what sin was. He argues that sin must be universal because death is universal. Sin is, after all, the whole reason people die. "Death [entered the world] through sin" (v. 12). "The wages of sin is death" (6:23). And everyone dies. That 100 percent statistic furnishes undeniable proof that everyone is a sinner.

Paul could also have argued from the standpoint of past judgments. God drowned the entire world in a massive flood because "the wickedness of man was great in the earth, and . . . every intent of the thoughts of his heart was only evil continually" (Gen. 6:5). The ruthlessness and extent of human evil was clearly enormous. And then, even after the flood had abated and Noah and family rebooted the human race, the Lord said, "The imagination of man's heart is evil from his youth" (Gen. 8:21). God subsequently destroyed the entire civilizations of Sodom and Gomorrah because "the men of Sodom were exceedingly wicked and sinful against the LORD" (Gen. 13:13).

Paul could have proved the universality of sin with an appeal to empirical evidence. The proof of sin's universality is everywhere. The fruits and frustrations of sin are inevitable aspects of the human experience. No sensible, rational person would ever claim to be guilt-free. Even those who might try to make that claim can easily detect the guilt of everyone else. And whether they know it or not, their guilt is obvious to all as well. This is one point of Christian doctrine that is not lacking for irrefutable evidence. Everyone sins. As the apostle John says, "The *whole world* lies under the sway of the wicked one" (1 John 5:19). Furthermore, "all that is in the world—the lust of the flesh, the lust of the eyes, and the pride of life—is not of the Father but is of the world" (1 John 2:16).

In short, history proves the universality of sin. Sociology proves it. The reality of death proves it. But the most potent and enduring proof of humanity's sinfulness is found in Scripture. Therefore having declared the truth about sin and the human dilemma, Paul proves it in the most conclusive way possible with a series of quotations from the Old Testament in Romans 3:10–18.

He introduces this section with the words, "As it is written," and everything that follows, through the end of verse 18, is either a direct quotation or a close paraphrase from Scripture. He draws from numerous Old Testament sources.

So this is God speaking through divine revelation about the exceeding sinfulness of sin. This is the coup de grace after Paul's long discourse on sin. He could have pointed to history; he could have applied a logical syllogism; he could have appealed to the reader's conscience. Paul was a great scholar. He might have manufactured a careful philosophical argument or quoted one of the ancient Greek poets.

Instead, he cites Scripture, because it is the Word of God. That, by the way, is the essential strategy underlying the gospel according to Paul with regard to how the good news is to be disseminated: "Preach the word! . . . in season and out of season. Convince, rebuke, exhort, with all longsuffering and teaching" (2 Tim. 4:2). That is precisely what Paul himself does at the culmination of his discourse about sin in Romans 3. This is the pinnacle of his presentation. He calls on God as the ultimate witness, by letting the Word of God speak to the question of sin's universality. And it is convincing. He quotes from or alludes to a long string of Old Testament sources, including Psalm 5:9; 10:7; 14:1–3; 36:1–3; 53:1–3; 140:3; Proverbs 1:16; Isaiah 59:7–8; and Jeremiah 5:16. All those texts authoritatively seal the case Paul has spent two chapters making.

The paradigm Paul uses is a classic legal pattern. He employs courtroom terminology and follows the course of a judicial proceeding. He puts the human race on trial. There is an arraignment. Then an indictment. And finally a verdict.

THE ARRAIGNMENT

We begin with the arraignment. A legal arraignment is where the accused is brought to court to answer formal charges. At this trial, the whole human race is brought before the eternal Judge. The charge against us is uttered in Romans 3:9: "What then? Are we better than they? Not at all. For we have previously charged both Jews and Greeks that they are all under sin."

"What then?" simply means, "What is the case? How are we to understand the situation?" What follows is the answer to that question, stated in God's own words.

Bear in mind the structure of the preceding context. In Romans 2:12 Paul states his point succinctly: "As many as have sinned without law will also perish without law, and as many as have sinned in the law will be judged by the law." That is all-inclusive. It encompasses each one of us—Jew and Gentile, male and female, bond and free.

Then Paul goes on to lay out the charge in meticulous detail. In Romans 2:14–16, he charges the Gentiles with sin, even though they were not directly given God's written law. In verses 17–29, he charges the Jews with sin as "transgressor[s] of the law" (v. 27). In 3:1–8, he defends the righteousness of God as Judge. Then in verse 9, just before launching into that long string of Old Testament references, he sums up what he has just said and reiterates the main point so no reader can possibly miss it: "We have previously charged both Jews and Greeks that they are all under sin." The whole world is "guilty before God" (v. 19).

That is his formal arraignment. The charge is universal guilt. No human being escapes that charge. Paul makes the universality of sin as plain and categorical as possible, refusing to exclude even himself: "Are we better than they?" (v. 9). "We" is a clear reference to Paul and his missionary companions—and by implication, it includes all Christians. The same pronoun ("we") is used in verse 8 ("we are slanderously reported"; "some affirm that we say"). The "we" in verse 9 clearly refers to the same people. It's a reference to those who proclaim the gospel. To paraphrase, *"Those of us who are making this charge, pointing out that Jews and Gentiles are hopeless sinners—are we saying we're a special case? Are we claiming to be better than everyone else?"* "Not at all." He uses an emphatic negative. *"In no way do we think that! We are wretched sinners too."* Elsewhere, in 1 Timothy 1:13, Paul describes himself as the chief of sinners—"formerly a blasphemer, a persecutor, and an insolent man." He retained a keen awareness of his own sin throughout his life. He was a mature, seasoned apostle when he wrote Romans 7:14: "I am carnal, sold under sin." And verse 24: "O wretched man that I am!"

So Paul very acutely feels his own fallenness. He's not setting himself up as a judge over the rest of humanity. He is merely stating the case. The entire human race is fallen and sinful, including Paul, his companions, and all believers. We all belong to the same sin-cursed race.

It's good to remember that Christians are nothing but redeemed sinners—saved from condemnation not because we are somehow better, smarter, more worthy, or more acceptable to God. As Paul himself testifies, "I know that in me (that is, in my flesh) nothing good dwells" (Rom. 7:18). "It is God who works in [us] both to will and to do for His good pleasure" (Phil. 2:13). Apart from Christ, we're all in the same guilty condition as the world's most dissipated human being. Without Christ, we would be completely under the command, control, dominion, and damning power of sin. As a matter of fact, we once did walk in step with the prince of the power of the air, Satan. Remember, in our natural, fallen state, we are "by nature children of wrath, just as the others" (Eph. 2:3).

That is the arraignment. Paul summons the entire Adamic race into court, and on the authority of God's Word, he reads the capital charge against us: "They are all under sin" (Rom. 3:9). The arraignment is complete.

THE INDICTMENT

In a legal arraignment, the document detailing the specific charges against the accused is called the *indictment.* This indictment could hardly be more grim or more imposing. It is a detailed accusation drawn entirely from an infallible source—Scripture. There are thirteen counts in Romans 3:10–17, and every one of them is a direct quotation from the Old Testament:

1. There is none righteous, no, not one.
2. There is none who understands.
3. There is none who seeks after God.
4. They have all turned aside.
5. They have together become unprofitable.
6. There is none who does good, no, not one.
7. Their throat is an open tomb.
8. With their tongues they have practiced deceit.
9. The poison of asps is under their lips.
10. Whose mouth is full of cursing and bitterness.
11. Their feet are swift to shed blood.
12. Destruction and misery are in their ways.
13. The way of peace they have not known.

Verse 18 then summarizes the indictment with one last Old Testament quotation: "There is no fear of God before their eyes."

It is a universal indictment of all humanity. Four times in this passage the word *none* is used. Twice that expression is underscored with the words *no, not one.* The word *all* is used in verses 9, 12, and 19; then twice more in verse 22; and a final time in verse 23—five times total in this discussion of the universality of sin. So this is a comprehensive statement. No one escapes the indictment.

The practice of stringing together verses and phrases drawn from diverse biblical sources was very common in rabbinic teaching. This is a didactic device known as *charaz* (literally, "string of pearls"). Paul draws from multiple Old Testament sources several parallel phrases about the universality of sin. And he strings them together like pearls—except that the result is not pretty. The full necklace is a choking indictment against every member of the human race.

This is no mere opinion of Paul's, nor is it dry theoretical doctrine. He purposely starts with the phrase "As it is written," in order to highlight the divine authority behind this indictment. He is using a phrase commonly used in rabbinical discourse to introduce biblical citations. It's an expression employed many times throughout the New Testament—often by Christ Himself.

Our Lord used it when He was being tempted by Satan. The Devil assaulted Jesus with three sinister dares. All three times Christ answered with direct quotations from the Old Testament, saying, "It is written . . . It is written *again* . . . *Away with you, Satan!* For it is written . . ." (Matt. 4:4, 7, 10). The phrase "it is written" is used more than sixty times in the New Testament. (It is used more than a dozen times in the Old Testament as well.) It is a formal appeal to the highest of all authorities, an implicit recognition that when Scripture speaks, God has spoken.

The Greek expression is a *perfect passive indicative*—meaning it describes a definitive action with abiding significance. The idea it conveys is, "This stands written as an eternal truth." The perfect tense is always significant in Koine Greek (the language of the New Testament). In this expression, the tense serves to underscore the finality and continuing authority of Scripture as the unchanging and eternal Word of God. What stands written is settled forever in heaven (Ps. 119:89). In Jesus' words, "Till heaven and earth pass away, one jot or one tittle will by no means pass from the law till all is fulfilled" (Matt. 5:18).

So this is God's definitive, authoritative Word on the hopeless depravity of fallen humanity.

Paul's indictment comes in three parts. The first deals with character, the second with conversation, and the third with conduct. In other words, the corruption of sin affects our very nature, it is revealed in what we say, and it is manifest in the way we act.

Sin Debauches Our Character

If we were using a medical metaphor, we might say this section of Paul's epistle includes a full examination of the sinner, beginning with a kind of spiritual MRI scan. Romans 3:10–12 reveals how corruption pervades the inner being—the very heart and soul of the sinner. In the words of Jeremiah 17:9, "The heart is deceitful above all things, and desperately wicked."

Paul says the same thing with a series of Old Testament references that make negative statements describing the debauched character of all people in their natural fallen state. Here Paul very bluntly spells out just how thoroughly corrupt we are because of our sin.

In verse 10, he says, "There is none righteous, no, not one." That is a paraphrase and summary of the first three verses of Psalms 14 and 53.

By the way, those two psalms closely follow the same thought-for-thought progression in nearly identical words. Psalm 53 uses *elohim* in four instances where Psalm 14 uses *YHWH*; and throughout Psalm 53 slightly different expressions are used to echo and convey various ideas in the exact same order as Psalm 14, using virtually identical rhythms. So these are clearly twin psalms. In all likelihood, Psalm 53 is an adaptation of Psalm 14, sung for a special occasion after a military victory—because the second half of verse 5 includes this: "God has scattered the bones of him who encamps against you; you have put them to shame, because God has despised them." That's the only line not echoed by both psalms, and it is unique to Psalm 53. Other than that, Psalm 53 follows Psalm 14 very closely.

The first three verses of both psalms contain several phrases that Paul will quote in Romans 3. Verse 1 of Psalm 14 says, "They are corrupt, they have done abominable works, there is none who does good." Psalm 53:1

says, "They are corrupt, and have done abominable iniquity; there is none who does good." Romans 3:10 is a shortened paraphrase of those two nearly identical verses, with these words added to the end: "No, not one." (That final phrase is borrowed from verse 3 in both psalms.)

Paul's choice of words in this paraphrase is deliberate. *Righteousness* is the central theme of Paul's entire epistle to the Romans. The word and its cognates appear at least thirty times. That's because the gospel according to Paul is a message about how sinners can be "righteous"—or right with God. At the very outset, therefore, he makes it clear that no one is righteous. And to make sure we don't miss the point or look for an escape hatch, he appends those words from the end of Psalms 14:3 and 53:3: *"No, not one."*

By the way, the Greek word translated "righteous" (here and elsewhere in the New Testament) is the same word translated "justified" just a few verses later, in Romans 3:20: "Therefore by the deeds of the law no flesh will be *justified* in His sight." No one is righteous and no one can become righteous through his own efforts—no matter how hard one applies oneself under the law of God.

Paul will restate this point as distinctly as possible in Romans 8:7–8: "The carnal mind is enmity against God; for it is not subject to the law of God, nor indeed can be. So then, those who are in the flesh cannot please God." In fact, the only standard acceptable to God is absolute perfection. In His famous Sermon on the Mount, Jesus said, "Unless your righteousness exceeds the righteousness of the scribes and Pharisees, you will by no means enter the kingdom of heaven" (Matt. 5:20). He went on to teach that anger is of the same nature as murder, and lust is the same flavor of sin as adultery. Then He set the standard as high as possible: "You shall be perfect, just as your Father in heaven is perfect" (v. 48). That is an echo of Leviticus 11:44, where God tells the Israelites, "You shall be holy; for I am holy." That command is repeated more than a dozen times throughout Scripture.

If we don't sense our lost condition when we read what Scripture has to say about sin, we certainly ought to feel it when we understand the nature of the holiness God demands of us. No mere mortal has ever attained that standard, nor do we have the potential even to come close.

Romans 3:11 continues this indictment of our character, now homing in on the sinfulness of the human intellect. He is following the order of Psalms 14 and 53. Verse 2 in both psalms says that God "looks down from heaven upon the children of men, to see if there are any who understand, who seek God." Paul notes the psalmist's reference to "understand[ing]" and states the conclusion plainly implied by the two psalms: "There is *none* who understands."

This is the reality of sin. It has a blinding effect even on the human intellect. Fallen humanity has no true perception of divine reality. Sinners have no right apprehension of God—and therefore they cannot even have a true perception of what righteousness looks like. Paul says the same thing in different words in 1 Corinthians 2:14: "The natural man does not receive the things of the Spirit of God, for they are foolishness to him; nor can he know them, because they are spiritually discerned."

This is a harsh indictment, but it is absolutely true. The entire human race is fallen and fleshly. In our natural state we lack righteousness, we lack even a proper understanding of righteousness, and we hate what we don't understand. Every one of us has been "foolish, disobedient, deceived, serving various lusts and pleasures, living in malice and envy, hateful and hating one another" (Titus 3:3). Elsewhere, Paul says fallen people go through life "in the futility of their mind, having their understanding darkened, being alienated from the life of God, because of the ignorance that is in them, because of the blindness of their heart; who, being past feeling, have given themselves over to lewdness, to work all uncleanness with greediness" (Eph. 4:17–19).

It's hard to see how the state of fallen humanity could be any worse.

But the reality *is* worse: "There is none who seeks after God" (Rom. 3:11, still echoing verse 2 of Ps. 14 and 53). No sinner naturally wants to know God. There simply is no such thing as a self-motivated seeker after God. "The wicked in his proud countenance *does not seek God*; God is in none of his thoughts" (Ps. 10:4).

This is a point people sometimes want to dispute. After all, there are many familiar verses in Scripture that invite sinners to seek God, promising that those who do seek will find. "Seek the LORD your God, and you will find Him if you seek Him with all your heart and with all your soul" (Deut. 4:29). "Let the hearts of those rejoice who seek the LORD!" (1 Chron. 16:10). "Seek the LORD while He may be found, call upon Him while He is near" (Isa. 55:6). "You will seek Me and find Me, when you search for Me with all your heart" (Jer. 29:13). "Ask, and it will be given to you; seek, and you will find; knock, and it will be opened to you" (Luke 11:9). "He who comes to God must believe that He is, and that He is a rewarder of those who diligently seek Him" (Heb. 11:6). There are literally more than a hundred verses in Scripture like those, urging sinners to seek God and promising blessing to those who do.

In recent years, many churches have based their entire ministry philosophy on the assumption that lots of unbelieving people are seeking God. These churches have refurbished their music, teaching, and public worship with the stated goal of being "seeker-sensitive." In order to achieve that goal, church leaders rely on opinion surveys and an almost obsessive fixation with cultural trends in order to gauge the tastes and expectations of unbelievers. Then every feature of their corporate gatherings is carefully reworked, dumbed down, or purposely desanctified in order to make unbelievers feel comfortable.

But people are not really seeking God if they are looking for a religious experience where the music, entertainment, and sermon topics are carefully vetted in order to appeal to popular preferences. That kind of "seeker" is just looking for a cloak of piety in a context where he or she will also get affirmation, self-gratification, and companionship with like-minded people.

The gospel according to Paul points the opposite direction. Paul fully understood the felt needs and cultural expectations of his diverse audiences: "Jews request a sign, and Greeks seek after wisdom" (1 Cor. 1:22). But the apostle's response was the polar opposite of "seeker-sensitivity": "We preach Christ crucified, to the Jews a stumbling block and to the Greeks foolishness" (v. 23). The Greeks who craved a philosophical discourse on wisdom heard a message Paul knew would sound to them like foolishness; and the Jews who demanded a sign instead got "a stumbling stone and rock of offense"

(Rom. 9:33). But both groups heard exactly the same message from Paul. Here again, we see that he knew only one gospel: "I determined not to know anything among you except Jesus Christ and Him crucified" (1 Cor. 2:2).

Seeking God is what fallen sinners ought to do, and God has every right to command them to do it. But they don't come. They disobey His commands—as is their common practice. In fact, they can't come, because they love their sin too much. Their attachment to sin amounts to a kind of bondage that would be impossible for them to break free of on their own. Jesus acknowledged this in John 6:44: "No one can come to Me unless the Father who sent Me draws him." He repeated the point again just a few verses later: "No one can come to Me unless it has been granted to him by My Father" (v. 65).

Paul clearly explains the problem in detail at the very beginning of his long discourse on sin:

> Although they knew God, they did not glorify Him as God, nor were thankful, but became futile in their thoughts, and their foolish hearts were darkened. Professing to be wise, they became fools, and changed the glory of the incorruptible God into an image made like corruptible man—and birds and four-footed animals and creeping things.
>
> Therefore God also gave them up to uncleanness, in the lusts of their hearts, to dishonor their bodies among themselves, who exchanged the truth of God for the lie, and worshiped and served the creature rather than the Creator, who is blessed forever. Amen.
>
> For this reason God gave them up to vile passions. For even their women exchanged the natural use for what is against nature. Likewise also the men, leaving the natural use of the woman, burned in their lust for one another, men with men committing what is shameful, and receiving in themselves the penalty of their error which was due.
>
> And even as they did not like to retain God in their knowledge, God gave them over to a debased mind. (Rom. 1:21–28)

They have sinned by suppressing basic truths that they knew to be true about God's existence and some of His attributes. That willful rejection brought judgment upon them. God gave them over to their own depravity. They are therefore judicially blind, dull of hearing, ignorant of the truth they themselves worked so hard to suppress, and hopelessly enslaved to their own lusts.

Some take their rebellion further than others, of course. But Paul's point here is that in our fallen condition, we are all guilty of turning away from God. No one by his or her own free will genuinely adores God and longs for His sovereign majesty to be put on display. Left to ourselves, no one naturally wants to feed on God's Word, live in His presence, obey His commands, pray to Him, trust Him in everything, and declare His praise. Given a free and unfettered choice, every one of us has already demonstrated that rebellion against God is bound up in our hearts.

So fallen humanity is in a desperate condition. No one is righteous. No one understands. And no one seeks God.

Romans 3:12 returns to Psalm 14 and quotes yet another phrase from verse 3, this time verbatim: "They have all turned aside." Or to put it another way, they've all gone off the track, no exceptions. They are deviant. The Greek expression is an active verb: *ekklinō*, meaning, "to deviate" or "to avoid." This isn't something that has happened to them; it's something they have done to themselves. They have diverged from the path of truth. They have fled. It's a word used in classical Greek to describe deserting soldiers who turned and fled at the height of the battle.

The whole human race has departed the way of God and deserted the narrow path of truth. "All we like sheep have gone astray; we have turned, every one, to his own way" (Isa. 53:6).

Paul is not finished. The next phrase in Romans 3:12 intensifies the indictment: "They have together become unprofitable." Both Psalm 14 and Psalm 53 say, "They have together become *corrupt*." The same Hebrew word translated "corrupt" is used in both psalms, and it's a word that would be used of milk that has gone sour. It speaks of that which is rancid or tainted. Or it could refer to a foul and festering wound. One possible translation of the word is "stinking." It is the psalmist's way of signifying moral corruption. The same word is used in Job 15:16, where Eliphaz describes the human race as "abominable and filthy, [drinking] iniquity like water!" Paul translates the thought with a Greek verb that means "to become useless." It's a word used nowhere else in Scripture, but Homer uses it in the *Odyssey* to refer to the senseless laughter of a moron. Paul's statement is in the passive voice (meaning now he is describing something that has happened to humanity rather than something we have done). This is the unplanned-for consequence of humanity's deliberate rebellion: the human race has been rendered "unprofitable"—like salt without savor, milk gone bad, or eggs turned rotten.

So much for the nobility of the human race. Paul's assessment is decidedly different from that of the typical anthropologist or religious guru.

And he's not even close to being finished yet.

Still following the line of logic in Psalms 14 and 53, he circles back to his starting point: "There is none who does good, no, not one" (Rom. 3:12). This is actually a whole new charge in the indictment. The idea in verse 10 was that no one *is* righteous. Here the point is that no one *does* what is moral and right.

This sixth allegation condemning the character of humanity is a sweeping, significant, grave condemnation: *fallen people don't do anything that is genuinely good.* The human character, in its fallen state, is *totally depraved.* (That's the common term theologians use to describe this aspect of biblical anthropology.) The point is not that people are as thoroughly evil as they could possibly be. Rather, it means that sin has infected every aspect of the human character—mind, will, passions, flesh, feelings, and motives. Nothing we do is completely free from the taint of sin. That includes our very best deeds of kindness or altruism.

This is perhaps one of the most difficult of all biblical doctrines for people to receive. We naturally want to think of ourselves as fundamentally good, praiseworthy, upright, compassionate, generous, and noble. Furthermore, Scripture does recognize and describe some astonishing examples of human virtue, like the kindness of the good Samaritan, or the compassion of Pharaoh's daughter when she rescued and adopted the infant Moses.

God graciously restrains the full expression of human depravity (Gen. 20:6; 31:7; 1 Sam. 25:26; 2 Thess. 2:7). The restraint of sin and the mitigation of sin's consequences are expressions of *common grace*, the benevolent care God extends to all his creation. Quite simply, things are not as bad as they could be in this fallen world because "the LORD is good to all, and His tender mercies are over all His works" (Ps. 145:9).

But again, Scripture also makes abundantly clear that even the best of our good works are not truly good enough to gain any merit with God. "We are all like an unclean thing, and all our righteousnesses are like filthy rags" (Isa. 64:6). Even the "good" things we do actually compound our guilt, because our motives are (at best) mixed with selfishness, hypocrisy, pride, a desire for the praise of others, or a host of other evil incentives. In order to portray ourselves or our works as "good," we have to allow for all kinds of leeway in our definition of what is good—and that exercise in and of itself is a diabolical transgression. Much of contemporary culture goes to the extreme of "call[ing] evil good, and good evil." They "put darkness for light, and light for darkness . . . bitter for sweet, and sweet for bitter" (Isa. 5:20). But when we understand that God's own absolute perfection is the only acceptable standard of good (Matt. 5:48), it's easy to understand why Scripture says "no one does good, not even one."

This is the starting point of biblical anthropology: humanity is fallen. The human creature is totally depraved, fundamentally wicked—ignorant, rebellious, wayward, and in and of ourselves worthless. Our character is debauched and defined by our sinfulness.

There's more.

Sin Defiles Our Conversation

Jesus said, "Out of the abundance of the heart the mouth speaks" (Matt. 12:34). James 3:3–10 compares the tongue to fire, spreading a conflagration of destruction and evil everywhere. Proverbs 10:32 says the mouth of the wicked speaks what is perverse. Proverbs 15:2 says, "The mouth of fools pours forth foolishness." Scripture frequently describes the mouth of the sinner as a fountain of evil. A person's speech reveals his or her true character. And worst of all, "no man can tame the tongue. It is an unruly evil, full of deadly poison" (James 3:8).

Paul makes that very point—and underscores the universal application—with a rapid-fire series of quotations from Psalm 5:9; 140:3; and 10:7. "'Their throat is an open tomb; with their tongues they have practiced deceit'; 'the poison of asps is under their lips'; 'whose mouth is full of cursing and bitterness'" (Rom. 3:13–14).

The sinner's wickedness is evident the moment he opens his mouth. And notice the progression, from the throat to the tongue to the lips—traversing a mouth that is full of cursing and bitterness. The next verse (Rom. 3:15) then shifts to the feet. It is as if he wants to portray the wickedness spewing forth from humanity like vomit.

Paul (like the psalmist before him) is painting a deliberately revolting picture: "Their throat is an open tomb" (Ps. 5:9). To a Jewish reader in particular, nothing would sound more abominable than an open grave with a rotting corpse putting out its staggering and unbearable stench. But this is not about bad breath; it's about something far more odious than that: an utterly corrupt soul with a decayed and still decaying heart. And because the grave is open, the evil is manifest, and the putrid foulness of it is pervasive.

And yet "with their tongues they have practiced deceit" (Rom. 3:13). Actually, they *keep practicing* deceit. That's what the Greek verb tense signifies. It's not merely that they have (in the past) been guilty of cunning and trickery. But as the NASB has it, "they keep deceiving." They are relentless with their insincerity and double-dealing. The idea includes everything from flattery (as the source text in Psalm 5:9 says) to the most cynical brands of fraud and treachery.

Furthermore, all that evil proceeding from the mouth is not merely unclean; it is ultimately deadly—like "the poison of asps." That is a direct quotation from Psalm 140:3. Vile, dishonest, unwholesome speech is viciously destructive, like poison. The imagery is apt. A deadly snake's fangs are usually invisible until the snake is ready to strike, but the bite it delivers can be destructive beyond measure. In a similar way, flattery and deception might briefly conceal the evil potential of wicked speech, but the cloak of dishonesty only makes the destructive power of such words that much more sinister.

Paul is not exaggerating for effect here. Words can literally be deadly. Many deadly conflicts have been started over words—ranging from wars between nations to conflicts that rip families asunder.

No one who listens to the speech that dominates today's world would deny that the human mouth "is full of cursing and bitterness"—angry, vile, filthy, blasphemous, proud, lustful, violent, lying, deceptive, destructive speech. In a way that is perhaps more conspicuous on the surface than any other aspect of human behavior, the topics and the tenor of human conversation provide irrefutable proof that the human heart is fallen and full of evil—thoroughly defiled by sin. There are certain gross evils most people would never *do* because of the consequences. But in today's culture people freely *speak* evil with little or no restraint.

Sin Debases Our Conduct

Paul's reading of the indictment turns next to the problem of human conduct: "'Their feet are swift to shed blood; destruction and misery are in their ways; and the way of peace they have not known.'" (Rom. 3:15–17). Citing Isaiah 59:7 ("Their feet run to evil, and they make haste to shed innocent blood"), he singles out the crime of murder and charges all humanity with the guilt of that crime.

The sin of murder is indeed woven into the fabric of human history. The first child born to Adam and Eve slew his own brother. A wicked bloodthirstiness infects the entire race. And if you wonder how the charge applies to all without exception, remember what Jesus said about murder. He cited the sixth commandment ("You shall not murder") and noted the penalty ("Whoever murders will be in danger of the judgment" [Matt. 5:21]). Then He said, "But I say to you that whoever is angry with his brother without a cause shall be in danger of the judgment. And whoever says to his brother, 'Raca!' shall be in danger of the council. But whoever says, 'You fool!' shall be in danger of hell fire" (v. 22). The apostle John made the point as explicit as possible: "Whoever hates his brother is a murderer" (1 John 3:15).

Humanity's penchant for hatred and violence has left a trail of destruction throughout history, and Paul notes that fact by returning once more to Isaiah 59:7–8: "Wasting and destruction are in their paths. The way of peace they have not known." The expression rendered "destruction and misery" in our version literally means "shattering calamity." The idea is more than mere wretchedness (though it certainly includes that). It signifies actual, painful, physical suffering. And there's no denying that manmade calamity and self-inflicted misery have always been at the center of human experience. In his classic commentary on Romans, early nineteenth-century Scottish commentator Robert Haldane wrote, "The most savage animals do not destroy so many of their own species to appease their hunger, as man destroys of his fellows, to satiate his ambition, his revenge, or cupidity [inordinate greed]."[3] "The way of peace they have not known."

Those are the thirteen charges.

Paul concludes and summarizes his indictment of the human race with one last phrase taken from the Psalms: "There is no fear of God before their eyes" (Rom 3:18). That is from Psalm 36:1, a psalm of David. It is (in David's words) "an oracle . . . concerning the transgression of the wicked." Here is both the motive underlying human guilt and the consummate expression of human depravity. Because the very essence of foolishness lies in a failure to fear God. "The fear of the LORD is the beginning of wisdom" (Ps. 111:10; Prov. 9:10). "The fear of the LORD is to hate evil" (Prov. 8:13). "And by the fear of the LORD one departs from evil" (Prov. 16:6). Of all the evils this string of Old Testament references attributes to fallen humanity, none is more despicable than the shameless, fearless, apathetic contempt people display toward their Creator and Judge. Of all the defects that mar fallen humanity, this is the most damnable of all.

The indictment is thus complete.

THE VERDICT

The conclusion of the matter is clear and inescapable: "Now we know that whatever the law says, it says to those who are under the law, that every mouth may be stopped, and all the world may become guilty before God" (Rom. 3:19). The guilty verdict is incontrovertible.

One thing is conspicuously missing here that would normally be found in any courtroom scene. The accused have offered no defense. That's because there is no defense. "By the deeds of the law no flesh will be justified in His sight, for by the law is the knowledge of sin" (v. 20). We stand guilty as charged. We have nothing even remotely credible to offer in our defense.

To borrow words from the prophet Isaiah: "Woe is me, for I am undone! Because I am a man of unclean lips" (Isa. 6:5). He was one of the best of the Old Testament prophets, and yet he had to confess that his throat was indeed an open sepulcher.

All of us stand guilty under the law of God and before the bar of divine justice. Every mouth is stopped. Meanwhile, a righteous judge has one responsibility: uphold the law.

This brings us back to that seemingly insoluble dilemma. God, the Lawgiver and perfect Judge, cannot simply overlook humanity's sin. "He who justifies the wicked, and he who condemns the just, both of them alike are an abomination to the LORD" (Prov. 17:15). God cannot lower the impossibly high standard of His own perfect righteousness in order to accommodate humanity's sin. Sin must be punished, and the wages of sin is death. Sinners have a debt they could never hope to pay.

If we stopped right there, no one would have any reason to think the gospel is good news. Thankfully, Scripture doesn't stop there. Starting in verse 21, the true glory of the gospel bursts on the scene.

THREE

HOW CAN A PERSON BE RIGHT WITH GOD?

If You, LORD, should mark iniquities,
O Lord, who could stand?

—PSALM 130:3

Paul's long, relentless discourse on human depravity culminates in a crushing verdict that leaves "every mouth . . . stopped, and all the world . . . guilty before God" (Rom. 3:19). He then punctuates that verdict by pointing out that the law of God offers no remedy for the human predicament: "By the deeds of the law *no flesh will be justified in His sight*, for by the law is the knowledge of sin" (v. 20).

For those inclined to think God in His mercy might simply set His law aside and overlook their sin, the law is replete with emphatic statements to the contrary. Although God is indeed "longsuffering and abundant in mercy, forgiving iniquity and transgression . . . *He by no means clears the guilty*" (Num. 14:18).

Reminders of this fact often came from God Himself. For example, as Moses stood atop Sinai, ready to receive the law engraved on tablets of stone, "the LORD passed by in front of him and proclaimed, 'The LORD, the

Lord God, compassionate and gracious, slow to anger, and abounding in lovingkindness and truth; who keeps lovingkindness for thousands, who forgives iniquity, transgression and sin; *yet He will by no means leave the guilty unpunished*' " (Ex. 34:6–7 NASB). In Exodus 23:7, God stated categorically, "I will not justify the wicked." Indeed, "He who justifies the wicked [is] . . . an abomination to the Lord" (Prov. 17:15).

Anyone who takes spiritual matters seriously will immediately understand how hopeless the plight of the sinner is. If God will not wink at sin or simply look the other way; if those who have sinned are already doomed and cannot possibly atone for their own sins; if fallen people cannot earn their way back into God's favor even by rigorously following God's law to the best of their ability—what hope is there for anyone?

JOB'S PERPLEXITY

Job, truly one of the most honorable people who ever lived, famously asked that very question: "How can a man be righteous before God?" (Job 9:2).

Although the book of Job is positioned near the middle of the Old Testament canon, it was probably the first book of Scripture to be written.* So Job's question is the original statement of a conundrum that resurfaces again and again at vital points throughout biblical history. It's the very same problem that explains Adam and Eve's failed attempts to cover their nakedness with fig leaves and hide from God's presence (Gen. 3:7–8). It's a question raised in various forms in the psalms and prophecies of the Old Testament: "If You, Lord, should mark iniquities, O Lord, who could

* The details of Job's story suggest that he must have lived in the time of the patriarchs. His long life is a major clue about what era he belongs to. He had ten adult children when his trial began, and he was still young enough to father more children at the end of his story, so he would have been between thirty-five and seventy years old when we first meet him in Scripture. Job 42:6 says he lived 140 years after his trials ended, meaning he must have been between 175 and 250 years old at his death. Based on the trajectory of human life spans given in the biblical genealogies, Job must have been a close contemporary of Abraham's. The generations of Abraham and Moses were separated by more than four centuries. (Galatians 3:17 says some 430 years passed between the Abrahamic covenant and the giving of the law at Sinai.) So if Job's story was committed to writing during or near Job's lifetime, it is the oldest book in our Bible.

stand?" (Ps. 130:3). "In [God's] sight no one living is righteous" (Ps. 143:2). "We are all like an unclean thing, and all our righteousnesses are like filthy rags" (Isa. 64:6).

Perhaps no one states the question with more soulful desperation than the prophet Micah. He asks, "With what shall I come before the LORD, and bow myself before the High God? Shall I come before Him with burnt offerings, with calves a year old? Will the LORD be pleased with thousands of rams, ten thousand rivers of oil? Shall I give my firstborn for my transgression, the fruit of my body for the sin of my soul?" (Micah 6:6–7).

The background of Job's story is instructive. Job 1:1 introduces him as the best of men, "blameless and upright, and one who feared God and shunned evil." God Himself twice uses those very words to extol Job's virtue (1:8; 2:3). But, as most readers will know, Job was put to the test by Satan in an effort to get him to curse God and deny his faith. Job's children all tragically died; his earthly possessions were taken from him; his body was ravaged "with sore boils from the sole of his foot unto his crown" (2:7 NASB); and Job "took for himself a potsherd with which to scrape himself [and] sat in the midst of the ashes" (v. 8), pondering the bitterness of all his misfortunes while he tried to make sense of the human dilemma.

Now, remember: Job was the very best of men. There was "none like him on the earth" (1:8). That is not to deny that he was a sinner. Indeed, like all truly spiritual people, Job was keenly conscious of his own sinfulness. He carefully offered the requisite sacrifices for sin, even taking pains to account for the possibility that the guilt of some thoughtless or accidental sin might bring God's displeasure on his family (1:5).

But Job had some friends who were sure his suffering was a sign that he was secretly guilty of some ultra-heinous sin against God. They pressed him with scolding accusations and gave him some spectacularly bad counsel. There must have been some monstrous, clandestine, unrepented sin in Job's life, they insisted. One of them, Bildad, voiced what they were all thinking: "If your sons have sinned against Him, He has cast them away for their transgression" (8:4). Then Bildad turned the spotlight of his suspicions against Job personally: "If you would earnestly seek God and make your supplication to the Almighty, if you were pure and upright, *surely* now He would awake for you, and prosper your rightful dwelling place" (vv. 5–6). After all, Bildad said, "God will not cast away the blameless" (v. 20).

Meanwhile, Job was clearly struggling to make sense of what his own conscience was telling him. He knew he was innocent of any unrepented evil or hypocritical coverup. And yet he also knew he was fallen and prone to sin.

Paul grappled with this very same problem. In 1 Corinthians 4:4, he wrote, "I know of nothing against myself, yet I am not justified by this; but He who judges me is the Lord." Job certainly would have echoed that famous groan of despair penned by Paul as the great apostle contemplated his own fallenness: "O wretched man that I am! Who will deliver me from this body of death?" (Rom. 7:24).

That same frustration prompts the question Job asks: "How can a man be righteous before God?" (Job 9:2). The question weighs heavily on Job's mind because there seems to be no satisfying answer. In fact, he later asks the question again in different words: "Who can bring a clean thing out of an unclean? No one!" (14:4).

Even Bildad finally gets the point, and a few chapters later he echoes Job's question. He even embellishes it with some graphic vermian imagery: "How then can man be righteous before God? Or how can he be pure who is born of a woman? If even the moon does not shine, and the stars are not pure in His sight, how much less man, who is a maggot, and a son of man, who is a worm?" (25:4–6). Bildad is hardly the world's most humble or thoughtful counselor, but this is one question he freely admits he has no answer for.

THE HUMAN DILEMMA

By now you realize that Job was asking the very question the gospel answers: *How can we be right with God?* The more carefully we ponder that question, the more we taste the bitterness of sin and human despair. Is it really possible for sinners to find favor with God—and if so, how?

No matter which gospel text we turn to, that same question arises. Indeed, it is impossible to understand the gospel at all without first considering the quandary of human fallenness—and candidly acknowledging all the seemingly impossible barriers sin puts between God and the sinner. Job's query calls to mind several adjunct questions about issues we have already touched on. Don't skim past this section just because it feels like we are approaching familiar ground. These are questions every sentient individual will inevitably need to face: If we're all guilty before God, without any excuse for our sin, how will anyone stand in the judgment? If works of righteousness cannot atone for our evil deeds, how could any sinner ever be saved from the guilt and bondage of sin? If God demands utter perfection and we are already irreparably imperfect, what hope is there for us? If divine justice absolutely requires that the wages of sin be paid in full, how could God ever justify a sinner without violating His own integrity? Indeed, He expressly says He "will not justify the wicked" (Ex. 23:7); so does that mean our doom is already sealed? *How could a just God justify the ungodly?*

Sound gospel answers to those questions go decidedly against the mainstream of popular opinion. Every belief system ever concocted by the human mind answers those crucial questions wrongly. In one way or another, all this world's religions (and all the major political ideologies and social theories, for that matter) teach that people need to earn righteousness for themselves through some kind of merit system. The means by which they seek to do this are as diverse as the many deities in the world's pantheon. Some put the emphasis on rites and rituals. Others stress self-denial and asceticism. In the postmodern West, people simply invent an imaginary deity for whom sin is really no big deal—thinking their "good" deeds will be taken into account in the judgment and their sins will simply be ignored. But at the opposite extreme are large numbers of people advocating jihad or some other outlandish expression of zealotry.

In the Old Testament, people sometimes burned their infants alive as a sacrifice to Molech, thinking that would gain the favor of an angry, iron-willed deity. And if you think such a heartless, self-serving atrocity belongs only to the ancient past, bear in mind that multitudes today actively favor abortion (the deliberate slaughter of unborn infants) simply because they want to be politically correct. They are desperate to appear "right" in the world's eyes.

All those things are the fruit of a relentless drive that lurks in every fallen human heart: a sinful need to justify oneself. By nature, all sinners have a depraved but powerful impulse to trust in themselves that they are righteous (cf. Luke 18:9). Even the most dogmatic secularists feel the need to be in the right. So they generally tell themselves that lavish philanthropy can atone for practically any evil. Or they might champion animal rights, the redistribution of wealth, or some other "progressive" notion of goodness. All of those ideas (the ancient religions and the novel ideologies alike) are fatally wrong. All of them are making the same fundamentally false assumption—foolishly believing that people can (and must) achieve a right standing for themselves.

That is the worst of all the lies people tell themselves. In fact, it's an eternally damning delusion to imagine that we can earn a righteousness of our own through any means. One of the most crystal-clear teachings of the Bible is that no one gains God's favor by self-effort—least of all those who self-identify as righteous. In fact, Paul said this was the very reason so many of his fellow countrymen remained in unbelief and under the condemnation of God: "Being ignorant of God's righteousness, [they were] seeking to establish their own righteousness" (Rom. 10:3).

There is simply no way for fallen people to extricate themselves from the bondage and guilt of sin, much less the disapproval of a holy God—the One whom they have sinned against. Those who think otherwise are guilty of arrogant overconfidence. Such hubris only deepens their condemnation. Whether they want to face it honestly or not, their plight is dark, dismal, and desperate. No human religion offers a good answer. Even the inspired law of God is powerless to redeem sinners. It merely reveals their sin and condemns them for it. This is precisely what makes Paul's universal "guilty" verdict so devastating: "By the deeds of the law no flesh will be justified in [God's] sight, for by the law is the knowledge of sin" (Rom. 3:20).

That verse is the culmination of Paul's whole argument about the devastating effects of sin. He has brought his readers to a point where they ought to be asking the same urgent question Job kept raising.

WHO THEN CAN BE SAVED?

It is the same question the disciples raised after Jesus' encounter with the rich young ruler: "Who then can be saved?" (Matt. 19:25; Mark 10:26; Luke 18:26). Everything we have seen so far in Paul's long discussion of humanity's sin problem would seem to make redemption an utter impossibility. And from the sinner's point of view, that is precisely the case. Jesus' answer to the disciples' question began by acknowledging the hopelessness of the sinner's plight: "With men this is impossible" (Matt. 19:26).

"But," our Lord continued, "with God all things are possible."

Paul says the same thing in a similar way in Romans 3. After his detailed discourse on the problem of sin, culminating in that resounding declaration about the hopelessness of the human dilemma, the apostle suddenly shifts both tone and direction in verse 21: *"But now . . ."*

The ugliness of those opening three chapters instantly gives way to hope. Just when we reach the point where it seems as if nothing helpful or encouraging could ever appear on such a bleak horizon, Paul takes a sudden turn, and we arrive at the reason the gospel is such good news: "But now the *righteousness of God apart from the law* is revealed" (v. 21).

Take some time to digest every phrase in that profound statement. This is about God's perfect righteousness, in contrast to the filthy rags of our own paltry and sin-stained works. It's a righteousness manifested "apart from the law," meaning it's something other than a simple restatement of the law's commandments. And it's not merely the legal justice that is woven into the law—the righteousness that requires full retribution for our sin.

"If there had been a law given which could have given life, truly righteousness would have been by the law" (Gal. 3:21). But the law can neither make us righteous nor give us life. The law is necessary to teach us what righteousness is, but it offers no help for sinners. It demands our full compliance. It condemns our disobedience. But it cannot make us righteous.

The gospel reveals a righteousness "apart from the law" that accomplishes the redemption of sinners. Under the terms of the law itself, redemption for sinners would seem impossible. But Paul is describing an amazing aspect of divine righteousness that accrues to the benefit (rather than the condemnation) of every believer. This was strongly suggested in the Old Testament, in texts like Genesis 15:6, Psalm 32:1–2, and Isaiah 61:10. Now it is fully unveiled in the gospel. It is "the righteousness of God, through faith in Jesus Christ, *to all and on all who believe*" (Rom. 3:22).

Notice that this righteousness comes down to us; it is not something we offer up to God. This righteousness is *imputed* (credited to the account of) to every sinner who renounces sin and trusts Christ as Savior. We know for a fact that's what Paul has in mind, because a few verses after this, he quotes Psalm 32, where "David . . . describes the blessedness of the man to whom God imputes righteousness apart from works" (Rom. 4:6). He also says the believing sinner's "faith is *accounted* for righteousness" (v. 5). The verbs *impute* and *account* are technical terms that describe a judicial transaction where the repentant sinner is formally credited with the perfect righteousness of God Himself.

This concept of imputation is crucial to understanding the gospel according to Paul. The word itself is a *forensic* term, meaning it describes a legal reckoning—such as the transfer of a debt or an asset from one person to another. The idea is not that God infuses or injects virtue into the soul, but that He fully credits believing sinners with a perfect righteousness that is not their own. It is not something earned or concocted through works they perform. It is an *alien* righteousness—the righteousness of another. Here Paul calls it "the righteousness of God." More specifically, it is the full perfection of divine righteousness as manifested in the man Christ Jesus. The full merit of Christ's righteousness is imputed to all who are united with Him by faith, in precisely the same way their guilt was imputed to Him (2 Cor. 5:21).*

---

* See chapter 5 for a detailed study of 2 Corinthians 5:21 and its implications.

That profound yet simple truth will resurface again and again as we examine the key Pauline texts on the gospel. There is no principle more vital to a sound understanding of justification by faith. And since the doctrine of justification is the linchpin of Paul's teaching on the gospel, it is simply not possible to understand or properly explain Pauline soteriology without recourse to the language and the principle of imputation.

NO MERIT OF MY OWN

With those truths in mind, look closely, phrase by phrase, at the implications of this pivotal statement: "But now the righteousness of God apart from the law is revealed, being witnessed by the Law and the Prophets, even the righteousness of God, through faith in Jesus Christ, to all and on all who believe" (Rom. 3:21–22).

"But now . . . is revealed"

First of all, Paul is saying that the gospel of Jesus Christ gives us a fuller, clearer understanding of the way of salvation than had ever been revealed before. The truth was there in the Old Testament, but it was concealed in shadows. For the most part, it was imbedded in typology and symbolism.

For example, the Old Testament sacrificial system was loaded with graphic depictions of substitutionary atonement. The vivid, bloody rituals reminded the faithful in a powerful way that sin's dire wages must be paid. Animal sacrifices pictured the death of a vicarious sin-bearer, showing that the penalty of sin could be borne by an appropriate substitute. But those offerings had to be made again and again, proving that animal sacrifices "can never take away sins" (Heb. 10:11). Old Testament sacrifices were merely symbolic, looking ahead to a greater, more suitable sacrifice that would be truly efficacious. "For it is not possible that the blood of bulls and goats could take away sins" (v. 4). But where could a truly acceptable substitute be found? Under the law, the answer to that question remained shrouded in mystery.

Furthermore, the sacrificial system was focused almost entirely on the *punishment* the law demanded. What about the *obedience* the law demanded? How was the perfect righteousness required by the law to be fulfilled? That question was another unanswered puzzle as far as Old Testament saints were concerned.

Both answers came in the incarnation of Christ: "What the law could not do in that it was weak through the flesh, God did by sending His own Son in the likeness of sinful flesh, on account of sin: He *condemned sin* in the flesh, *that the righteous requirement of the law might be fulfilled*" (Rom. 8:3–4).

The phrase "but now" in Romans 3:21 refers to the era that was inaugurated with the incarnation of Christ. This was literally the turning point of history and the pivotal juncture in God's plan of redemption. Galatians 4:4–5 describes it this way: "When *the fullness of the time* had come, God sent forth His Son, born of a woman, born under the law, to redeem those who were under the law."

Specifically, the birth of Christ was the portent of a new era of revelation in which the answers to Job's conundrum and all those related questions would become clear. Throughout Christ's earthly ministry and through the God-breathed words of the New Testament, the veil was lifted from these Old Testament mysteries. Many things that had always been shadowy and obscure were suddenly made clear. The writer of Hebrews stresses the superiority of New Testament revelation in his opening sentence: "God, who at various times and in various ways spoke in time past to the fathers by the prophets, has in these last days spoken to us by His Son" (1:1–2). Paul likewise acknowledges that "the mystery which [was] hidden from ages and from generations . . . has been revealed to His saints" (Col. 1:26). It "has now been revealed by the appearing of our Savior Jesus Christ" (2 Tim. 1:10).

"The righteousness of God"

"Now," in an unprecedented and marvelous way, "the righteousness of God *apart from the law* is revealed, being witnessed by the Law and the

Prophets" (Rom. 3:21). The expression "the Law and the Prophets" in a context like this is simply a common shorthand expression signifying the entire Old Testament canon. Who or what was foretold throughout the Old Testament?

The answer is clear. Paul is talking about Jesus Christ, who, of course, because He is God incarnate, embodies divine righteousness. The entire Old Testament bears Him witness (John 1:45; 5:39, 46).

Furthermore, having come to earth as a true man, born under the law, Jesus lived a sinless life, thus becoming the perfect embodiment of human righteousness as well. He (and He alone) is therefore perfectly suited to be a "Mediator" between God and men, our Great High Priest (1 Tim. 2:5). He is also uniquely qualified to offer Himself as a perfect sin offering—the spotless "Lamb of God who takes away the sin of the world" (John 1:29). Indeed, "this Man . . . offered one sacrifice for sins forever, . . . [and thus] by one offering He has perfected forever those who are being sanctified" (Heb. 10:12, 14).

How does Jesus Christ perfect those who believe in Him? Obviously, His death pays in full the penalty of their sin, thereby cleansing their guilt and erasing the debt. But in addition, His flawless righteousness—the only human righteousness that could ever stand alongside the perfect righteousness of God—is granted to believers by imputation.

"Through faith in Jesus Christ, to all and on all who believe"

This is the only possible solution to our sin. A righteousness must come down to us, a righteousness that is alien to us. "Rain down, you heavens, from above, and let the skies pour down righteousness; let the earth open, let them bring forth salvation, and let righteousness spring up together. I, the LORD, have created it" (Isa. 45:8).

This imputed righteousness is the sole ground of the sinner's justification. God accepts sinners not because of something good or praiseworthy He finds in them. Remember, "we are all like an unclean thing, and all our righteousnesses are like filthy rags" (Isa. 64:6). Our good works contribute nothing at all to our righteous standing. Once more: if your trust is in your own goodness, you are doomed (Luke 18:8). God accepts only absolute perfection, which does not exist in the human realm, except in Christ.

But here's the good news: true believers are united with Christ "through faith" (Eph. 3:17), and therefore they too are "in Christ" (Rom. 12:5; 1 Cor. 1:30). God accepts them and blesses them on that basis (Eph. 1:6). That is how He "justifies the ungodly" (Rom. 4:5). He credits them with a righteousness that is not their own—an alien righteousness, reckoned to their account.

Paul prominently features this truth in his own testimony. His heart's desire, he said, was to "be found in [Christ], not having my own righteousness, which is from the law, but that which is through faith in Christ, the righteousness which is *from God* by faith" (Phil. 3:9).

Notice what Paul is confessing: God Himself had to come to the rescue. He alone can save. The very One who gave the law that condemns us also supplies the righteousness needed to save us. And that is the only merit we need to have a right standing before Him.

This is "the light of the gospel of the glory of Christ" (2 Cor. 4:4). And it's the only way a person can be right with God.

FOUR

SOLA FIDE

Abraham believed in the LORD, and He accounted it to him for righteousness.

—GENESIS 15:6

Before leaving Romans 3, we need to get a bird's-eye view of the section where Paul explains the heart of his gospel: verses 21–26. This is a potent passage, and it is absolutely vital for an accurate understanding of the gospel according to Paul. But it's also a text that presents some formidable interpretive challenges. Here's the complete paragraph in one bite:

> But now the righteousness of God apart from the law is revealed, being witnessed by the Law and the Prophets, even the righteousness of God, through faith in Jesus Christ, to all and on all who believe. For there is no difference; for all have sinned and fall short of the glory of God, being justified freely by His grace through the redemption that is in Christ Jesus, whom God set forth as a propitiation by His blood, through faith, to demonstrate His righteousness, because in His forbearance God had passed over the sins that were previously committed, to demonstrate at the present time His righteousness, that He might be just and the justifier of the one who has faith in Jesus.

One of the distinctive features of Paul's writing style is the way he injects short excursive comments. Here, for example, immediately after introducing the gospel's good news ("Now the righteousness of God apart from the law is revealed"), he reverts straightaway to the bad news. He inserts a single-sentence digression that neatly reiterates, summarizes, and reemphasizes the vital point he has been carefully expounding for two and a half chapters: "For there is no difference; for all have sinned and fall short of the glory of God" (vv. 22–23). It's a brief interjection, deliberately added at the very point where Paul transitions into an explanation of why the gospel is truly good news. He wants to make sure readers don't quickly set aside the difficult truth that constitutes the gospel's essential starting point.

Once we realize that sentence is a rhetorical digression—just an abbreviated recap of Paul's first point—the text's inspired logic becomes crystal clear. It turns out the truth in this passage is both simple and profound. Here is the gist of it: *Because "the righteousness of God apart from the law" is imputed to "all who believe," they are "justified freely by His grace through the redemption that is in Christ Jesus."*

That is the doctrine of justification by faith—the core and touchstone of the gospel according to Paul. Although he considered himself "the least of the apostles" (1 Cor. 15:9), it is significant that among all the New Testament writers, Paul was the chief one the Holy Spirit used to proclaim this principle clearly, expound it thoroughly, and defend it fiercely when the gospel came under attack from false teachers and legalists. The proliferation of so many false teachers and gospel-denying doctrines in the earliest years of church history is remarkable, and it shows how determined the Devil is to sow tares among the wheat (Matt. 13:24–30).

"NOT BY WORKS OF RIGHTEOUSNESS"

Paul presents in Romans 3:21–26 the definitive feature of his teaching on the gospel. He restates it succinctly a few verses later with these words:

"God imputes righteousness apart from works" (4:6). This is the principle the Reformers labeled *sola fide* (Latin for "faith alone").

Faith as the sole instrument of justification is a doctrine the Roman Catholic Church has formally and emphatically anathematized since the Council of Trent in the mid-sixteenth century.* Apologists for the Roman position often claim they can't find this doctrine anywhere in Scripture.

But here it is in plain terms. In fact, it's the first point Paul makes as he shifts from the bad news about the human predicament to the gospel's good news: for those "who *believe*," God Himself supplies all the righteousness necessary for their justification (Rom. 3:22).

Critics of *sola fide* are fond of pointing out that Paul doesn't use the precise words "faith alone." But there's no escaping his meaning; the immediate context makes it plain. Remember that final, devastating point in Paul's lengthy discourse on sin: "By the deeds of the law no flesh will be justified in His sight, for by the law is the knowledge of sin" (v. 20). In other words, works are worthless for justification. Paul's very next statement is that "the righteousness of God, through faith in Jesus Christ, [is granted] to all and on all who believe" (v. 22). That is a clear affirmation of the principle of *sola fide.*

Most Roman Catholic theologians (and a fairly recent strain of nominal Protestants** who reject the principle of *sola fide*) have claimed that when Paul speaks of "the deeds of the law," he means only the formal rituals and

* Canon IX, from the Sixth Session of the Council of Trent, declares, "If any one saith, that by faith alone the impious is justified; in such wise as to mean, that nothing else is required to co-operate in order to the obtaining the grace of Justification, and that it is not in any way necessary, that he be prepared and disposed by the movement of his own will; let him be anathema." Philip Schaff, ed., *The Creeds of Christendom,* 3 vols. (New York: Harper, 1877), 2:112.

** The three leading representatives of the so-called New Perspective on Paul—E. P. Sanders, James D. G. Dunn, and N. T. Wright—are all ecumenists who self-identify as Protestants, and over the past two decades their views (Wright's opinions in particular) have gained considerable influence among American evangelicals. One of the central tenets of their hypothesis is a vigorous denial that the apostle Paul's teaching on justification by faith bore any resemblance to the Reformation principle of *sola fide.* This was the material principle of the Protestant Reformation—the very doctrine all the fuss was originally about. The Reformers and their evangelical heirs have always defended this principle fiercely. Advocates of the New Perspective either downplay or deny it. Indeed, the most controversial aspect of New Perspective teaching has been that movement's redefinition of the doctrine of justification—an innovation that seems to be driven mainly by the ecumenical impulse.

other ceremonial features of the law—circumcision, rules governing ceremonial cleanness, and such.* But Paul's use of this phrase simply cannot be narrowed down that way, in a heretical effort to give sinners some credit for their salvation.

In Romans 7, for example, when Paul wanted to illustrate the law's utter inability to justify sinners, the one precept he chose to single out as an example is the tenth commandment: "You shall not covet" (v. 7; cf. Ex. 20:17). Coveting is arguably the least of all the sins named in the Decalogue. It deals with desire. Resisting or committing that sin is not something that entails any kind of action. So when Paul speaks of "the deeds of the law," he is using that expression in the broadest possible sense. His meaning cannot be limited to the rituals and ceremonial features of the law. Quite the contrary: the expression "deeds of the law" as Paul consistently employs it would include any thought, action, or attitude that aims to gain God's approval through a show of obedience to the Old Testament's 613 commandments. No matter how rigorously the sinner tries to follow the law, seeking justification before God that way is a futile exercise.

Scripture is perfectly clear on this. No good work of any kind contributes anything meritorious to the sinner's justification before God. All human righteousness (other than the perfect righteousness of Christ incarnate) is a product of fallen flesh and is therefore fatally flawed. Yet again: "We are all like an unclean thing, and all our righteousnesses are like filthy rags" (Isa. 64:6).

By this point in his epistle to the Romans Paul has repeatedly stressed that truth, and he will continue to bring it up. Immediately after the passage we are examining, Paul argues that justification by faith leaves no one with any ground for personal pride—and he expressly contrasts *works*

* N. T. Wright, for example, insists that when Paul speaks of "works of the law," these "are not . . . the moral 'good works' which the Reformation tradition loves to hate. They are the things that divide Jew from Gentile." *Justification: God's Plan & Paul's Vision* (Downer's Grove: InterVarsity, 2009), 117. Wright insists that for Paul, justification is an ecumenical principle, and it is not about personal salvation at all. Much less is Paul trying to refute the idea of salvation by works of righteousness. Wright says, "This way of reading Romans has systematically done violence to that text for hundreds of years, and . . . it is time for the text itself to be heard again. . . . Paul may or may not agree with Augustine, Luther, or anyone else about how people come to a personal knowledge of God in Christ; but he does not use the language of 'justification' to denote this event or process." *What Saint Paul Really Said* (Grand Rapids: Eerdmans, 1997), 117.

with *faith*: "Boasting . . . is excluded. By what law? Of works? No, but by the law of faith" (Rom. 3:27). Then he reiterates the central point: "We conclude that a man is justified by faith apart from the deeds of the law" (v. 28). Though he might not use the precise expression "faith alone," he is plainly defending the principle of *sola fide.* He makes the same point again in Romans 4:5: "To him who *does not work but believes* . . . his faith is accounted for righteousness." That is as clear a statement of *sola fide* as any of the Protestant Reformers ever affirmed.

So it's remarkable that anyone would believe a sinner's own works can play a role in his or her justification—but the iron grip of humanity's predisposition for self-justification is powerful and hard to break. That's why, as we noted in chapters 2 and 3, all the major world religions (including Roman Catholicism) insist that some measure of justifying righteousness or divine approval must be merited by a person's own good works.

Paul powerfully argues otherwise. Indeed, for Paul, this is virtually the distilled essence of gospel truth: "Not by works of righteousness which we have done, but according to His mercy He saved us" (Titus 3:5).

Despite all the papal anathemas and dubious works of ecumenical scholarship that have joined forces against the principle of *sola fide,* there's simply no legitimate way around the plain fact that this is the most distinctive feature of the gospel according to Paul: "If by grace, then it is no longer of works; otherwise grace is no longer grace. But if it is of works, it is no longer grace; otherwise work is no longer work" (Rom. 11:6). Any religion that tells people they can earn merit for a right standing before God is teaching a false gospel. And those who corrupt the truth in that way only seal their own damnation (Gal. 1:8–9).

JUST BY FAITH

By now the monumental importance of justification by faith and the prominent role this doctrine plays in Paul's teaching about the gospel should be obvious. The whole substance of Paul's epistle to the Romans is a systematic explanation of the gospel and its implications. The justification of sinners dominates the discussion from start to finish. In other epistles too—in every context where Paul undertakes to explain or defend the gospel—he always focuses on this doctrine. That's because every major attack on the true gospel ultimately either subtly undermines or overtly attacks the principle of justification by faith alone. It's a truth that has always been firmly denied by legalists and sacramentalists of every variety—from the original false teachers who were troubling the churches of Galatia to the Roman Catholic Church and Protestant liberalism of today. It is blown out of shape by antinomians. It is often attacked in the academic realm by proud scholars who have an insatiable appetite for novelty and hold every expression of orthodoxy in high contempt. It is targeted by virtually every pseudo-Christian cult. And it is sadly neglected by most in the mainstream of today's evangelical movement.

But for Paul, this was the gospel's capital doctrine: "We maintain that a man is justified by faith apart from works" (Rom. 3:28 NASB). The original Protestant Reformers and all their true spiritual heirs likewise would say that among all the cardinal precepts of Christianity, none is more important than the doctrine of justification by faith. It's what Martin Luther was referring to when he wrote, "If this article stands, the church stands; if this article collapses, the church collapses."* Luther also said, "One cannot go soft or give way on this article, for then heaven and earth would fall."[1] John Calvin called the doctrine of justification "the principal ground on which religion must be supported."[2]

Simply defined, the biblical doctrine of justification teaches that God graciously declares believing sinners perfectly righteous for Christ's sake. He not only forgives their sins, but He also imputes to them the full merit of Christ's unblemished righteousness. They therefore gain a right standing with God, not because of any good thing they have done (or will do), but solely because of Christ's work on their behalf.

The Westminster Confession of Faith was ratified by the Westminster

* "Quia isto articulo stante stat Ecclesia, ruente ruit Ecclesia." From the Weimar edition of Martin Luther's works 40/III.352.1–3.

Assembly in 1646 and has stood ever since as the most important and most influential of all the classic Protestant confessions. It explains this vital doctrine in similar terms:

> Those whom God effectually calleth he also freely justifieth; not by infusing righteousness into them, but by pardoning their sins, and by accounting and accepting their persons as righteous: not for any thing wrought in them, or done by them, but for Christ's sake alone: nor by imputing faith itself, the act of believing, or any other evangelical obedience to them, as their righteousness; but by imputing the obedience and satisfaction of Christ unto them, they receiving and resting on him and his righteousness by faith; which faith they have not of themselves, it is the gift of God.[3]

That is precisely what Paul means when he says sinners are "justified freely by [God's] grace" (Rom. 3:24). As always with Paul, the stress is on the gospel's lavish grace. Justification is a gift, not a wage or a reward.

Therefore, every lesson we can legitimately learn from biblical soteriology points to the glory of God, not the self-esteem of the sinner. The paragraph we are concerned with here in Romans 3 gives four ways the justification of sinners—by grace alone through faith alone—extols the glory of God.

JUSTIFICATION DEMONSTRATES GOD'S RIGHTEOUSNESS

All creation declares the glory of God in "His eternal power and Godhead" (Rom. 1:20). In other words, "what may be known of God" by way of His omnipotent greatness and deity is obvious from the testimony of nature alone to anyone whose conscience is not totally seared, "for God has shown it to them" (v. 19).

But what of His perfect righteousness? It's true that the basics of moral law are inscribed on the human heart, so some sense of divine righteousness is intrinsic in the human consciousness (Rom. 2:14–15). But nature alone cannot even begin to convey the depth and richness of divine righteousness—including not only God's fierce hatred of evil but also His love of mercy and grace. Those truths were partially revealed in the Old Testament scriptures, of course, but (as we noted in the previous chapter) much remained shrouded in mystery under the dispensation of law.

"But now the righteousness of God apart from the law is revealed," Paul says (Rom. 3:21). The gospel uniquely puts God's righteousness on display in a way that erases all the mystery that remained under the law. It sounds strangely paradoxical on several levels, but God best demonstrates His own righteousness by declaring sinners righteous.

The New Testament verb translated "to justify" is the Greek word *dikaioç*, meaning precisely that: "to declare righteous," or "to justify." Words derived from the same root include the noun *dikaiosunē* ("righteousness" or "justification") and the adjective *dikaios* ("just" and "righteous"). Those terms pepper all the Pauline discussions of the gospel, and Romans 3 is thick with them. The verb form has obvious forensic, or legal, overtones. It signifies a formal decree, as when a judge in the courtroom pronounces a "not guilty" verdict.

As we have seen, the believing sinner is declared righteous because of the alien righteousness that is imputed by divine reckoning. The sinner's own good deeds are counted as worthless rubbish (Phil. 3:7–8). So nothing about justification exalts the sinner. "Christ Jesus . . . became for us wisdom from God—and righteousness and sanctification and redemption—that, as it is written, 'He who glories, let him glory in the LORD'" (1 Cor. 1:29–31). In short, "boasting . . . is excluded" (Rom. 3:27).

Meanwhile, God's righteousness is gloriously put on display in the act, demonstrating an aspect of divine righteousness the law could never reveal (v. 21). In this way, the Lord Himself gets all the glory in our salvation. We owe it all to His righteousness, not our good works. As redeemed sinners, "we are His workmanship, created in Christ Jesus for good works, which God prepared beforehand that we should walk in them" (Eph. 2:10).

JUSTIFICATION MAGNIFIES GOD'S GRACE

The justification of sinners furthermore exalts God "to the praise of the glory of His grace" (Eph. 1:6).

Again, whenever Paul deals with the gospel, there is always a heavy emphasis on divine grace. Here in Romans 3, he makes the point that while all of us fall far short of the glory of God, those who turn to Him in faith are "justified freely by His grace" (v. 24). The term *grace* usually denotes God's favor, but it is a multifaceted word with a depth of meaning that is hard to convey in any single English word. The word in the Greek text is *charis*, sometimes translated "favor" (Luke 1:30; 2:52; Acts 7:46). It can also denote a gift or a benefit. It has connotations of well-meant kindness, delight, and mercy. Normally in the New Testament (and in standard, technical, theological usage) the word draws from all those shades of meaning and signifies the merciful favor of God, freely given to believing sinners who in reality deserve nothing but wrath and righteous retribution.

There's a dynamic aspect of grace too, as we shall observe in future chapters. Grace trains and empowers us to "live soberly, righteously, and godly" (Titus 2:12; see also Phil. 2:13). Elsewhere I have spoken of grace as "the free and benevolent influence of a holy God operating sovereignly in the lives of undeserving sinners."[4]

In Romans 3:24, Paul adds the adverb *freely*, so the clear stress is on the fact that God's favor is completely unmerited by the redeemed sinner. Reject the principle of *sola fide*, and in effect you have denied that sinners are "justified *freely*." Reject the principle of *sola fide*, and you have no option other than to seek justification by works. The result is devastating. Those who do that are "estranged from Christ . . . fallen from grace" (Gal. 5:4).

To put it in the plainest possible language, the idea that a sinner's own works can contribute anything meritorious for justification is an arrogant and devilish notion. It's not merely errant doctrine; it is anti-Christian and gospel-nullifying. Such a belief demeans the grace of God and illegitimately exalts the sinner. Its fruit is damnation rather than justification (Gal. 1:8–9). That was Paul's main point in his epistle to the Galatians: "I do not set aside the grace of God; for if righteousness comes through the law, then Christ died in vain" (2:21).

Grace is the whole reason, in a single word, why the gospel is such good news. Here, also, is why Paul devoted so much space to the indictment "charg[ing] both Jews and Greeks that they are all under sin" (Rom. 3:9). It was not because he took some perverse delight in belaboring the bad news. But that long discourse on sin and human depravity establishes a pitch-black backdrop against which the glory of the gospel shines with infinite brightness.

Moreover, the hopeless reality of sin is what forces believers to turn to the grace of God as their only hope (cf. Luke 18:13–14). "The Scripture has confined all under sin, that the promise by faith in Jesus Christ might be given to those who believe" (Gal. 3:22). Thus the grace of God is magnified.

Of course, God's willingness to forgive, His lovingkindness, and His mercy to those who repent were major themes in the Old Testament as well, but it is the gospel that puts every facet of divine grace in close, sharp focus, as under a powerful magnifying glass, and unveils its glory in a whole new light.

Remember, in the Old Testament, it wasn't clear how a just God could justify sinners. In the previous chapter, you'll recall, we considered some questions suggested by Job's predicament. The question voiced by Job himself in Job 9:2 ("But how can a man be righteous before God?") is clearly and definitively answered by the forgiveness of sin and the imputation of divine righteousness.

So is the answer to the other side of the question the same? *If justice demands vengeance against sin, how can a just God justify the ungodly?* How can *God* be righteous if He justifies us? As glorious as God's grace appears, is it truly righteous? If it is an abomination to condemn the just or justify the wicked, does the justification of sinners violate God's own law?

We considered those questions in chapters 1 and 3. They come up frequently in Paul's teaching about the gospel because they were very much at the heart of what mystified him as an unregenerate Pharisee, when he was struggling to earn God's favor by obeying the law's demands for himself. And the answer to those questions clearly delighted and amazed him as a believer. Paul's own conversion brought him to the profound discovery that all those questions are thoroughly and satisfactorily answered by the doctrine of justification.

JUSTIFICATION VINDICATES GOD'S JUSTICE

As we've mentioned previously, Paul was not the only student of the Old Testament who struggled with the question of how God could pass over the sins of His saints, pardoning guilty souls and covering their misdeeds with lavish forgiveness, without compromising or diminishing His own righteousness. One of the distinguishing characteristics of Scripture is its utter lack of any qualms or camouflage when it comes to reporting the transgressions of its own heroes. The sins of the saints are recounted as frankly as their virtues. And all of them were sinners. With very few exceptions, we are told about specific sins committed by practically every major character in the Old Testament.

And many of them were egregious sinners. Even the great Hall of Faith in Hebrews 11 is well salted with people who were guilty of gross acts of shocking unrighteousness. Moses murdered an Egyptian (Ex. 2:12). Rahab made her living as a harlot (Josh. 2:1). Samson (not to mention most of the other judges) frequently let fleshly lusts get the better of him and nearly lost his usefulness completely because of his foolish behavior (Judg. 16). David committed adultery with Bathsheba and had her husband, Uriah, killed (2 Sam. 11:15). If "God is a just judge . . . [who] is angry with the wicked every day," how could He pass over the willful moral failures of these people (Ps. 7:11)?

Furthermore, it is evident that the Lord sometimes permits believing people who live basically righteous lives to suffer while wicked unbelievers prosper. The prophet Habakkuk pointed out this conundrum with great passion: "You are of purer eyes than to behold evil, and cannot look on wickedness. Why do You look on those who deal treacherously, and hold Your tongue when the wicked devours a person more righteous than he?" (Hab. 1:13). Even unbelievers in Malachi's time noticed the apparent inequity, saying, "'Everyone who does evil is good in the sight of the LORD, and He delights in them,' or, 'Where is the God of justice?'" (Mal. 2:17).

Hebrews 11 likewise acknowledges that those who would seem to be most deserving of God's blessing often get trouble and persecution instead. After all, many of the most faithful people in Scripture

> were tortured, not accepting deliverance, that they might obtain a better resurrection. Still others had trial of mockings and scourgings, yes, and of chains and imprisonment. They were stoned, they were sawn in two, were tempted, were slain with the sword. They wandered about in sheepskins and goatskins, being destitute, afflicted, tormented. . . . They wandered in deserts and mountains, in dens and caves of the earth.
>
> And all these, having obtained a good testimony through faith, did not receive the promise. (vv. 35–39)

Those facts raised serious questions, even in the minds of the faithful, about how God would finally balance the scales of justice. The prevailing expectation was that when Messiah came, He would conquer the evildoers and establish a kingdom where He would rule in perfect righteousness. Everything wrong would be made right.

That is why when Christ appeared and people began to realize that He had all the right credentials, they were prepared to "take Him by force to make Him king" (John 6:15). After all, He had demonstrated His absolute power to heal the sick, raise the dead, cast out demons, feed the multitudes, and silence His enemies. And He embodied true righteousness. It's no wonder Peter and the disciples simply could not fathom that He would "be delivered into the hands of sinful men, and be crucified" (Luke 24:7).

The crucifixion of Christ was the most evil act ever carried out by the hands of lawless men: the unjust murder of God's own sinless Son—the very One of whom God Himself had testified, "This is My beloved Son, in whom I am well pleased" (Matt. 3:17). Here was a truly innocent victim suffering unfathomable pain, unbearable indignities, unwarranted mockery, and a totally undeserved death. Death, after all, is the "wages" of sin; but Christ was "holy, harmless, undefiled, separate from sinners" (Rom. 6:23; Heb. 7:26).

And yet this very act put the righteousness of God on display more vividly than if God had sent a catastrophe that wiped all evil from the face of the earth forever.

How? Why?

Paul sums up the answer in a few familiar words: Christ made "*propitiation* by His blood" (Rom. 3:25). Remember our discussion of that word in chapter 1. It speaks of an appeasement offered to placate the wrath of an offended deity. Christ's death on the cross was the payment of a penalty that fully satisfied the wrath and righteousness of God, and that is what makes it possible for believing sinners to be justified apart from any merit of their own.

The mere mention of the word *propitiation* will provoke a fierce argument in some circles. This doctrine comprises all the major factors that make the cross of Christ "a stone of stumbling and a rock of offense" (Rom. 9:33; 1 Cor. 1:23). Liberal theologians absolutely despise the concept. Anyone whose thinking is shaped by humanism rather than Scripture will balk at it. Indeed, one of the first principles to be categorically rejected by virtually everyone who denies the authority of Scripture is Hebrews 9:22: "Without shedding of blood there is no forgiveness" (NASB).

Candidly, it's not hard to see the difficulties this truth poses for anyone lacking an understanding of (and commitment to) the biblical doctrine of atonement. The idea of appeasing an angry deity was a prominent feature in most ancient Middle Eastern pagan religions. And the means of appeasement were often monstrous. Those who worshiped Molech, you'll remember, believed they needed to appease their god by the sacrifice of live infants on an altar of fire. Scripture repeatedly condemns that kind of superstition. The Old Testament also goes to great lengths to differentiate the character of the true God from the ruthless savagery and temperamental capriciousness of the Philistine and other pagan deities.

It is nevertheless a fact that blood sacrifices were both essential and prominent in Old Testament Judaism. "According to the law almost all things are purified with blood" (Heb. 9:22). That is not because God Himself is bloodthirsty, full of rage, or reluctant to forgive. On the contrary, the Old Testament continually stresses His willingness to forgive: "The LORD is gracious and full of compassion, slow to anger and great in mercy. The LORD is good to all, and His tender mercies are over all His works" (Ps. 145:8–9). Even on Sinai, as the Lord prepared to inscribe the stone tablets with His law and formalize the covenant, "The LORD passed before [Moses] and proclaimed, 'The LORD, the LORD God, merciful and gracious, longsuffering, and abounding in goodness and truth, keeping mercy for thousands, forgiving iniquity and transgression and sin' " (Ex. 34:6–7).

So the reason a propitiation is necessary is clearly not to make God willing to forgive. He is no enraged deity needing something to calm Him. His wrath against sin is a judicial loathing of all evil; it is not a bad mood He needs to be coaxed out of. The "satisfaction" offered in the atonement is a payment of the legal penalty of sin. It eliminates the sinner's debt to justice and therefore removes every obstacle to forgiveness. It means God can be favorably disposed to the sinner without compromising His own righteousness or overturning the demands of His law. It is in that sense that His wrath against sin is turned away. That is how, as our passage says, Christ's work of propitiation demonstrates God's righteousness, so "that He might be just and the justifier of the one who has faith in Jesus" (Rom. 3:26).

That in turn answers the lingering question of how and why a perfectly righteous God "in His forbearance . . . passed over the sins that were previously committed" (v. 25).

The sins passed over in the Old Testament included not only the transgressions of the elect (which were forgiven), but also most of the evils committed by wicked people, which God "endured with much longsuffering" (Rom. 9:22). As Paul explained to the philosophers of Athens, God overlooked the "times of ignorance" (Acts 17:30). "He, being full of compassion, forgave their iniquity, and did not destroy them. Yes, many a time He turned His anger away, and did not stir up all His wrath; for He remembered that they were but flesh, a breath that passes away and does not come again" (Ps. 78:38–39). He delayed His judgment against the wicked. He forgave the sins of the faithful. He manifested great mercy and longsuffering, even when it wasn't clear how a truly righteous Judge could be so lenient.

But now ("at the present time") God's righteousness has been clearly demonstrated "through the redemption that is in Christ Jesus" (Rom. 3:24). Paul is making the point that Christ's crucifixion shows us that God's patience ("pass[ing] over the sins that were previously committed") was always rooted in legal justice, because He Himself had foreordained the plan by which full atonement for sin would be secured through the propitiatory sacrifice of Christ. This is the ground of saving grace for all the elect, from Adam to the last soul redeemed. It is even the basis of common grace for the reprobate—the whole reason God's judgments are so often delayed.

Notice carefully what Paul is saying: "God set forth [His own Son] as a propitiation by His blood" (Rom. 3:25). The sacrifice Christ rendered was not only offered *to* God; it was initiated *by* Him as well. "In this the love of God was manifested toward us, that *God has sent His only begotten Son into the world*, that we might live through Him. . . . He loved us and *sent His Son to be the propitiation for our sins*" (1 John 4:9–10). Far from needing to mollify an irate and reluctant deity, we are saved entirely at God's loving initiative. The cross embodies and illustrates His eagerness to forgive (even at infinite cost to the Godhead). It also puts on display the holiness that moved Him to secure an atonement for our sin that would make it possible for Him to maintain His justice while justifying sinners (to "be [both] just and the justifier of the one who has faith in Jesus" [Rom. 3:26]).

Thus the righteousness of God is fully vindicated. "Mercy and truth have met together; righteousness and peace have kissed" (Ps. 85:10). God is both supremely gracious and supremely just. That's the denouement of *propitiation* in Christian doctrine.

JUSTIFICATION UPHOLDS GOD'S LAW

It's important for believers not to evade, gloss over, or attempt to explain away the biblical principle of propitiation, even though it is one of the major reasons the cross constitutes a stumbling block to so many. Most people (including, I fear, many who self-identify as Christians) speak of God's forgiveness as an unconditional, no-strings-attached amnesty in which God simply ignores or abrogates the demands of His own law. *If God is willing to forgive,* they reason, *no atonement should be needed.* They think pardon and payment are incompatible concepts; sins can either be forgiven or atoned for, but not both.

That may sound reasonable to someone's intuitive sense of justice, but it is a patently unbiblical notion. It is a flat contradiction of everything Scripture teaches about atonement, as distilled in Hebrews 9:22: "Without the shedding of blood there is no forgiveness of sins" (ESV).

Forgiveness without atonement would require the total annulment of God's law. As we've just discussed, the atoning work of Christ makes full and free forgiveness possible in a way that upholds and even establishes the law of God. Romans 3 closes with the apostle Paul making that very point: "Do we then make void the law through faith? Certainly not! On the contrary, we establish the law" (Rom. 3:31).

I hope you can see why (to paraphrase Calvin) justification by faith is the principal hinge of all religion—and the central theme of Paul's gospel. This one doctrine brings together and brightly illuminates all the major features of gospel truth—God's righteousness, His grace, His justice, and His law. It demonstrates His righteousness; it reconciles His mercy with His wrath against sin; and it provides full and free forgiveness while perfectly fulfilling the demands of God's law. Every facet of this truth prompts profound awe and adoration.

I love what the crucifixion of Christ accomplished for sinners. But it is even more profound and thrilling to consider all that the cross accomplished from God's perspective—in its expression of His love, the demonstration of His righteousness, the magnification of His grace, the vindication of His justice, and the upholding of His law. This is the gospel according to Paul.

FIVE

THE GREAT EXCHANGE

What does the Scripture say? "Abraham believed God, and it was accounted to him for righteousness." . . . Now it was not written for his sake alone that it was imputed to him, but also for us. It shall be imputed to us who believe in Him who raised up Jesus our Lord from the dead, who was delivered up because of our offenses, and was raised because of our justification.

—ROMANS 4:3, 23–25

In the opening words of Paul's first epistle to the Corinthians, he wrote, "Christ did not send me to baptize, but *to preach the gospel*" (v. 17). Just a few verses later, he wrote, "We preach *Christ crucified*" (v. 23). Then a paragraph or two after that, he wrote again, "I determined not to know anything among you except *Jesus Christ and Him crucified*" (2:2).

Thus Paul neatly summarized the gist of the gospel: it is a declaration about the atoning work of Christ.

In the preaching of Christ and the apostles, the gospel was always punctuated by a clarion call to repentant faith. But it is not merely a summons to good behavior. It's not a liturgy of religious ceremonies and sacraments. It's not a plea for self-esteem and human dignity. It's not a manifesto for culture warriors or a rallying cry for political zealots. It's not a mandate for earthly dominion. It's not a sophisticated moral philosophy seeking to win admiration and approval from the world's intellectual elite, or a lecture about the evils of cultural and racial division. It's not an appeal for "social justice." It's not a dissertation on gender issues or a prescription for "redeeming culture." It's not the kind of naive, indiscriminate congeniality that is content to sing "Kumbaya" to the rest of the world.

Within the past half decade I have seen every one of those ideas touted as "the gospel" in various books, blogs, and sermons. They are all deviations or distractions from the true gospel as proclaimed by Paul.

The cross of Jesus Christ is the sum and the focus of the gospel according to Paul: "We preach Christ crucified" (1 Cor. 1:23). "God forbid that I should boast except in the cross of our Lord Jesus Christ" (Gal. 6:14). And in Pauline theology, the cross is a symbol of atonement. "Christ crucified" is a message about redemption for sinners.

How vital is that truth, and how crucial for the messenger to stay on point? To make the gospel about anything else is to depart from biblical Christianity. Paul's teaching is not the least bit ambiguous about this. It's the very definition of what he meant when he spoke of "my gospel." Quite simply, *the gospel is good news for fallen humanity regarding how sins are atoned for, how sinners are forgiven, and how believers are made right with God.*

THE OFFENSE OF THE CROSS

That may not sound very elegant or fashionable. It is certainly not a message suited to appeal to the frivolous fads or cultural concerns of the present age. But our Lord did not commission His disciples to proclaim a pliable message that would need to be overhauled every generation. And the mission of the church is not to win the world's admiration.

Many of today's best-known evangelical strategists and the leading practitioners of "missional" methodology seem not to grasp that simple point. They constantly encourage young evangelicals to "engage the culture" and defer to the rules of political correctness. When they translate that counsel into concrete, practical plans of action, it often turns out to mean little more than trying to stay in step with fashion—as if being perceived as cool were the key to effective ministry.*

You won't find anything like that in Paul's exhortations to young ministers. On the contrary, as we've discussed, Paul candidly acknowledges that the gospel is "a stumbling block to Jews and folly to Gentiles" (1 Cor. 1:23 ESV). Indeed, "the message of the cross is *foolishness* to those who are perishing, but to us who are being saved it is the power of God" (v. 18). Therefore, he says, "We preach Christ crucified" (v. 23).

What, precisely, is "the message of the cross"? How did Christ's death make atonement for sin? Bad theologians for generations have assaulted the correct answer to that question. Several competing "theories of the atonement" have been proposed.**

For the record, I despise the weak word *theory* in this connection, because the Bible presents the doctrine of atonement in terms that are anything but optional or conjectural. As we have noted, the imagery of atonement in Scripture is both vivid and violent. "One may almost say, all things are cleansed with blood" (Heb. 9:22 NASB). The New Testament repeatedly tells us that all the bloody pageantry of those Old Testament animal sacrifices symbolized and foreshadowed the work of Christ on the cross. "Every priest stands ministering daily and offering repeatedly the same sacrifices, which can never take away sins. But this Man, [Jesus,] after

* Here's a typical example: An article at the *Christian Post* website describes "a New Jersey megachurch's latest effort to better engage with culture by embracing some of pop culture's most popular songs. . . . Liquid Church is using songs like Adele's 'Rolling in the Deep' and Bruno Mars' 'Grenade' as part of its 'Pop God' sermon series." Brittany Smith, "Secular Music in the Church Endangers Sacredness?" Christianpost.com, February 15, 2012, http://www.christianpost.com/news/secular-music-in-the-church-endangers-sacredness-69590/. That is by no means novel or unusual. Sermon series based on the latest movies (or other themes borrowed from pop culture) are commonplace today. Indeed, judging from what gets the most publicity and promotion in evangelical circles, it seems shallow homilies dealing with cultural artifacts vastly outnumber serious sermons featuring biblical exposition. Churches that base their ministries on whatever is trendy are not "redeeming" or "engaging" culture, they are absorbing its fashions and values.

** See appendix 1 in the present volume. Also, appendix 1, "How Are We to Understand the Atonement?" in John MacArthur, *The Freedom and Power of Forgiveness* (Wheaton: Crossway, 1998), 193–204.

He had offered one sacrifice for sins forever, sat down at the right hand of God" (Heb. 10:11–12). "You were not redeemed with corruptible things, like silver or gold, . . . but with the precious blood of Christ, as of a lamb without blemish and without spot" (1 Peter 1:18–19).

Those texts (and others like them) are clear. Christ's death purchased atonement for His people's sins. But the connotations of blood atonement are grossly offensive to the genteel sensitivities of those who fancy themselves more refined than Scripture. (It is the same squeamish attitude that causes "progressive" minds to shudder at the term *propitiation.*) Several writers and theologians have therefore proposed spurious theories of the atonement. Most of them deliberately attempt to eliminate, as much as possible, the offense of the cross. All of them offer some kind of false alternative to the truth that Christ's death was an offering to God meant to satisfy and placate His righteous anger against sin.

What are these aberrant theories?* There's the *moral influence theory*—the belief that Christ's death was merely an example of personal sacrifice and self-giving love and not at all the payment of a redemption price. This is the view most theological liberals hold. For reasons that should be obvious, their perspective on the atonement inevitably breeds works-oriented religion. If Christ's work is merely a model to follow, and not a substitutionary sacrifice, salvation must somehow be earned through one's own effort.

The *ransom theory* (a belief that was common in the post-apostolic era in the first century) is the notion that Christ's death was a ransom paid to Satan for the souls of the faithful. There's no biblical warrant for such a view, of course. It was originally based on a misunderstanding of the biblical term *ransom*, which simply means "redemption price." But this view fails to take into account all the biblical data. Scripture makes abundantly clear that Christ's death on the cross was "an offering and a sacrifice *to God*" (Eph. 5:2; cf. Heb. 9:14).

The *governmental theory* was proposed by Hugo Grotius, a Dutch legal

* For a more in-depth overview of various theories of the atonement and the history of opinion on these issues, I recommend Archibald Alexander Hodge, *The Atonement* (Philadelphia: Presbyterian Board of Publication, 1867).

expert from the early seventeenth century. He said the cross was not a ransom at all; it was merely a vivid symbolic display of God's wrath against sin—and therefore it stands as a public vindication of God's moral government. Grotius's view was adopted by American revivalist Charles Finney. It was shared by other leading New England theologians of the eighteenth and nineteenth centuries. And has been brought back into the limelight recently by a certain class of radical Arminians. They typically favor this view because it does away with the idea that Christ died as anyone's substitute—a truth they consider unjust (even though Scripture stresses the fact that Christ voluntarily took that role).

Another opinion that has been steadily gaining popularity for the past quarter century is the *Christus victor theory.* This idea is favored by many new-model theologians (including most of the architects of the now-failed Emerging Church movement).* In their view, Christ's death and resurrection signified nothing more than His triumph over all the foes of fallen humanity, including sin, death, the Devil, and especially the law of God. They want to scale down the significance of Christ's atoning work to a very narrow spectrum of what He actually accomplished. It is certainly true enough that Christ "wiped out the handwriting of requirements that was against us, which was contrary to us," and "disarmed principalities and powers" (Col. 2:14–15). But the theme of victory over the enemies of the human race simply doesn't do full justice to everything the Bible says about the cross. It's a man-centered and severely truncated view of the atonement.

Those who adopt the *Christus victor* theory favor triumphal language, and they eschew biblical terms like *sacrifice for sin* or *propitiation.* Most who hold this view would emphatically deny that Christ offered Himself to God on the cross. At the end of the day, this is just another unbiblical view that pretends to exalt and ennoble the love of God by overturning and eliminating the law's demand for justice.

All those theories attempt to sidestep the biblical principle of

* "[This] atonement theory in particular has exploded in popularity, in fact." Mark Galli, "The Problem with Christus Victor," *Christianity Today,* April 7, 2011. For an explanation and critique of the Emerging Church movement, see John MacArthur, *The Truth War* (Nashville: Nelson, 2007).

propitiation. Most of them do it on purpose, because they are rooted in a skewed view of divine love. People are drawn to these views by a common false assumption—namely, that God's mercy is fundamentally incompatible with His justice. They believe God will forego the demands of justice in order to forgive. They conclude that divine righteousness needs no satisfaction; God will simply set aside His own righteousness and erase whatever debt is owed to His justice because of sin. Given those faulty presuppositions, the death of Christ must then be explained in terms that avoid any suggestion of retributive justice.

The *doctrine of penal substitution* is the only view that incorporates the full range of biblical principles regarding atonement for sin. In chapter 1 of this book, near the end of a section dealing with the atonement, I used that expression one time, but I didn't pause at that point to explain the terminology. *Penal substitution* may sound like an arcane technical term, but it is actually quite simple. The word *penal* denotes punishment—a penalty that is inflicted because an offense has been committed. *Substitution* speaks of a replacement or a proxy. *Penal substitutionary atonement* is therefore a straightforward exchange wherein one person bears the penalty someone else deserves. Christ's death on the cross was a penal substitution. He bore the guilt and punishment for His people's sins.

This is not a "theory." It is the plain teaching of Scripture. In virtually every text where the New Testament writers mention the relevance of Christ's death, they prominently feature the language of substitutionary atonement. "Christ died for the ungodly" (Rom. 5:6). "While we were still sinners, Christ died for us" (v. 8). He "was delivered up for our trespasses and raised for our justification" (4:25 ESV). He "died for our sins according to the Scriptures" (1 Cor. 15:3). He "gave Himself for our sins" (Gal. 1:4). "In Him we have redemption through His blood, the forgiveness of sins" (Eph. 1:7). "Christ was offered once to bear the sins of many" (Heb. 9:28). He "bore our sins in His own body on the tree" (1 Peter 2:24). He "suffered once for sins, the just for the unjust, that He might bring us to God" (3:18). "He Himself is the propitiation for our sins" (1 John 2:2). "He laid down

His life for us" (3:16). "In this is love, not that we loved God, but that He loved us and sent His Son to be the propitiation for our sins" (4:10). All the New Testament writers agree on this: Christ was our sinless Substitute, and He died to pay the penalty for our sins.

A KEY PASSAGE ON PENAL SUBSTITUTION

One of my favorite gospel-oriented passages in the New Testament epistles is 2 Corinthians 5:18–21. Of all the places where Paul boils the gospel message down to a verse or two, few are more potent than the closing sentence of these verses:

> Now all things are of God, who has reconciled us to Himself through Jesus Christ, and has given us the ministry of reconciliation, that is, that God was in Christ reconciling the world to Himself, not imputing their trespasses to them, and has committed to us the word of reconciliation.
>
> Now then, we are ambassadors for Christ, as though God were pleading through us: we implore you on Christ's behalf, be reconciled to God. *For He made Him who knew no sin to be sin for us, that we might become the righteousness of God in Him.*

That emphasized verse explains how Paul viewed the atonement. It establishes the principle of penal substitution. It shows why the doctrine of justification is so crucial to a right understanding of the gospel. It reveals the source of the righteousness imputed to believers. And it helps clarify the significance of Christ's life as well as His death.

Reconciliation is obviously the key term in that passage. The word or one of its cognates is used five times in the span of three verses. This was the whole purpose for Christ's coming to earth: "to seek and to save that which was lost" (Luke 19:10); to "save His people from their sins" (Matt. 1:21). And the way this mission of salvation was accomplished is by *reconciling sinners to God.* This is not about paying a ransom to Satan. It is not about merely giving lost people new guidelines or a good example to emulate. The reference to "reconciliation" in this context has nothing to do with breaking down racial, ethnic, or religious barriers. It is about "God . . . in Christ reconciling the world to Himself" (2 Cor. 5:19).

The passage turns our attention again to a familiar truth. The dominant theme of this passage—and the proper keynote of the gospel itself—is a declaration about what God has done for sinners (not vice versa). God, in the Person of His incarnate Son, has intervened on behalf of sinful humanity to reverse our estrangement from Him. As Paul says elsewhere, "You, who once were alienated and enemies in your mind by wicked works, yet now He has reconciled in the body of His flesh through death" (Col. 1:21–22).

Paul is describing the atoning work of Christ.

In the process, he gives an ingeniously crisp summary of the gospel. It is a compact overview of evangelical principles, weighted differently from the longer, more systematic approach he took in Romans. But all the essential features of gospel truth are here—some implied and others expressly stated. The passage presupposes, for example, the problem of sin. We know that all humanity is fallen, lost, and at enmity with God, because we saw how meticulously Paul labored to establish that doctrine in Romans 1–3. Here the horrible truth of human depravity is implicit in the argument, so this time he doesn't devote any effort to proving it.

Also, we find here again some clear statements about the principle of imputation. The topic is first mentioned by name in verse 19, where Paul makes the point that the trespasses of those who have been reconciled to God are not imputed to them. (That's a clear echo of Psalm 32:2 and Romans 4:6–8.) And then in verse 21, he describes the positive imputation of the believer's sin to Christ and the reckoning of Christ's righteousness to the believer. Even though he doesn't employ any of the classic accounting terminology, everything Paul says in that verse clearly hinges on the principle of imputation. (We'll return to this point when we get to that part of the text.)

Consider now what stands out most clearly on the face of this passage.

THE WILL OF GOD

Remember what the dominant theme is in this section of Scripture: salvation is a creative work of God, not a do-it-yourself project for sinners. Second Corinthians 5:17 is a commonly quoted verse that illustrates this: "If anyone is in Christ, he is a new creation; old things have passed away; behold, all things have become new." The point of that statement should be clear: salvation is accomplished solely and sovereignly by God. Making "a new creation" by definition is something God does; it is not the fruit of the sinner's own self-reform. "We are *His* workmanship, created in Christ Jesus" (Eph. 2:10).

So Paul begins this passage on penal substitution by expressly underscoring that truth: "Now all things are of God, who has reconciled us to Himself" (2 Cor. 5:18). God is the One who reaches out, initiates, and accomplishes the redemption of fallen creatures who have set themselves at enmity against Him. Without God's sovereign intervention, no sinner could ever be saved. He does for them what they could never do for themselves.

Consider what this says about believers. All Christians are former adversaries of God who have been made right with Him. "When we were enemies we were reconciled to God" (Rom. 5:10). But our salvation is not our own doing. Redemption is not something we purchase for ourselves. Even our faith is a gift from God, not an independent, free-will choice we make on our own. "To you it has been granted on behalf of Christ . . . to believe in Him" (Phil. 1:29). God is the One who grants repentance to sinners, "so that they may know the truth" (2 Tim. 2:25). Paul therefore reminds those who have responded positively that even the faith that energizes their daily walk is a gracious gift from God: "It is God who works in you both to will and to do for His good pleasure" (Phil. 2:13).

Scripture always stresses the sovereignty of God in salvation. Believers are born again, "not of blood, nor of the will of the flesh, nor of the will of man, but of God" (John 1:13). "*Of His own will* He brought us forth by the word of truth, that we might be a kind of firstfruits of His creatures" (James 1:18). Jesus Himself repeatedly affirmed the sovereignty of God in salvation. He said the redeemed believe because they are elect, not vice versa.

To His disciples, He said, "You did not choose Me, but I chose you and appointed you" (John 15:16). To hardened unbelievers, He said, "You do not believe, because you are not of My sheep" (10:26). On the other hand, He said, "All that the Father gives Me will come to Me" (6:37).

No New Testament author emphasizes God's sovereignty more often or more clearly than the apostle Paul. It's one of his main talking points every time the subject of the gospel comes up. This is why he often starts with the subject of sin—to make the point that all men and women in their fallen state are "aliens from the commonwealth of Israel and strangers from the covenants of promise, having no hope and without God in the world" (Eph. 2:12). Unregenerate people are absolutely enslaved to sin (Rom. 6:20; John 8:34). They have trespassed against God and made themselves His enemies, and therefore they have absolutely no way of redeeming themselves. "The natural man does not receive the things of the Spirit of God, for they are foolishness to him; nor can he know them, because they are spiritually discerned" (1 Cor. 2:14).

If sinners are to be saved, it must therefore be by God alone, no thanks to their own efforts and totally apart from any merit of their own. "So then it is not of him who wills, nor of him who runs, but of God who shows mercy" (Rom. 9:16).

Even though Paul is fully aware that this is a doctrine sinners naturally tend to discount or deny, he doesn't hesitate to say it plainly. In fact, he stresses this truth at every opportunity. For Paul, the conviction that the salvation of sinners is entirely God's work, done in accord with His own sovereign will, is absolutely vital to a proper understanding of the gospel.

> We ourselves were also once foolish, disobedient, deceived, serving various lusts and pleasures, living in malice and envy, hateful and hating one another. But when the kindness and the love of God our Savior toward man appeared, *not by works of righteousness which we have done, but according to His mercy He saved us,* through the washing of regeneration and renewing of the Holy Spirit, whom He poured out on us abundantly through Jesus Christ our Savior. (Titus 3:3–6)

Never does Paul teach that salvation is a joint effort between God and the sinner. "Because the carnal mind is enmity against God; for it is not subject to the law of God, nor indeed can be. So then, those who are in the flesh cannot please God" (Rom. 8:7–8). Left to themselves, all sinners would continue indefinitely in their rebellion. The stubborn will and self-deceiving heart of a fallen creature has no capacity for self-reform. A sinner can no more reform his own heart than a leopard could change his spots or an Ethiopian alter his skin color (Jer. 13:23). Jesus Himself was emphatic about this: "No one can come to Me unless the Father who sent Me draws him" (John 6:44); "No one can come to Me unless it has been granted to him by My Father" (v. 65). God's will is the determinative factor in bringing sinners to Christ.

THE WORD OF RECONCILIATION

Nevertheless, the gospel message includes an open invitation—a general call to faith—that is extended indiscriminately to all who come under the sound of the message. In fact, Paul uses much stronger words than *call* or *invitation*. He says it is "as though God were *pleading* through us: we *implore* you on Christ's behalf, be reconciled to God" (2 Cor. 5:20).

The Greek word translated "pleading" is *parakaleo parakale?*. It speaks of an exhortation, admonishment, or entreaty. The word translated "implore" (*deomai*) is stronger yet. It has the connotation of begging. It is a common word in Scripture, often used to describe passionate prayer. It is the same word used by the father of a demon-possessed boy in Luke 9:38, pleading with Jesus for help: "Teacher, I *beg* You to look at my son" (NASB).

That is the proper tone of the gospel's invitation, what Paul refers to as "the word of reconciliation" (2 Cor. 5:19). This is how God commissions His ambassadors to preach: "We *beg* you on behalf of Christ, be reconciled to God" (v. 20 NASB). It is not a dispassionate suggestion, or even a stern command. It is an earnest, urgent plea extended with God's own authority, tenderly entreating the sinner to respond with repentant faith.

It is the duty of every believer to make this message known to the world. God "has given us the ministry of reconciliation" (v. 18). That is why it is crucial for Christians to understand the gospel correctly and be able to present it clearly and persuasively. God has commissioned us as His ambassadors not only to proclaim *the fact* "that God was in Christ reconciling the world to Himself, not imputing their trespasses to them" (v. 19); but also to be persistent with *the appeal* to "be reconciled to God" (v. 20). In this capacity we are "ambassadors for Christ," speaking "on Christ's behalf" and "as though God were pleading through us."

Don't miss the rich significance of the word *ambassadors*. An ambassador is an officially delegated emissary tasked with delivering a message on behalf of the government he represents. When he speaks, he does so with the full authority of the rightful head of state. He doesn't get to craft the message to suit his own (or his audience's) tastes and personality. He is not an editor or script doctor. He is given a message to convey, and he is not entitled to rewrite it, abridge it, amend it, or alter it in any way. He has no authority to omit parts of the message that might not be to his liking, and he can't dress it up with his own personal opinions. His task is to deliver the message exactly as it was given to him.

We have every reason to be faithful in fulfilling this vital and extremely urgent task. For one thing, the cross of Christ clearly demonstrates the gravity of divine judgment. "Knowing, therefore, the terror of the Lord, we persuade men" (2 Cor. 5:11). Furthermore, "the love of Christ compels us" (v. 14). No threat or hardship can dissuade us—not rejection, persecution, or the world's utter contempt. We must entreat sinners as persuasively as we can: "Be reconciled to God."

In the Greek text, the word translated "reconciliation" is *katallag*. Like its English counterpart, it signifies restored favor, goodwill, and friendly relations between two parties formerly at odds with one another. The Greek term was commonly used in financial transactions with a slightly different shade of meaning. In such contexts it signified an exchange—like the making of change. Every purchase involves such an exchange; in return for the money a customer gives a merchant, he receives whatever goods or services he is purchasing plus enough change to equal the value of his money. Thus with the completion of the transaction, the two parties were said to be reconciled. We use the English verb in a similar fashion to speak of reconciling accounts, such as when a checkbook register is balanced.

The exchange by which God reconciled sinners to Himself is remarkable. It involves a transaction no mere human mind ever would have conceived. Indeed, it runs counter to everything human intuition would normally think about how sinners might be reconciled with God. As we have seen repeatedly, the idea is not that the sinner purchases God's favor by good works (or by any other asset the sinner brings to the table). In fact, the sinner is on the sidelines while "God . . . *in Christ* reconcil[es] the world to Himself" (2 Cor. 5:19).

Of course, the guilt of sin must be dealt with and removed, because that is the cause of the sinner's alienation. And as we have seen, God does not forgive by sleight of hand. For the sake of His righteousness and the honor of His holy law, a real transaction involving actual punishment had to take place. Unless sin was dealt with, He could not righteously forego imputing trespasses to guilty sinners (cf. v. 19). The wages of sin—the death penalty—had to be administered (Rom. 6:23). God's holy nature required that His wrath against sin had to be fully satisfied.

It was such an awful price that no mere mortal would ever be able to pay it for himself. An eternity in hell is not enough for a sinner to erase his or her own debt. Therefore, the infinitely holy Son of God voluntarily took the place of sinners and paid that infinite price on their behalf.

In 2 Corinthians 5:21, Paul recounts the transaction that took place. His description is absolutely shocking: "[God] made Him who knew no sin to be sin for us, that we might become the righteousness of God in Him." This was the exchange that bought reconciliation with God for all believers: Christ traded His righteousness for our sin.

On the surface, that is not an easy statement to comprehend. God made His sinless Son "to *be* sin." What does it mean?

It cannot mean that Christ was made sinful or tainted in any way with personal guilt. God would never make His beloved Son into a sinner.

Besides, Christ had no capacity to sin. He is God. He did not relinquish His deity in order to become human. And Scripture says God is "of purer eyes than to behold evil, and cannot look on wickedness"—meaning, of course, that He cannot regard sin with approval or indifference (Hab. 1:13). "It is impossible for God to lie" (Heb. 6:18). "He cannot deny Himself" (2 Tim. 2:13). Therefore He could never sin.

Furthermore, it is perfectly clear that He didn't sin. Scripture everywhere asserts that Christ "offered Himself without spot to God" (Heb. 9:14). He is "holy, harmless, undefiled, separate from sinners" (7:26). He "committed no sin, nor was deceit found in His mouth" (1 Peter 2:22). Even here in 2 Corinthians 5:21, the text speaks of Christ as "Him who knew no sin."

That means, of course, that He knew nothing of sin through personal experience. He certainly knew all *about* sin. He lived His earthly life in a world cursed because of sin. His preaching was filled with instruction and exhortations against sin. He even had "power on earth to forgive sins" (Luke 5:24). But throughout His whole earthly life He remained perfectly sinless, and nothing that took place at the cross altered that fact.

This can only mean that Christ was "made . . . to be sin" by imputation. Paul has just stated in 2 Corinthians 5:19 that "God was in Christ reconciling the world to Himself, not imputing their trespasses to them." Since we already know that God does not simply look the other way or wink at evil, Paul's meaning is simple and obvious: the legal obligation stemming from sin's guilt was transferred to Christ, and He bore its full penalty.

In a solemn, judicial sense—*by imputation*—Christ took on Himself all the guilt of all the sins of all the people who would ever believe. He bore not only their misdemeanors and accidental indiscretions, but also their grossest, most deliberate sins. He stood in the place of countless fornicators, idolaters, adulterers, homosexuals, thieves, covetous people, drunkards, revilers, and extortioners (1 Cor. 6:9–10), and He took the punishment for those sins. Imagine all that guilt consolidated into one horrific indictment. Christ stood as a proxy for His people at the bar of divine justice—before "God the Judge of all" (Heb. 12:23). He answered every charge against them, pleaded guilty, and bore the full penalty of their sin.

"He was wounded for our transgressions, He was bruised for our iniquities; the chastisement for our peace was upon Him" (Isa. 53:5). Thus He became the living embodiment of every evil the fallen human heart is capable of imagining. He became "sin *for us*"—as our Substitute. That is precisely what Scripture means when it says, "Christ died for our sins" (1 Cor. 15:3). The principle of ***penal substitution*** is the only doctrine that makes sense of all the relevant texts.

THE WORK OF CHRIST

Today's evangelicals often speak about the gospel as if it were a means of discovering one's own purpose, a message about how to have a happy and prosperous life, or a method of achieving success in one's relationships or business. In the minds of many, the best starting point for sharing the gospel is an announcement that "God loves you and has a wonderful plan for your life."

All those ways of presenting the gospel have become such common clichés among contemporary Christians that most people in the church today do not flinch when they hear the gospel framed in such language. They don't notice how profoundly all those narratives deviate from the gospel Paul proclaimed and defended. A major problem with all of them is the way they turn the gospel into a message about "you"—your life, your purpose, your prosperity. *You* become the center and subject of the story.

Those are concepts that would have appalled and outraged Paul. One truth that should stand out boldly in every text we have looked at is that the central figure in the gospel according to Paul is always "Jesus Christ and Him crucified" (1 Cor. 2:2). The apostle takes great care never to let the narrative drift.

Here in our text (2 Cor. 5:18–21), Paul's intention is to explain *how* "God . . . has reconciled us to Himself through Jesus Christ" (v. 18). He mentions both Christ and God in every verse. In the span of those four verses, he mentions God by name at least once in every verse (five times total). Three additional times he refers to God with pronouns (*Himself* twice and *He* once). He uses the Messianic title *Christ* four times. And in that final verse he refers to Christ twice with the pronoun *Him*. The entire passage is decidedly God-centered, not man-centered. That should be the case any time we talk about the gospel. It's first of all a message about God's purpose in the work of Christ; the sinner's own purpose in life is secondary. That, of course, is the point we started with in this chapter: *the gospel is a declaration about the atoning work of Christ.*

Nevertheless, we are by no means left entirely out of the picture. "He made Him who knew no sin to be sin *for us*" (2 Cor. 5:21). Christ is the subject of this narrative; His people are the objects. All told, pronouns referring to redeemed people are used nine times in the passage. People from every tongue, tribe, and nation constitute "the world" whom Christ has reconciled to God.* Everything Christ did, He did on our behalf.

Why? Not for our comfort or self-aggrandizement, but for His glory. So "that we might become the righteousness of God in Him" (v. 21).

In what sense do believers "become" righteousness? The answer again is simple and obvious. This is the mirror image of how Christ was "made . . . sin." Just as the sins of His people were imputed to Him, His righteousness is imputed to them. They "become the righteousness of God" by imputation, through their union with Christ.

Notice the expression "in Him" in 2 Corinthians 5:21. It's an echo of verse 17: "If anyone is *in Christ*, he is a new creation." The expression speaks of a spiritual union that occurs at salvation, when the Holy Spirit takes residence in the believer and thereby makes us spiritually one with Christ. "By one Spirit we were all baptized into one body—whether Jews or Greeks, whether slaves or free—and have all been made to drink into one Spirit" (1 Cor. 12:13). That's true of every believer. We are "in Christ," or as Paul

---

* Paul isn't suggesting that every individual who ever lived will be reconciled to God. Both Jesus and Paul emphatically reject universalism (Matt. 7:21–23; Rom. 2:5–9). "The world" in this context refers to humanity as a race, regardless of gender, class, or ethnic distinctions (Gal. 3:28).

says in Ephesians 5:30, "We are members of His body."* The church—the fellowship of true believers—is metaphorically spoken of as "His body, the fullness of Him who fills all in all" (Eph. 1:23). In that sense, believers embody the very righteousness of God.

So 2 Corinthians 5:21 is describing a double imputation—believers' sins are imputed to Christ, and He pays the due penalty in full. His righteousness is imputed to them, and they are rewarded for it. Our Lord's perfect righteousness is like a glorious mantle that covers all His people's imperfections and gives them a right standing before God. "He has clothed me with the garments of salvation, He has covered me with the robe of righteousness" (Isa. 61:10).

In other words, *God treated Christ as if He sinned all the sins of everyone who would ever believe, so that He could treat them as if they had lived Christ's perfect life.* That's a fitting paraphrase of 2 Corinthians 5:21. Christ, as our perfect Substitute, not only died for our sins and thereby "canceled out the certificate of debt" (Col. 2:14 NASB); He also embodied the perfect righteousness God requires for entry into the kingdom of heaven (Matt. 5:20). Both His life and His death therefore count vicariously for all those whom He reconciles to God.

THE WAY OF SALVATION

We have stressed the sovereignty of God in salvation because that doctrine stands out prominently on the face of this text. It's an amazing and counterintuitive truth. After all, God is the offended deity. But reconciliation for sinners comes at His instigation, through an atonement that He sovereignly provides.

Even the language Paul uses stresses the efficacy of God's saving work.

* The King James and New King James Versions add the phrase "of His flesh and of His bones" to the end of Ephesians 5:30. Those words aren't found in the earliest Greek texts. That phrase is a gloss, probably added by a scribe who intended to write a marginal comment echoing Genesis 2:23, where Adam says of Eve, "This is now bone of my bones and flesh of my flesh." Obviously, our membership in the body of Christ is not a physical flesh-and-bones union.

The point is not that God began a work that sinners must now complete. It's not that God took a step in our direction, hoping we would come the rest of the way. Rather, "*all* these things are from God, who reconciled us to Himself" (2 Cor. 5:18). The salvation of sinners is entirely God's doing. And Christ is both "the author and finisher of our faith" (Heb. 12:2 KJV). Nothing sinners can do would in any way exculpate their sins or earn them any merit.

Yet sinners are not passive in the process. The gospel confronts every sinner with a duty. That's why this passage includes an urgent plea: "We implore you on Christ's behalf, be reconciled to God" (2 Cor. 5:20).

God's sovereignty does not eliminate human responsibility. God holds us responsible for what we do and don't do, and it is perfectly just for Him to do so. He doesn't control human actions by constraint. As the Westminster Confession of Faith says, "Neither is God the author of sin, nor is violence offered to the will of the creatures."[1] In other words, although "the king's heart is in the hand of the LORD, . . . [and] He turns it wherever He wishes," God does not exercise His sovereignty over the human will by force or coercion (Prov. 21:1). He doesn't manipulate people's actions like some kind of cosmic puppet master. When we sin, we do it willingly. And when God draws a sinner to Christ, He does it by attraction, not by force. He regenerates the heart and soul, so that Christ becomes irresistible to that person. Therefore, when a person is saved, God gets all the credit. And when we sin, the responsibility and the blame belong entirely to us.

That seems to be one of the most difficult truths to wrap the human mind around. We naturally want credit when we do good, and we want to avoid blame when we sin. So in all candor, we don't really want to see both sides of this truth. Charles Spurgeon, the great nineteenth-century Baptist preacher,* made some helpful observations about the dilemma:

> That God predestines, and yet that man is responsible, are two facts that few can see clearly. They are believed to be inconsistent and contradictory

* See also appendix 4: "Paul's Glorious Gospel," featuring material drawn from Spurgeon's sermons analyzing Paul's protective mind-set with regard to the defense and proclamation of the gospel.

> to each other. If, then, I find taught in one part of the Bible that everything is fore-ordained, that is true; and if I find, in another Scripture, that man is responsible for all his actions, that is true; and it is only my folly that leads me to imagine that these two truths can ever contradict each other. I do not believe they can ever be welded into one upon any earthly anvil, but they certainly shall be one in eternity. They are two lines that are so nearly parallel, that the human mind which pursues them farthest will never discover that they converge, but they do converge, and they will meet somewhere in eternity, close to the throne of God, whence all truth doth spring.[2]

Just as God's sovereignty doesn't eliminate the sinner's responsibility, likewise the plea for sinners to "be reconciled to God" poses no actual contradiction to the fact that God is the One who sovereignly draws those who do respond to the plea.

Paul believed as strongly as anyone in the sovereignty of God. But his point here is that the plea is an essential feature of the gospel message. God is not indifferent to the plight of lost humanity. He has no pleasure in the death of the wicked (Ezek. 18:23, 32; 33:11). Therefore to omit the passion and urgency of the entreaty ("we *beg* you . . . be reconciled to God") is to fail to preach the gospel as it should be proclaimed.

How can a sinner be reconciled with God? In Acts 16:30, the jailer in Philippi asked that question of Paul: "What must I do to be saved?"

Paul's answer to the Philippian jailer was the same one he gives in all his gospel summaries: "Believe on the Lord Jesus Christ, and you will be saved" (v. 31).

He was certainly not suggesting to the jailer that faith is a meritorious work summoned out of the sinner's own free will in order to earn salvation. As noted earlier, faith itself is a gift. God is the only one who can "give to you the spirit of wisdom and revelation in the knowledge of Him" (Eph. 1:17). It was, after all, the Lord who opened Lydia's heart to heed the things spoken by Paul (Acts 16:14).

Nevertheless, God "commands all people everywhere to repent" (Acts

17:30 ESV). And no one is excluded from His plea for reconciliation. We'll return to the difficult subjects of predestination and divine sovereignty in the following chapter, but the point to grasp here is that no one is compelled by force or coercion to reject the gospel message. They do it freely, by their own choice. Those who turn away in unbelief are therefore wholly responsible for putting themselves under God's condemnation (John 3:18). "They have no excuse for their sin" (John 15:22). "Because what may be known of God is manifest in them, for God has shown it to them. For since the creation of the world His invisible attributes are clearly seen, being understood by the things that are made, even His eternal power and Godhead, so that they are without excuse" (Rom. 1:19–20). Both unbelief and indifference are sins (John 16:9; Heb. 2:3; 12:25). Furthermore, unbelief is blasphemy, because "he who does not believe God has made Him a liar, because he has not believed the testimony that God has given of His Son" (1 John 5:10).

Full reconciliation with God is there in Christ for all who do respond to the plea. Dear reader, if you understand that you are hopelessly in bondage to sin and therefore you sense your desperate need for God's grace, then simply "ask, and it will be given to you; seek, and you will find; knock, and it will be opened to you. For everyone who asks receives, and he who seeks finds, and to him who knocks it will be opened" (Matt. 7:7–8). Those who come will not be cast out (John 6:37).

Six

ALIVE TOGETHER WITH CHRIST

Awake, you who sleep, arise from the dead,
and Christ will give you light.

—Ephesians 5:14

Of all the short gospel summaries Paul penned, few are more frequently quoted than Ephesians 2:8–9. This is one of the first passages many new Christians memorize: "For by grace you have been saved through faith, and that not of yourselves; it is the gift of God, not of works, lest anyone should boast."

The immediate before-and-after context of those two verses is not quite so well known, but the entire paragraph (Eph. 2:1–10) makes an instructive and highly edifying study in the gospel according to Paul. It's a rich text, drawing several vital gospel themes together. In these few short verses Paul teaches some profound truths about human depravity, divine grace, God's sovereignty, regeneration, justification, sanctification, and the walk of the true believer.

But the central point of the passage is simple and straightforward. Paul is explaining to the saints at Ephesus that their conversion to Christ was quite literally a miracle analogous to Christ's resurrection from the dead and His ascension into heaven.

This theme was first introduced in the epistle's opening chapter, where Paul was describing how he prayed for the Ephesian church (Eph. 1:17–23). One of his specific prayer requests was that they might know "what is the exceeding greatness of [God's] power toward us who believe, *according to the working of His mighty power which He worked in Christ when He raised Him from the dead and seated Him at His right hand in the heavenly places*" (vv. 19–20). The opening paragraph of Ephesians 2 is a detailed explanation of that emphasized clause. It is Paul's exegesis of his own prayer request. It is his answer to readers who might ask, "What *is* the exceeding greatness of His power toward us who believe?" After all, we are talking about the power that brought Christ up from the grave and then carried Him into the heavenlies—miraculous power that not only defeats death but literally transcends all earthly power. What relevance does "the power of His resurrection" (Phil. 3:10) have "toward us who believe"—not just at the final resurrection but in our present experience?

To answer those questions, Paul goes back to the familiar starting point of his gospel presentation—the bad news of humanity's sin problem. The first three verses of Ephesians 2 constitute Paul's bleakest, most frightful description of the sinner's predicament. This time he isn't focused on the evil depravity of sin or the diabolical bondage that enslaves sinners. Here, in order to stress how utterly hopeless the human situation really is, he likens unbelievers to dead people.

This is not a flippant metaphor. It's not really a metaphor at all. Paul truly means that sin has inflicted a fatal wound on the whole human race, and sinners in their fallen state are already *spiritually* dead, insensible to divine reality, lacking any righteous impulse, "having no hope and without God in the world" (Eph. 2:12). He expounds on those chilling words ("dead in trespasses and sins" [2:1]) for the next three verses.

But then, when it seems perfectly clear that the sinner's utter reprobation is hopelessly irreversible, the tone changes abruptly, just as it did in Romans 3:21. Paul goes on to explain how those who are redeemed have been spiritually raised from the dead by God Himself, and they have been granted a lofty privilege—a perfectly righteous standing before the eternal

Judge. It is as if they had ascended into heaven, and were seated in a place of honor there beside Christ (Eph. 2:6).

This passage is full of themes that should be very familiar by now. That is because these are the cardinal themes of Paul's gospel: death and resurrection; sin and grace; faith rather than works; and salvation as a free gift from God, leaving the Christian with absolutely no reason to boast. So although we are turning to a fresh passage, once more our study requires us to revisit some themes we have already encountered. Because these are such vital doctrines, the repetition will be helpful to our understanding. These truths are certainly rich enough to justify going over them again and again. Moreover, of all the major Pauline gospel texts, Ephesians 2:1–10 brings the vital themes together with supreme clarity and gives us a unique opportunity to review them from a fresh perspective. Here is the full text of the passage in question:

> And you He made alive, who were dead in trespasses and sins, in which you once walked according to the course of this world, according to the prince of the power of the air, the spirit who now works in the sons of disobedience, among whom also we all once conducted ourselves in the lusts of our flesh, fulfilling the desires of the flesh and of the mind, and were by nature children of wrath, just as the others.
>
> But God, who is rich in mercy, because of His great love with which He loved us, even when we were dead in trespasses, made us alive together with Christ (by grace you have been saved), and raised us up together, and made us sit together in the heavenly places in Christ Jesus, that in the ages to come He might show the exceeding riches of His grace in His kindness toward us in Christ Jesus. For by grace you have been saved through faith, and that not of yourselves; it is the gift of God, not of works, lest anyone should boast. For we are His workmanship, created in Christ Jesus for good works, which God prepared beforehand that we should walk in them.

Don't rush past the main point of that passage: whenever a sinner turns to Christ for salvation, it is because God has done a miracle of spiritual resurrection. The common theological term for this is *regeneration*, or the new birth. This is the same thing Jesus was speaking of when He told Nicodemus, "Most assuredly, I say to you, unless one is born again, he cannot see the kingdom of God" (John 3:3). Our Lord went on to describe redeemed people—all true believers—as those who have been "born of the Spirit" (v. 8). Elsewhere He said, "It is the Spirit who gives life" (6:63). Paul likewise said believers are saved "through the washing of regeneration and renewing of the Holy Spirit" (Titus 3:5).

Here, then, is a simple definition: *regeneration is a miracle wrought by the Holy Spirit, whereby He gives life to a spiritually dead soul.* This life-giving act of God is a complete spiritual rebirth unto eternal life, no less a miracle than a literal bodily resurrection from the dead.

By the way, resurrection and rebirth are kindred concepts, and the Bible uses both of them in reference to the risen Christ. He is "the firstborn from the dead" (Col. 1:18; Rev. 1:5). "Now Christ is risen from the dead, and has become the firstfruits of those who have fallen asleep" (1 Cor. 15:20). Both rebirth and resurrection are likewise apt descriptions of the miracle that takes place when God regenerates a spiritually dead sinner and gives that person the gift of salvation.

Let's trace that theme through this brief passage and observe carefully as Paul deals with several vital truths about regeneration.

WE HAVE BEEN RESURRECTED FROM DEATH

There is no sunny way to describe the picture Paul paints of the sinner in thrall to sin. "You . . . were dead in trespasses and sins" (Eph. 2:1). He is not addressing these comments to a narrow class of former rogues and scoundrels whose sins were extraordinarily diabolical. What the apostle says here describes all of us. That comment was addressed to every individual believer in the Ephesian assembly, and he unmistakably applies the same dismal assessment to all "the rest of mankind" (v. 3 ESV). All fallen people are "*by nature* children of wrath."

For genuine believers, this is Paul's description of our former state, of course. For *un*believers, the obvious implications of this text are grave and horrifying—and still a present-tense reality. It should provoke somber self-examination with a trembling heart. The unbeliever is dead to God—in every sense of that expression. The unbeliever is devoid of spiritual life, and he subsists in a state of total condemnation (John 3:18). Paul doesn't dither or back away from the harshness of that truth. Indeed, he will return to it in Ephesians 4:17–19 and say it with even more emphasis, describing unbelievers as those who "walk, in the futility of their mind, having their understanding darkened, being alienated from the life of God, because of the ignorance that is in them, because of the blindness of their heart; who, being past feeling, have given themselves over to lewdness, to work all uncleanness with greediness."

Note the phrase "alienated from the life of God." That is another way of describing spiritual death. In every sense that pertains to spiritual vitality and understanding, unbelievers are hopelessly cut off from God, who is the true source of all life.

Dead people have no ability to respond to any stimulus. A corpse can't feel pain and doesn't hear the pleading of a loved one. One of the most heartbreaking scenes I have ever witnessed was the grief of a young mother whose infant had been discovered dead in a crib. She held the child's body, spoke to it, wept over it, tenderly touched its face, and desperately tried to awaken that baby. When the coroner arrived, she was reluctant to hand the body over—as if more earnest pleading might eventually awaken the little one. But nothing short of a divine miracle could have brought that child back from the dead. As poignant as that grieving mother's loving caresses and tender pleadings were, the child no longer had any ability to feel and respond.

That is exactly the case with those who are spiritually dead. They have no capacity on their own to perceive (much less respond to) the truth of God's Word or the generous overtures of the gospel call. "The natural man does not receive the things of the Spirit of God, for they are foolishness to him; nor can he know them, because they are spiritually discerned"

(1 Cor. 2:14). Furthermore, "the god of this world [Satan] has blinded the minds of the unbelieving so that they might not see the light of the gospel of the glory of Christ, who is the image of God" (2 Cor. 4:4 NASB).

Death is not a pleasant subject to think about, and in modern Western culture we go to great extremes not to have to deal with it. In the part of the country where I live and minister, when someone dies it is quite common nowadays for the loved ones to have a simple memorial service rather than a traditional funeral with a graveside service. No casket is present; there is no viewing of the body and no procession to the grave site. Mourners are shielded as much as possible from the harsh reality of death.

That's certainly understandable. Something intrinsic to our human nature compels us to memorialize the dead, but we don't want visible reminders of death constantly confronting us with the cold reality of our own mortality. Abraham, negotiating with the Hittites for the meager plot of land that he needed as a final resting place for his beloved wife, said "Give me property for a burial place among you, that I may bury my dead *out of my sight*" (Gen. 23:4).

Death is a loathsome reality. It's hard to think of anything that is more universally feared, hated, and mourned. Death is inevitable, and we are powerless in its wake. The dead feel nothing, hear nothing, and respond to no stimulus. Furthermore, we all have an appointment with death. "It is appointed for man to die once, and after that comes judgment" (Heb. 9:27 ESV). We can't avoid it; we can't change it; and once it happens, we have no remedy for it. No human power can reverse rigor mortis.

Likewise, those who are spiritually dead are in a hopeless state that no human power can remedy. The light of truth has no effect on them because they are impervious to spiritual things (Matt. 13:13). The lovingkindness of God, which ought to produce heartfelt shame and repentance (Rom. 2:4), elicits no appropriate response because a carnal mind is utterly incapable of responding rightly to God (Rom. 8:6–8).

But unlike a physically dead person, unbelievers are animate. They are dead while they live (1 Tim. 5:6)—spiritually dead, but still "walk[ing] according to the course of this world" (Eph. 2:2). One nineteenth-century

Scottish Presbyterian commentator observed, "In this sleep of death there is a strange somnambulism . . . death-walking."[1] In more contemporary terms, we might say that Paul is describing spiritual zombies—the ungrateful dead. They don't even know they are dead, and they are still going through the motions of life.

Paul says the unregenerate are in this condition "by nature" (Eph. 2:3). It's not as if they were born totally innocent, undefiled by sin, but then they fell sometime after they became aware of right and wrong and began to sin willfully. They didn't become sinners somewhere in the course of life. They are natural-born sinners. They are members of a fallen race. It is their very nature to be oblivious to spiritual realities and unmoved by spiritual truth. All humanity was plunged into this guilty condition because of Adam's sin. "By one man's disobedience many were made sinners" (Rom. 5:19). This is the doctrine of *original sin*, a truth that is expounded by Paul at length in Romans 5:12–19.[2] In 1 Corinthians 15:22, he sums up the doctrine in three Greek words. It translates into four English words, but none of the impact is lost: "In Adam all die."

This doctrine is affirmed as an essential tenet of orthodoxy in all major Christian traditions. Nevertheless, questions always arise about whether it's fair for the whole human race to be condemned because of the actions of one man. That argument might have some weight if it had ever been made by a person who didn't deliberately defy God's law. We prove our willing complicity in Adam's rebellion every time we sin. And since no one other than Jesus has ever lived a sinless life, no one is really in a position to doubt the doctrine of original sin, much less deem it unjust.

G. K. Chesterton referred to original sin as "the only part of Christian theology which can really be proved."[3] He decried the extreme illogic of liberals in the church who gave lip service to truths "which they cannot see even in their dreams. But they essentially deny human sin, which they can see in the street."[4] Ample evidence of sin's wickedness and universality is all around us. We see it on the news every night, reminding us just how hopelessly fallen and depraved the human race is.

It would indeed be a completely hopeless predicament except for the rich mercy and great love of God. In verse 4, Paul's tone shifts abruptly: "But God, who is rich in mercy, . . . raised us up" (Eph. 2:4–6). Again we see that God is the instigator, the architect, and the executor of our salvation.

D. Martyn Lloyd-Jones, pastor of London's Westminster Chapel from 1943 to 1968, spent eight years preaching verse by verse through the book of Ephesians. He preached some 230 sermons on this epistle. Those messages, and the commentary series that grew out of them, are some of the twentieth century's finest examples of biblical exposition. They are renowned for their insight and clarity. But the most talked-about sermon in the whole series was the one Lloyd-Jones preached when he came to Ephesians 2:4. He devoted an entire sermon to those first two words: "But God . . ." He titled that message, "The Christian Message to the World."[5] He said,

> With these two words ["But God . . . "] we come to the introduction to the Christian message, the peculiar, specific message which the Christian faith has to offer to us. These two words, in and of themselves, in a sense contain the whole of the gospel. The gospel tells of what God has done, God's intervention; it is something that comes entirely from outside us and displays to us that wondrous and amazing and astonishing work of God that the apostle goes on to describe and to define in the following verses.[6]

That is precisely Paul's point. The salvation of sinners is "not of yourselves" (Eph. 2:8); it is entirely God's work, beginning with an act of spiritual resurrection that only God could accomplish. The life-giving power of the One who spoke the universe into being instantly gives life to a spiritually dead soul, hearing to spiritually deaf ears, and sight to spiritually blind eyes. As we said earlier, regeneration is no less supernatural than Christ's own resurrection from the dead. Indeed, it is wrought by the very same divine power by which "He raised Him from the dead and seated Him at His right hand in the heavenly places" (1:20).

As a matter of fact, the regeneration of a sinner is the result and a constant reminder of every believer's participation in Christ's resurrection and ascension to heaven. God "made us alive together with Christ . . . and raised us up together, and made us sit together in the heavenly places in Christ Jesus" (Eph. 2:5–6). Notice that Paul doesn't use the future tense. When he speaks of being seated in heaven with Christ, he is not describing a promise of some reward yet to come. This is a present reality for every believer, the immediate and direct result of God's saving work. It's a spiritual reality, of course. This is Paul's description of our spiritual union with Christ and the high place of honor that we gain through justification.

We must understand verses 5 and 6 in that light. Those two verses bring together the truths of regeneration, justification, and the believer's union with Christ. God "made us alive" through regeneration. He elevated us to a position of highest privilege (seating us in a place of supreme honor "in the heavenly places") through justification. All of this—our participation with Christ in His resurrection and our standing with Him before God—is possible because of our spiritual union "in Christ Jesus."

WE HAVE BEEN RESURRECTED BY GRACE

Twice in Ephesians 2:1–10 Paul repeats the phrase "by grace you have been saved" (vv. 5, 8). That, in a nutshell, is the whole theme of the passage and a suitable summary of the gospel according to Paul. Have you noticed that God's grace is a dominant theme in every context where the apostle Paul explains the gospel? No wonder. Grace is the fountain from which every feature of our salvation flows. Spurgeon wrote,

> Because God is gracious, therefore sinful men are forgiven, converted, purified, and saved. It is not because of anything in them, or that ever can be in them, that they are saved; but because of the boundless love, goodness, pity, compassion, mercy, and grace of God. Tarry a moment, then, at the well-head. Behold the pure river of water of life as it proceeds out of the throne of God and of the Lamb. What an abyss is the grace of God! Who can fathom it?[7]

If one truth emerges clearly from Ephesians 2, it is the fact that our salvation is not earned or deserved in any degree. Salvation is not a reward for something good God detects in the sinner. The exact opposite is true. He freely bestows His redeeming love on sinners who deserve total condemnation. That, as you know already, is the very definition of *grace*.

"But God, who is rich in mercy, *because of His great love with which He loved us*, even when we were dead in trespasses, made us alive" (vv. 4–5). God's grace is the originating cause of regeneration; the sinner's faith is the immediate effect.

Unfortunately, many Christians think and speak as if it worked the other way around—as if a free-will act of faith from the sinner were the determining factor that enables God to bestow His saving grace. In other words, they think faith is the cause and regeneration is the effect. Here in Ephesians 2, the apostle Paul is making the polar opposite point. This is about the primacy of God's grace as the root cause of the sinner's spiritual awakening. Paul's point is not at all obscure: *the person who is spiritually dead has no capacity for faith.*

To put the same point in different words, the hopelessness of human depravity explains why divine grace is an absolute necessity. It also points us to the truths of God's sovereignty and the doctrine of election. If God did not intervene to save His elect, no one would ever be saved. Corpses don't raise themselves.

Many Christians recoil from the language and the concept of divine election, but the doctrine is thoroughly biblical. Scripture refers to believers as "the elect of God" (Col. 3:12; Luke 18:7; Rom. 8:33). The elect are chosen, not (as many suppose) because God looks down the corridors of time to foresee who might be worthy of His favor. Rather, they are "predestined according to the purpose of Him who works all things according to the counsel of His [own] will" (Eph. 1:11). Paul specifically points to God's own free and sovereign purpose in answer to the question of how the elect are chosen. He says God "predestined us to adoption as sons by Jesus Christ to Himself, according to *the good pleasure of His will*" (v. 5).

If the sinner's own free-will choice rather than God's electing grace were the determining factor in salvation, no one would ever be saved. "So then it is not of him who wills, nor of him who runs, but of God who shows mercy" (Rom. 9:16). That is why when Luke recorded the conversion of Gentiles in Pisidian Antioch, he did not say that those who believed were therefore appointed to eternal life. Instead, he wrote, "As many as had been appointed to eternal life believed" (Acts 13:48). Repeatedly the Word of God tells us that the source and the reason for regeneration is purely God's grace, not the sinner's own faith. We must not confuse the effect with the cause.

Those who struggle with the doctrine of election and the principle of divine sovereignty have not thought deeply enough about the horror of human depravity and what it means to be "dead in trespasses and sins." No one but God could ever rescue a sinner from that condition and then elevate that person to a place of privilege in heavenly places. Who else could ever accomplish that? After all, the resurrection and rebirth of a spiritually dead soul

> is a creation. Who can create but he who spake and it was done? It is a resurrection. Who but God can raise the dead? . . . The soul thus raised is then illuminated, and who but he who commanded light to shine out of darkness can shine into our minds, "to give the light of the knowledge of the glory of God, in the face of Jesus Christ" [2 Corinthians 4:6]?[8]

It would be impossible to overstress the importance of divine grace in the salvation of sinners. Again, every aspect of salvation—beginning with regeneration, including the sinner's faith and good works—*all of it*—is purely by grace. It is done for us freely. "It is the gift of God, not of works, lest anyone should boast" (Eph. 2:8–9). God's grace does not merely start us on the road to salvation and leave us to finish the project. From our predestination in eternity past, through our calling and justification in this life, all the way into the infinite future of eternal glory, God sovereignly guarantees the triumph of His grace in every stage of our salvation (Rom. 8:29–30). "What then shall we say to these things? If God is for us, who can be against us?" (v. 31).

Don't lose track of the reality that if we received what we deserved we'd be damned for all eternity. Yet God does not merely grant believers a reprieve from the judgment we deserve; He exalts us to an unfathomably high position in Christ. This is no temporary benefit, but an eternal blessing, done so "that in the ages to come He might show the exceeding riches of His grace in His kindness toward us in Christ Jesus" (Eph. 2:7). God certainly "*is* rich in mercy" toward sinners (v. 4).

Think of that when you hear the hymn "Amazing Grace." God's grace is vastly more amazing than you could ever imagine with a finite mind. The English word *rich* in Ephesians 2:4 only hints at the sense of the original. The word actually suggests spectacular, overabundant wealth. (The noun form of that same word is used in verse 7 with a superlative modifier that accents the lavish grandeur—"exceeding riches"—of divine grace.) The truth is, no human language could adequately convey the concept. Grace is amazing indeed. God saves unworthy sinners in order to honor them forever "in Christ Jesus."

WE HAVE BEEN RESURRECTED THROUGH FAITH

If we were responsible—even partly—for our own salvation, we would receive some of the glory for it. But all the work necessary to gain our salvation was done to perfection by Christ alone. That work is now complete, with nothing for the sinner to add. That's why, just before He gave up His spirit on the cross, Jesus said, "It is finished!" (John 19:30).

Here in our text, we have Paul's familiar, explicit statement that salvation is "not of yourselves . . . not of works, lest anyone should boast" (Eph. 2:8–9). No matter which phrase of our passage we examine, everything points to one very clear truth; namely, that salvation "is the gift of God" (v. 8), and therefore the redemption of a sinner is not creditable in any way to the sinner's own works or worthiness.

Does that mean sinners are totally passive in the process?

Not at all. Faith is the essential instrument by which redeemed sinners lay hold of justification. Faith adds nothing meritorious to salvation; it is simply the channel through which the blessing is received.

But some measure of practical righteousness is the inevitable fruit of saving faith. Faith is not bare assent; real faith engages the whole person—mind, heart, and will.* And far from being inert or uninvolved, sinners are saved "for good works" (Eph. 2:10). God is, after all, transforming and conforming them to the image of His Son (Rom. 8:29; 2 Cor. 3:18). Indeed, authentic faith absolutely guarantees that the believer will not be completely barren, totally passive, or ultimately apostate (Matt. 7:17–19; Luke 6:44; James 2:14–20; 1 John 2:19; 1 Peter 1:5). We'll return to that aspect of the text before closing this chapter, but the point here is that faith does not produce passivity.

And yet faith is not a human work. It is important to think rightly about this. As we noted in chapter 5, faith itself is a gift from God. Here in Ephesians 2:8–9, Paul confirms that salvation is "through faith . . . not of yourselves . . . not of works." Paul not only contrasts faith with works; he is also emphatically denying that faith is generated by sinners themselves out of their own free will.

The phrase "that not of yourselves; it is the gift of God" has been fiercely debated by theologians and commentators. In almost any English translation, it would appear the antecedent of the demonstrative pronoun *that* is the immediately preceding noun. Hence it would mean "that [*faith* is] not of yourselves; it is the gift of God." That's true enough, because as we have already seen, Romans 12:3 makes it absolutely clear that God is indeed the gracious source of every believer's faith: "God has dealt to each one a measure of faith."

But the Greek pronoun (*touto*, "that") in Ephesians 2:8 is neuter, and the immediately antecedent noun (*pisteos*, "faith") is feminine. So the claim is often made that the pronoun cannot be referring to the word *faith*,

* Faith consists of knowledge, assent, and trust. For a discussion of how this engages the mind, emotions, and will, see John MacArthur, *The Gospel According to the Apostles* (Nashville: Nelson, 1993), 44–45.

because the genders of the two words do not match. Faith, according to this rationale, is not "the gift of God."

There are two answers to that. The first one points out that in Greek grammar (and throughout Paul's epistles) neuter demonstrative pronouns do sometimes refer to feminine nouns. That is precisely the case in Philippians 1:28, for example, where Paul speaks of "salvation, and that from God." The grammar in that text is precisely the same as Ephesians 2:8. The neuter pronoun (*that*) can only refer to the feminine noun (*salvation*). This is not an uncommon grammatical construction, even in more formal classical Greek.

A second point must be made as well: there is no neuter noun preceding *touto* in Ephesians 2:8 or any of the verses immediately before it. If the pronoun doesn't refer specifically to "faith," the only other option would be to interpret the word *that* as a reference to the entire preceding clause. Hence Paul's meaning would be that salvation—every aspect of it—is a gift from God to the sinner. Thus each phase of the sinner's transformation that is named or implied in verses 1–8 (including regeneration, justification, grace, faith, and our ultimate glorification)—all of it combined—constitutes "the gift of God." Indeed, that interpretation would be perfectly consistent with the point of the whole passage. Paul adds in verse 10 that even the good works that are faith's fruit were "prepared beforehand" by God.

So there's no escaping the fact that Paul regards saving faith as a gift from God, not a human work.

To put Paul's point as simply as possible, you can breathe spiritually only because God slapped you on the backside to make you breathe. You can hear with the ear of faith because God unstopped your ears. If you are a believer, your faith is not the product of your own free will, any more than your salvation is the result of your confirmation, baptism, communion, church attendance or membership, giving to the church or to charity, keeping the Ten Commandments, living by the Sermon on the Mount, believing in God, being a good neighbor, or living a respectable life. Such things add no merit and play no role in anyone's salvation. "For *by grace* you have been saved *through faith*."

It is quite true that genuine faith involves all the faculties of your mind, will, and emotions. Certainly no one believes for you. No one forces you to believe against your will. Much less does someone else's faith count for you. But at the end of the day, you still cannot take credit for having believed, because even the faith with which you lay hold of Christ is God's gift, "not of works, lest anyone should boast."

To anyone prone to boast, Paul asks, "For who makes you differ from another? And what do you have that you did not receive? Now if you did indeed receive it, why do you boast as if you had not received it?" (1 Cor. 4:7). Every good thing about us, including our faith, is a gift from God, so we cannot righteously congratulate ourselves for being believers. Pride is contrary to the entirety of the gospel message.

WE HAVE BEEN RESURRECTED WITH A PURPOSE

Our salvation is for God's glory, not our own. We become partakers of His glory because we are spiritually united with Christ. Our union with Christ puts us in such a high position of privilege that Paul says we are "[seated] together in the heavenly places in Christ Jesus" (Eph. 2:6). From there we also get to see and enjoy God's glory, because of "God who commanded light to shine out of darkness, who has shone in our hearts to give the light of the knowledge of the glory of God in the face of Jesus Christ" (2 Cor. 4:6). And the greatest honor of all is to reflect that glory. In 2 Corinthians 3, Paul compares it to the glow of divine glory on Moses' face when he got a glimpse of God's glory on Sinai. The reflected radiance was so bright "that the children of Israel could not look steadily at the face of Moses because of the glory of his countenance, which glory was passing away" (v. 7). So he had to put a veil over his face until the glow finally faded. But the glory of Christ shines from within the Christian, and it doesn't fade; it steadily increases. "We all, with unveiled face, beholding as in a mirror the glory of the Lord, are being transformed into the same image from glory to glory" (v. 18).

But it is nevertheless God's glory, not our own. God's glory is the ultimate end for which we were created. It's the purpose for our salvation. It is quite literally the reason for everything.*

Only the most carnal person would imagine that by removing all grounds for human boasting Paul has somehow diminished the blessings or benefits of salvation for the sinner. Notice how the eternal plan of God plays out in our salvation. He saves us so "that in the ages to come He might show the exceeding riches of His grace in His kindness toward us in Christ Jesus" (Eph. 2:7). That is how God displays His glory throughout all eternity—and we are the beneficiaries, by His amazing grace alone.

WE HAVE BEEN RESURRECTED FOR GOOD WORKS

Paul makes a final point in this passage that must not be overlooked or discounted. God is also glorified through the righteousness wrought by His grace in us. "For we are His workmanship, created in Christ Jesus for good works, which God prepared beforehand that we should walk in them" (Eph. 2:10). We touched on that part of the passage a few pages ago. Now let's come back to it for a closer look.

Too many people quote Ephesians 2:8–9 and put all the emphasis on full pardon and free forgiveness we receive when we are justified—as if that were the end, rather than the beginning, of the many blessings we lay hold of by faith. People also misuse the word *grace* as if it were a license for sin. That has always been an opinion favored by wolves in sheep's clothing and people whose profession of faith in Christ is either false or merely superficial. The epistle of Jude was written to warn early Christians about dangerous false teachers who had crept unnoticed into the fellowship of true believers. Jude described them as "ungodly men, who turn the grace of our God into lewdness" (v. 4). Peter said of them, "While they promise . . . liberty, they themselves are slaves of corruption" (2 Peter 2:19). He urged Christians not to use their liberty as a cloak for vice (1 Peter 2:16).

* See appendix 3, "The Reason for Everything."

Paul likewise cautioned believers not to "use liberty as an opportunity for the flesh" (Gal. 5:13). The apostle obviously had encountered the common notion that grace somehow gives us permission to sin boldly.* He regarded that kind of thinking as utterly ludicrous. "What shall we say then? Shall we continue in sin that grace may abound? Certainly not! How shall we who died to sin live any longer in it?" (Rom. 6:1–2).

In the first nine verses of Ephesians, Paul repeatedly makes it clear that good works are not meritorious, nor are they a prerequisite for faith. Then in verse 10 he makes it equally clear that good works are nevertheless the expected fruit of regeneration.

In fact, the point is even stronger than that. Because God is sovereign (one of the central points of this passage), good works are inevitable in the lives of those who are saved. After all, good works are what we are "created in Christ Jesus *for*." God Himself ordained our good works "beforehand [i.e., in eternity past] that we should walk in them" (Eph. 2:10). So good works are not eliminated in the gospel according to Paul; they are simply put in their proper place.

Here is the point of verse 10: God's grace produces good works in true believers just as surely as grace was the source of their faith in the first place. None of it is meritorious. The only righteous merit in the gospel belongs to Christ. Believers lay hold of Christ (and thus gain credit for

---

* The expression "sin boldly" refers to a letter Martin Luther wrote to Philip Melancthon in August 1521, during Luther's time of exile in the Wartburg Castle. This was less than a year after Luther burned a papal bull that had been issued against him and was therefore formally excommunicated by the pope. Luther, for whom the doctrine of justification by faith was still a fairly recent discovery, was encouraging Melancthon with the truth of Romans 8:38–39, that "[nothing] shall be able to separate us from the love of God which is in Christ Jesus our Lord." Luther injudiciously wrote, "Sin, and sin boldly, but let your faith be greater than your sin. . . . Sin cannot destroy in us the reign of the Lamb, although we were to commit fornication and to kill a thousand times a day." Cited in Jean Marie Vincent Audin, *History of the Life, Writings, and Doctrines of Martin Luther* (Philadelphia: Kelly, 1841), 178. Context is crucial, and to be fair, Luther wrote that letter to chide Melancthon for his reluctance to stand with Luther on the matter of celibacy. Luther pointed out that the apostle Paul said mandatory celibacy is a doctrine of demons (1 Tim. 4:1–3). Therefore, Luther told Melancthon, Catholic priests' vows of celibacy were not binding. Melancthon wasn't convinced, and Luther regarded his friend's fear as superstitious. So Luther was actually urging Melancthon to do something Luther himself did not regard as sinful. His words must be read in that light. Unfortunately, Luther's remark is often cited by antinomians as justification for a lax attitude toward sin.

His righteousness) by faith. The Christian's own good works, foreordained and prepared by God, are faith's inevitable fruit. Even the motivation and power for those works is graciously supplied by God (Phil. 2:13). Every genuine believer should therefore be *zealous* for good works.

That truth is highlighted and explained in the passage we will look at in the next chapter.

SEVEN

THE LESSONS OF GRACE

The night is far spent, the day is at hand.
Therefore let us cast off the works of darkness,
and let us put on the armor of light.

—ROMANS 13:12

On trial before the Sanhedrin in Acts 23, Paul told the council, "I am a Pharisee, the son of a Pharisee" (v. 6).* He was born and bred to be a member of that sect, and his zeal was unsurpassed. All his energies were devoted to a strict application of Jewish law, religious ceremony, and the Pharisees' own exacting traditions. They paid particularly close attention to the formal and ceremonial minutiae of Moses' law, often neglecting the more important moral precepts. They were obsessed with the law's external features (ritualism, symbolism, formalism, and anything else that involved visible tokens of piety). They loved to pray standing in the synagogues and on the corners of the streets so they could be seen (Matt. 6:5). Jesus said,

* Acts 21:27–36 describes how a riot broke out when some of Paul's adversaries falsely accused Paul of bringing Trophimus, a Gentile, into the temple. Roman authorities intervened to stop the mob from beating Paul to death, and they took Paul into their custody. But they weren't sure what the charges were against him and didn't know quite what to do with him when he revealed that he was a Roman citizen (22:22–30). So they brought him before the Sanhedrin to answer the charges.

"*All* their works they do to be seen by men. They make their phylacteries broad and enlarge the borders of their garments. They love the best places at feasts, the best seats in the synagogues, greetings in the marketplaces, and to be called by men, 'Rabbi, Rabbi'" (23:5–7).

Yet they were careless or even contemptuous of the hidden virtues and righteous character qualities commanded by the law—godly values such as mercy, compassion, integrity, and purity of heart. In short, they cared more about receiving honor than they did about being honorable. Jesus harshly condemned them for that, saying, "Woe to you, scribes and Pharisees, hypocrites! For you pay tithe of mint and anise and cummin, and have neglected the weightier matters of the law: justice and mercy and faith" (Matt. 23:23). Mocking their pathological fixation on ceremonial trivialities, He called them "blind guides, who strain out a gnat and swallow a camel!" (v. 24).*

LEGALISM: THE FOLLY OF PHARISAISM

The standard pharisaical assumption seemed to be that they could merit God's favor and thus inherit eternal life if their zeal and devotion to the fine points of pharisaical tradition exceeded the piety of their neighbors. This, of course, made them aggressive, ambitious, and arrogant—proud of themselves and contemptuous of everyone else. They "trusted in themselves that they were righteous, and despised others" (Luke 18:9).

Their whole belief system was rooted in the pernicious error of *legalism*, the notion that people earn favor with God by what they do or don't do. And the Pharisees' unique brand of legalism was the worst kind—a graceless, harsh, uncharitable style of artificial holiness that fostered a condescending contempt for pretty much everyone other than themselves. It was a systematic, self-righteous infringement of the Second Great Commandment, "You shall love your neighbor as yourself" (Lev. 19:18; Matt. 22:39).

After his conversion, the apostle had nothing but contempt for legalism

* Gnats were the smallest creatures listed as ceremonially unclean in Moses' law (Lev. 11:23); camels were the largest (v. 4).

of every flavor. It was not that he came to despise the law per se. In fact, he wrote, "The law is holy, and the commandment holy and just and good" (Rom. 7:12). To those who would abolish the law in the name of grace, Paul replied, "Do we then make void the law through faith? Certainly not! On the contrary, we establish the law" (Rom. 3:31). Paul was no antinomian.

Nevertheless, he emphatically rejected the Pharisees' beliefs about the law. They saw the law as a means to life. In reality, all the law can do for sinners is condemn them to death (Rom. 7:10). "The law brings about wrath; for where there is no law there is no transgression" (4:15). In fact, the law's central purpose was to show sinners the exceeding sinfulness of sin (7:13), strip them of self-confidence (v. 18), and thereby drive them to dependence on the grace of God, pointing them in the direction of justification by faith (Gal. 3:24).

But the Pharisees placed all their confidence in their own knowledge of the law, their lip service to its moral principles, and their fanatical obsession with its ceremonial features. By fastidiously cultivating a devout veneer, they thought they could earn for themselves exalted status among men, special honor from God, and eternal life in the final judgment. They had totally inverted the law's chief lessons.

Once Paul's spiritual eyes were opened, he became an ardent foe of every kind of legalism. The themes of divine grace and Christian liberty permeate almost everything he ever wrote. "Where the Spirit of the Lord is, there is liberty" (2 Cor. 3:17).

The issue came up frequently in his writings because he kept having to defend the doctrines of divine grace and justification by faith alone (*sola fide*) from endless attacks by false teachers. The early church was invaded by a party of pseudo-Christians who were determined to subvert Paul's gospel with legalistic doctrines. We know very little about the men who started and led this cult, except that they were former Pharisees from Judea (Acts 15:1, 4). They apparently professed conversion to Christianity, but then they set out to spread their distinctively pharisaical brand of legalism from one end of the Roman Empire to the other. They targeted Paul in particular. They seemed to follow him everywhere. After he planted a new church and moved on, they moved in to challenge his apostolic authority and spread vicious lies about him. They sometimes succeeded in turning his own companions, disciples, and spiritual children against him (Gal. 4:11–20).

These legalists insisted that Gentiles could not be saved unless they first became Jewish proselytes. Since Paul was specifically commissioned to minister among the Gentiles (Rom. 11:13), the churches he planted were filled with non-Jewish converts. The legalists told them, "Unless you are circumcised according to the custom of Moses, you cannot be saved" (Acts 15:1). And the false teachers were not content merely with demanding circumcision. They claimed it was "necessary" for Christian churches to instruct their Gentile members to keep the whole law of Moses (v. 5). Their message was pure law, not gospel.

Paul opposed that error with every fiber of his being. His epistle to the Galatians is an emphatic denunciation of the legalists' doctrine, followed by an extended refutation of it. He starts by twice cursing the heretics and their false gospel (Gal. 1:8–9). He never eases off in his critique or softens his condemnation of the false teachers. Finally, near the end of the epistle, he tells the members of those churches, "Stand fast therefore in the liberty by which Christ has made us free, and do not be entangled again with a yoke of bondage. Indeed I, Paul, say to you that if you become circumcised, Christ will profit you nothing" (5:1–2).

As someone saved out of Pharisaism, Paul clearly hated every hint of legalism. He could not have been any more clear about it. "If you are led by the Spirit, you are not under the law," he told the Galatian Christians (v. 18). His writings are full of anti-legalistic exhortations like that. One of the best-known texts in the whole Pauline corpus is Romans 6:14: "You are not under law but under grace."

ANTINOMIANISM: THE DOMINANT ERROR OF THE PRESENT AGE

Unfortunately, statements like those are often ripped from their contexts and used as proof texts for various flavors of modern and postmodern antinomianism—as if Paul meant that Christians are free from any kind of moral injunction, legal imperative, or rule governing our conduct. This is an increasingly popular way of interpreting those texts among evangelical libertines and spiritual libertarians. Some of today's evangelical trend-setters will bristle and complain every time someone cites any of the Bible's commandments or reminds Christians "that those who have believed in God should be careful to maintain good works" (Titus 3:8). I frequently encounter professing Christians who seem to think it's a sin rather than a duty "to stir up one another to love and good works" (Heb. 10:24).

"That's law, not grace," they protest—as if any mention of the Bible's imperatives is inherently legalistic. Some of today's antinomians seem determined to discover pietistic moralism practically everywhere. They are worried because they fear other Christians are too worried about being right and doing right. They seem to think the whole point of the gospel is to eliminate the sinner's concern about righteousness altogether. One popular author says,

> The good news is that Christ frees us from the need to obnoxiously focus on our goodness, our commitment, and our correctness. Religion has made us obsessive almost beyond endurance. Jesus invited us to a dance . . . and we've turned it into a march of soldiers, always checking to see if we're doing it right and are in step and in line with the other soldiers. We know a dance would be more fun, but we believe we must go through hell to get to heaven, so we keep marching.[1]

It's quite true that when someone is obsessed with "correctness" because he thinks it will gain merit with God or honor for himself, he is guilty of a form of legalism not substantially different from Pharisaism. The selfish fruit of such an evil motive—not merely the desire to be righteous—makes such thinking "obnoxious." But it is spiritually irresponsible and dangerous to suggest that it is inherently moralistic to cultivate a hunger and thirst for righteousness (cf. Matt. 5:6). When the motives for obedience are true love for Christ and a desire to honor Him, it is unjust and uncharitable to belittle a believer's concern for holiness and zeal for good works by branding those desires with the label of "pietism." Jesus Himself said, "If you love Me, keep My commandments" (John 14:15), and He was no moralistic pietist. (It may be worth mentioning, too, that the imagery of soldiers engaged in spiritual warfare is one of the ways the New Testament describes the church. The dance-party analogy is not.)

The spiritual weakness of today's evangelical megachurches and their leaders ought to convince any honest believer that the most imminent threat to our gospel witness at the moment is hardly an unhealthy fixation with being correct. Indifference about personal holiness, apathy about sound, biblical doctrine, and an easygoing susceptibility to worldly values are far more pressing problems.

GRACE AND LAW ARE NOT ADVERSARIES

Obviously grace and law are vastly different principles. In some ways they contrast starkly. Though both are found throughout Scripture, law was the dominant theme in the Old Testament; grace is the central message of the New Testament. "The law was given through Moses, but grace and truth came through Jesus Christ" (John 1:17). The law judges sinners guilty, but grace grants believers forgiveness. The law pronounces a curse; grace declares a blessing. The law says, "The wages of sin is death." Grace says, "The gift of God is eternal life" (Rom. 6:23).

Furthermore, as we have said from the beginning, the gospel is not a call for sinners to save themselves. It is not advice about something the sinner must do to gain salvation. It is not about the sinner's own self-betterment. The gospel is a message about God's work on behalf of the sinner. It is an account of what God does to save sinners. It is about how God justifies the ungodly.

That is precisely what makes the true gospel so starkly different from almost every counterfeit version of the Christian message. That's why the gospel is good news. It is a glorious message about liberty from the law's curse and condemnation (Rom. 8:1). It sets us "free from the law of sin and death" (v. 2).

Sound doctrine therefore demands that a clear distinction be made between law and grace. But if you imagine that grace establishes a new standard of righteousness that *contradicts* the law, or if you think of the law itself as an evil influence, then you have not listened carefully enough to what Paul and the other apostles taught. "Is the law sin? Certainly not! On the contrary, I would not have known sin except through the law" (Rom. 7:7). After all, "sin is lawlessness" (1 John 3:4)—meaning the law shows us what sin is. The law also defines righteousness for us (Deut. 6:25).

Grace speaks more benignly than law, but the two do not disagree about what constitutes sin and righteousness.

And don't imagine that the principle of justification by faith renders obedience unnecessary for Christians. The fact that Christ's righteousness is imputed to believers does not give them license to live *un*righteously; it motivates them and gives them a constant desire to pursue practical righteousness.

Although our own good works, obedience, and holy living are not in any way the ground of our justification, they are nevertheless inevitable fruits of genuine faith and one of the vital tests by which saving faith can be distinguished from mere pretense. "Every good tree bears good fruit. . . . Therefore by their fruits you will know them" (Matt. 7:17, 20). As we saw in the previous chapter, believers are saved "*for* good works, which God prepared beforehand that we should walk in them" (Eph. 2:10).

GRACE AND GOOD WORKS

Grace not only brings salvation; it also instructs and motivates believers to live righteous lives. Paul says so expressly in a brief discourse on grace in Titus 2:11–14:

> For the grace of God that brings salvation has appeared to all men, teaching us that, denying ungodliness and worldly lusts, we should live soberly,

> righteously, and godly in the present age, looking for the blessed hope and glorious appearing of our great God and Savior Jesus Christ, who gave Himself for us, that He might redeem us from every lawless deed and purify for Himself His own special people, zealous for good works.

Clearly, then, grace is far more than bare forgiveness. It is not a vacuous get-out-of-hell-free token. Grace is active and dynamic. It has past, present, and future implications for every believer.

Paul portrays grace as an instructor, "teaching us." This goes well with the imagery he applied to the law in Galatians 3:24: "The law was our tutor." The Greek word translated "tutor" is a unique expression, *paidagçgos.* It refers to a child's guardian. It is derived from two words meaning "boy-leader." This was a caretaker tasked with supervising a nobleman's son. He was custodian of a wealthy family's children (not a "schoolmaster," as in the KJV). He did indeed act as a tutor to the children, especially in matters of behavior and morality, but he was not their formal instructor. In fact, one of his tasks was to bring the children to school. That is precisely how Paul portrays the law in Galatians 3:24—the law's tutorial function was "to bring us to Christ, that we might be justified by faith."

So the law is more like a nanny or a child-care specialist; grace is the master teacher. Titus 2:11–14 highlights three major lessons that grace teaches.

A LESSON FROM THE PAST: SALVATION CAME THROUGH GRACE, NOT LAW

The first lesson points back to the dawn of the New Covenant era and the incarnation of Christ: "For the grace of God that brings salvation has appeared to all men" (Titus 2:11). Paul is referring to the incarnation and first advent of Christ. That is when grace began to be manifest most clearly. As we noted earlier, John 1:17 says, "The law was given through Moses, but grace and truth came through Jesus Christ."

That, of course, does not mean Moses gave the law as a means of salvation for people living in Old Testament times. It also isn't suggesting that grace was an unknown concept prior to the time of Christ. The theme of justification by grace alone through faith alone is traceable back into the early chapters of Genesis and the record of Abraham, who "believed in the LORD, and He accounted it to him for righteousness" (Gen. 15:6). An alien righteousness was imputed to him. In that sense Abraham's salvation embodied all the same principles we learn from the gospel according to Paul. Paul himself makes that point repeatedly: "What then shall we say that Abraham our father has found according to the flesh? For if Abraham was justified by works, he has something to boast about, but not before God. For what does the Scripture say? 'Abraham believed God, and it was accounted to him for righteousness'" (Rom. 4:1–3; cf. Gal. 3:6–7).

So God's lavish forgiveness was by no means unknown or inactive prior to the birth of Christ. In Isaiah 1:18, the Lord invites sinners to be reconciled with Him: "Come now, and let us reason together. . . . Though your sins are like scarlet, they shall be as white as snow; though they are red like crimson, they shall be as wool." He issues the invitation again in Isaiah 55:1 and 7: "Ho! Everyone who thirsts, come to the waters. . . . Let the wicked forsake his way, and the unrighteous man his thoughts; let him return to the LORD, and He will have mercy on him; and to our God, for He will abundantly pardon."

In fact, the Old Testament is full of praise to God for the many blessings of His benevolent mercy:

> *Bless the LORD, O my soul,*
> *And forget not all His benefits:*
> *Who forgives all your iniquities,*
> *Who heals all your diseases,*
> *Who redeems your life from destruction,*
> *Who crowns you with lovingkindness and tender mercies.*
> (Ps. 103:2–4)

The theme of divine grace is thus woven throughout the Old Testament. But to some degree it is overshadowed by all the elaborate detail and emphasis given to the commandments—and by the curses that were essential features of the Mosaic covenant.

When John writes, "The law was given through Moses," he means not only that the Ten Commandments (and the rest of Israel's law code) were handed down from God through Moses at Sinai, but also that Moses was the human mediator through whom the Old Covenant was inaugurated (John 1:17). Moses was the human author who wrote the *Torah*—the principal books of Old Testament law (also known as the *Pentateuch*, the first five books in the biblical canon). There was no more towering figure in the history of the Jewish religion.

But when Christ, God incarnate, came to earth, He quite literally personified grace and truth. John says, "We beheld His glory, the glory as of the only begotten of the Father, full of grace and truth" (John 1:14). He brought God's grace to light with new clarity and in a way that grace had never been manifested before.

Under Moses, law was the primary feature and grace was a subplot. With Christ, the order is reversed. Grace is the dominant theme, and the law takes its proper, subservient role in the drama of redemption. Again, this is not to suggest that the way of salvation changed. No one was ever saved through the law. Nor should we imagine that the law, when used rightly, is hostile to grace. "Is the law then against the promises of God? Certainly not!" (Gal. 3:21). But because we are sinners already, grace (obtained through "faith in Jesus Christ") is the only means by which we can have eternal life (v. 22).

Now, Paul says, grace has been brought out from under the shadow of the law and put on display in its full luster. "The grace of God has appeared, bringing salvation for all people" (Titus 2:11 ESV). He is not suggesting that "all people" will be saved. Jesus Himself made it abundantly clear that "narrow is the gate and difficult is the way which leads to life, and there are few who find it" (Matt. 7:14). He further said, "Many will say to Me in that day, 'Lord, Lord, have we not prophesied in Your name, cast out demons in Your name, and done many wonders in Your name?' And then I will declare to them, 'I never knew you; depart from Me, you who practice lawlessness!'"

(Matt. 7:22–23). "He will also say to those on the left hand, 'Depart from Me, you cursed, into the everlasting fire prepared for the devil and his angels. . . . And these will go away into everlasting punishment" (25:41, 46).

"All people" in Titus 2:11 (ESV) refers to all kinds of people—not all people without exception, but all people without distinction. Paul had just catalogued a list of various people types among whom Titus had pastoral oversight: older men, older women, young women, young men, and bondservants (vv. 2–9). "The grace of God that brings salvation" reaches all categories of humanity (v. 11). No social class, race, or age group is excluded.

"The grace of God . . . brings salvation." That is the central idea, one we have seen from the pen of Paul many times before. A chapter later, Paul will repeat the point yet again: "When the kindness and the love of God our Savior toward man appeared, not by works of righteousness which we have done, but according to His mercy He saved us" (Titus 3:4–5). As always, Paul ascribes all the glory to God. "It is of faith that it might be according to grace" (Rom. 4:16). God "has saved us and called us with a holy calling, not according to our works, but according to His own purpose and grace which was given to us in Christ Jesus" (2 Tim. 1:9).

Grace, not law, has *always* been the sole means of salvation for sinners. But with the coming of Christ, through His teaching, by His death, and in His resurrection, the gospel of grace has now been fully articulated so that it can be understood with absolute clarity. This is the central lesson of His atoning work, and it stands out as if written in bold headlines throughout the New Testament: *Salvation is only by grace.*

A LESSON FOR THE PRESENT: GRACE INSPIRES ZEAL, NOT APATHY

We've discussed the dangers of legalism and the fact that believers are "not under law" (Rom. 6:14). What Paul means by that statement is fairly simple. Believers are free from the law's sentence of condemnation (Rom. 8:1). We have been redeemed from the law's curse (Gal. 3:13). We are not trying to earn any part of our own justification through the works of the law. We know precisely what Paul meant when he spoke of being "under the law," because he wrote his epistle to the Galatians to confront the error and correct the confusion of people in those churches who were placing themselves back under the law. He addressed them in Galatians 4:21: "Tell me, *you who desire to be under the law*, do you not hear the law?" He addressed them again in 5:4: "You have become estranged from Christ, *you who attempt to be justified by law*." So to be "under law" in the Pauline sense is to be seeking one's justification (on the whole or in part) through legal means, by one's own works.

But remember, grace does not render the law entirely moot. "What then? Shall we sin because we are not under law but under grace?" (Rom. 6:15). Paul's answer to that question is unequivocal and full of passion: "Certainly not!" The grace of God does not breed spiritual apathy or indifference in the heart of someone whose faith is authentic. In fact, this is the whole thrust of grace's instruction—"teaching us that, denying ungodliness and worldly lusts, we should live soberly, righteously, and godly in the present age, . . . [being] *zealous* for good works" (Titus 2:12, 14).

Remember that the work of grace in a believer's experience begins with "the washing of regeneration and renewing of the Holy Spirit" (Titus 3:5). The Holy Spirit implants a whole new heart and spirit within the believer: "I will give you a new heart and put a new spirit within you; I will take the heart of stone out of your flesh and give you a heart of flesh. I will put My Spirit within you *and cause you to walk in My statutes*" (Ezek. 36:26–27). Good works are not the ground of our justification, but they are the inevitable consequence of our regeneration.

The salvation wrought by grace is full-orbed; it does not stop with our justification. It continues to instruct us through the present age and conveys us all the way to glory, teaching us along the way to pursue sobriety, righteousness, and godliness. Anyone who thinks God is blithely indifferent to the sins of His people hasn't understood the first thing about grace. Likewise, the notion that grace gives believers permission to be careless about or tolerant of their own transgressions is a pernicious lie.

That is not to suggest that as believers we will not struggle with sin or temptation. Just the opposite. As believers, we wage continual war against sin, always seeking to mortify it, never to dance with it. "The flesh lusts against the Spirit, and the Spirit against the flesh; and these are contrary to one another, so that you do not do the things that you wish" (Gal. 5:17). Because sin is such a tenacious enemy, our own righteous desires are frequently frustrated. Paul clearly understood this, and he described the frustration in passionate terms in Romans 7. Elsewhere, he acknowledged, "I do not count myself to have apprehended" (Phil. 3:13). Though he embodied the traits of spiritual maturity and devotion to Christ, like all of us, Paul was still far from perfect, and he knew it. "But," he said, "I press on, that I may lay hold of that for which Christ Jesus has also laid hold of me" (v. 12).

Grace trains believers to have that perspective. This earthly life is a long struggle toward the goal of sanctification, whereby we are being gradually conformed to perfect Christlikeness. It's a process driven and empowered by grace. There is a negative aspect to it as well as a positive aspect.

On the negative side, grace is teaching us "to deny ungodliness and worldly desires" (Titus 2:12 NASB). That is a practical, day-to-day expression of the same self-denial Jesus called for: "If anyone desires to come after Me, let him deny himself, and take up his cross, and follow Me" (Matt. 16:24). This, of course, is the fruit of God's grace in us, not something we summon from within ourselves by a free-will act of self-determination. The mortification of our sin may feel like difficult self-effort, but the desire to wage war against the lust of our own flesh and the temptations that assault us is nevertheless produced by grace. Paul perfectly described the tension between the effort we put forth and the grace that empowers that effort: "By the grace of God I am what I am, and His grace toward me was not in vain; but I labored more abundantly than they all, yet not I, but the grace of God which was with me" (1 Cor. 15:10).

Specifically, it is the power of Christ, through the indwelling of the Holy Spirit, that enables us to renounce and resist sin. To be under grace and out from under the condemnation of law means that "sin shall not have dominion over you" (Rom. 6:14). It does not mean Christians no longer need to resist the coercive power of sin. It means grace equips them with the strength and the will to resist temptation. "It is God who works in you both to will and to do for His good pleasure" (Phil. 2:13).

On the positive side, grace teaches us that "we should live soberly, righteously, and godly in the present age" (Titus 2:12). Having a right standing before God because Christ's righteousness is imputed to us, it is only fitting that we should seek to honor that perfect righteousness and seek (by God's grace) to conform ourselves to it. How could grace teach otherwise? "Shall we continue in sin that grace may abound? Certainly not! How shall we who died to sin live any longer in it?" (Rom. 6:1–2). For Paul, the idea that someone who had been redeemed from judgment and transformed by God's grace could blithely or willfully continue in sin was absolutely unthinkable.

In other words, grace does not deliver us from hell without also delivering us from our bondage to sin. Those who teach otherwise don't exalt the principle of grace; they denigrate it.

When someone shows no evidence of sanctification (sober, righteous, and godly living), there is no reason to assume that person has received grace. Likewise, the person who has never repented of sin has never known the grace of God. The greatest danger of antinomianism is that it obscures (or denies) this truth and thereby gives false assurance to people who give lip service to Christ but are still under condemnation, having never really been partakers of God's grace.

Sanctification is not an optional part of the Christian experience. All believers are "predestined to be conformed to the image of [God's] Son" (Rom. 8:29). Because He is sovereign and His grace is always effectual, there is no possibility that any believer will utterly fail to bear the fruit of good works. God's grace transforms the Christian's whole life, not merely his religious credo.

A LESSON ABOUT THE FUTURE: WE CAN LIVE IN HOPE, NOT FEAR

Although law and grace operate with the same moral standard, the *eschatology* of grace—what it teaches us about things to come—is infinitely brighter than the eschatology of law. Indeed, the eternal future of those under grace holds nothing but unending glory and blessings. But the only thing the future holds for those who remain under the law is death and eternal damnation.

Here is the fundamental difference between law and grace. The law makes no promise to sinners other than the guarantee of judgment. For those still under the law, the return of Christ will signal the final outpouring of the judgment to come, and it is a terrifying prospect. But God's saving grace teaches us to be "looking for the blessed hope and glorious appearing of our great God and Savior Jesus Christ" (Titus 2:13). Law threatens judgment and pronounces a death sentence. Grace grants forgiveness and promises eternal blessings. The law points to the sinner's past, filling the guilty heart with fear and regret. Grace points to the believer's future and fills the forgiven heart with gratitude and hope.

The difference could not be more stark, and far from luring us into a kind of apathetic passivity—rather than eliminating our desire to be and do good—it should motivate us to pursue holiness with all our passions and energies. This, after all, is what Christ died for: to "redeem us from every lawless deed and purify for Himself His own special people, *zealous for good works*" (Titus 2:14). Zeal for good works is not inherently legalistic or hostile to the spirit of grace. This is precisely the attitude grace instructs us to cultivate.

Grace produces a holy hatred of sin in every true believer. It fills our hearts and minds with a sacred dislike for everything that dishonors God. Although our flesh is still susceptible to sin's enticements, in our innermost soul we "abhor what is evil" (Rom. 12:9). Indeed, hatred for evil is a necessary expression of love for God (Ps. 97:10), and this is the believer's motive for "denying ungodliness and worldly lusts" (Titus 2:11). Its positive flip side is an enduring hunger and thirst for righteousness—the incentive that prompts us to "live soberly, righteously, and godly in the present age" (v. 12).

The "glorious appearing of our great God and Savior Jesus Christ" (v. 13) is the blessed hope we look forward to precisely because Christ's appearing in glory will mean the total and permanent removal of sin from our experience, and we will instantly be transformed and perfected.

For the moment, we groan, together with all creation (Rom. 8:22), but it is not a hopeless complaint, nor is it a cry of defeat. We are "eagerly waiting for the adoption, the redemption of our body" (v. 23). "Beloved, now we are children of God; and it has not yet been revealed what we shall be, but we know that when He is revealed, we shall be like Him, for we shall see Him as He is" (1 John 3:2).

That is the end and the culmination of the gospel according to Paul. That is the glorious hope that makes all the sufferings and hardships of this life seem insignificant by comparison. "For I consider that the sufferings of this present time are not worthy to be compared with the glory which shall be revealed in us" (Rom. 8:18). "Our light affliction, which is but for a moment, is working for us a far more exceeding and eternal weight of glory" (2 Cor. 4:17).

We began our study in the opening verses of 1 Corinthians 15. It's fitting to end on the same point Paul was leading to:

> Behold, I tell you a mystery: We shall not all sleep, but we shall all be changed—in a moment, in the twinkling of an eye, at the last trumpet. For the trumpet will sound, and the dead will be raised incorruptible, and we shall be changed. For this corruptible must put on incorruption, and this mortal must put on immortality. So when this corruptible has put on incorruption, and this mortal has put on immortality, then shall be brought to pass the saying that is written: "Death is swallowed up in victory."
>
> *"O Death, where is your sting?*
> *O Hades, where is your victory?"*
>
> The sting of death is sin, and the strength of sin is the law. But thanks be to God, who gives us the victory through our Lord Jesus Christ.
>
> Therefore, my beloved brethren, be steadfast, immovable, always abounding in the work of the Lord, knowing that your labor is not in vain in the Lord.
>
> (1 Cor. 15:51–58)

Epilogue

PAUL'S TESTIMONY

If I must boast, I will boast in the things which concern my infirmity.

—2 Corinthians 11:30

The gospel was no sideline for the apostle Paul. As we have seen from the beginning, "Jesus Christ and Him crucified" was the principal theme of everything the apostle taught or preached (1 Cor. 2:2). If he spent a great deal of time on any other doctrine, such as that long discourse on sin in Romans 1–3, it was only to lay the necessary groundwork for what he really wanted his readers to get; namely, the good news. If he waded chin-deep into a doctrinal controversy—as he did in Galatians, for example, and 1 Corinthians 15—it was because the gospel was under attack. Whenever he wrote anything that sounded like self-defense, what he was really concerned about was guarding the clarity and authority of "my gospel." In the end, he literally gave his life "for [Christ's] sake and the gospel's" (Mark 8:35).

He always came back to the gospel, like a theological homing pigeon. If I wanted this book to be twenty times longer, there are dozens more passages we could examine where the apostle explains and reiterates the way of salvation by grace through faith in the life, death, and resurrection of

Christ. But perhaps there is no better example to end the book with than Paul's own brief account of his life and conversion in Philippians 3:4–11:

> If anyone else thinks he may have confidence in the flesh, I more so: circumcised the eighth day, of the stock of Israel, of the tribe of Benjamin, a Hebrew of the Hebrews; concerning the law, a Pharisee; concerning zeal, persecuting the church; concerning the righteousness which is in the law, blameless.
>
> But what things were gain to me, these I have counted loss for Christ. Yet indeed I also count all things loss for the excellence of the knowledge of Christ Jesus my Lord, for whom I have suffered the loss of all things, and count them as rubbish, that I may gain Christ and be found in Him, not having my own righteousness, which is from the law, but that which is through faith in Christ, the righteousness which is from God by faith; that I may know Him and the power of His resurrection, and the fellowship of His sufferings, being conformed to His death, if, by any means, I may attain to the resurrection from the dead.

That is a remarkable testimony because of the way Paul weaves in several of his favorite gospel themes: the worthlessness of human works as means of gaining merit with God; the pivotal role of faith; the principles of grace and imputed righteousness; the death and resurrection of the Savior; and above all, the supreme value of knowing Christ over any earthly benefit, privilege, or treasure.

It was rare for Paul to talk about his life prior to conversion or speak of his accomplishments as a scholar and a Pharisee. He despised anything that smacked of boasting. "It is doubtless not profitable for me to boast," he wrote in 2 Corinthians 12:1. In fact, when he had no choice but to talk about himself and his accomplishments, he often did so in self-effacing ways. In 2 Corinthians 12, for example, he was forced to defend his apostolic authority for the gospel's sake. Specifically, he needed to answer the false teachers' claim that they themselves were "super-apostles," because they had supposedly received some gnostic-flavored secret revelation that was the real key to all truth. In reply, Paul described how he had been caught up into paradise. But he told the story in third person, as if it had happened to someone else. Then in verse 11 he wrote, "I have become a fool in boasting."

Indeed, to boast shamelessly in any self-aggrandizing way would be a violation of the definitive pride-killing principle Paul himself often underscored when he spoke of grace: "Where is boasting then? It is excluded" (Rom. 3:27). "Your glorying is not good" (1 Cor. 5:6). Under the gospel, no one has any legitimate grounds for boasting (Eph. 2:9). "No flesh should glory in [God's] presence. . . . 'He who glories, let him glory in the LORD' " (1 Cor. 1:29, 31).

This refusal to boast was proof that Paul had renounced Pharisaism. The Pharisees had virtually made spiritual swagger into a religious sacrament. As we saw in that last chapter, their distinctive religious symbols and works of charity were designed mainly "to be seen by men" (Matt. 23:5). Their most visible trademarks were ostentatious robes and large *phylacteries* (leather boxes containing Scripture that were bound to their foreheads and arms, in a literal and superficial application of Deuteronomy 6:8). If they did any simple works of charity (such as giving to the needy), they performed the deed in such a pretentious manner that Jesus characterized it as "sound[ing] a trumpet" to announce what they were doing. He said the only real purpose for all the Pharisees' exaggerated ploys and symbols was to gain praise for themselves (Matt. 6:2). It was a way of boasting without actually saying anything.

There was much Paul could have boasted about, if he were so inclined. Remember, he was better educated, more literate, more adept at handling Scripture, more knowledgeable about Old Testament history, more well-versed in philosophy, and more skilled in linguistics than any of his critics. Moreover, Paul was an apostle, recognized and fully affirmed by all the other apostles, possessing the full authority of the apostolic office. He was the human instrument by which the Holy Spirit wrote a significant portion of the New Testament, and he was a close companion to Luke, who penned more of the inspired text than any other New Testament author. The risen Christ in the brightness of His glory had shown Himself to Paul on the road to Damascus (Acts 9:1–6, 17; 26:14–18). In fact, Paul was the last person to whom Christ personally appeared after rising from the dead (1 Cor. 9:1; 15:8). Paul had even seen heaven (2 Cor. 12:2–4). So he had far more to boast about than practically any other figure in the New Testament.

Yet when he lists his credentials in Philippians 3, he does so only so that he can formally disavow all his own past religious accomplishments. He dismisses them as "rubbish." The Greek word in that verse is *skubalon.* It's a strong and coarse-sounding term that is used nowhere else in the New Testament. The King James Version gives a more literal translation of the original: "I . . . do count them but dung" (v. 8).

Paul is like the man in the parable of Matthew 13:44, who gives up everything he has in order to obtain a field where treasure is hidden, or the merchant in verses 45–46, who dissolves all his assets to obtain the pearl of great price.

The point of those parables is not to suggest that sinners can purchase salvation in exchange for their own sacrifice. What's preeminent in the parables is that the man with the field and the merchant with the pearl gladly gave up everything they had ever treasured or trusted.

Paul wasn't saying, "I had something good, but this is better." He was declaring the utter worthlessness of his own accomplishments. He was agreeing with Jeremiah, who said, "We are all like an unclean thing, and all our righteousnesses are like filthy rags" (Isa. 64:6). He was quite literally saying that his own best features and highest achievements were not assets; they were liabilities. Rather than gaining because of them, he was losing. "What profit is it to a man if he gains the whole world, and loses his own soul?" (Matt. 16:26). "What things were gain to me, these I have counted loss for Christ" (Phil. 3:7).

For all his life as a Pharisee, Paul had believed eternal life would be won through ritual, race, rank, religion, and right living. His religious credentials were second to none, according to how the Pharisees ranked advantages. He was "a Hebrew of the Hebrews" (Phil. 3:5)—maintaining the Hebrew language and customs, even though he was born in a Gentile region dominated by Hellenized Jews. He came from an especially noble tribe. (Benjamin was one of only two tribes that did not join the rebellion against the House of David after Solomon's death.) He was born into the household of a Pharisee and circumcised as an eight-day-old—precisely as commanded in Genesis 17:12. In other words, he was still a newborn infant when his parents started him on a course of fastidious observance to the ceremonial law. He never overtly defiled the Sabbath or violated the Pharisees' traditions regarding the sacrifices, washings, or other ceremonial law works. He had thus managed to keep his reputation unblemished, so in his own estimation, and from the perspective of any devoted Pharisee, he was "blameless." The proof of his pharisaical zeal was his savage persecution of the church. Any Pharisee would be deeply impressed with such a pedigree.

But when he met Christ, Paul saw that both his ancestry and his accomplishments were permanently and irreparably flawed. It was nothing but one large mass of liabilities.

Therefore, he trashed it all in order to gain Christ (Phil. 3:8). Paul was not saying he gave up *doing* good works, of course, but that he realized first that those were not really good works at all, since there was nothing truly righteous about him. So he gladly gave up *trusting* that his own tainted, pharisaical "good works" might earn merit with God. Merely adding Christ to his religion would not have sanctified it. Remember, he said he counted it as *excrement*. Decorating *skubalon* doesn't alter the reality of what it is.

So Paul put all his faith solely in Christ. His only aim from then on was to "be found in [Christ], not having my own righteousness, which is from the law, but that which is through faith in Christ, the righteousness which is from God by faith" (Phil. 3:9).

He is, of course, describing justification by faith and the principle of imputed righteousness. If anyone tries to tell you Paul never spoke of the imputation of Christ's righteousness,* point out that it is the focus of his

* N. T. Wright, for example, says of 1 Corinthians 1:30, "It is the only passage I know where something called 'the imputed righteousness of Christ,' a phrase more often found in post-Reformation theology and piety than in the New Testament, finds any basis in the text." *What St. Paul Really Said* (Oxford: Lion, 1997), 123.

own personal testimony. To be found *in Christ* is to be clothed in Christ's own righteousness, "not . . . my own righteousness . . . but that which is through faith in Christ" (Phil. 3:9). This establishes the most intimate imaginable relationship between the believer and his Lord. It is an inviolable spiritual union.

What motive could possibly take a devoted, overzealous Pharisee like Saul of Tarsus and persuade him gladly to abandon his lifelong efforts and convictions, labeling them all "dung"?

Paul himself gives the answer to that question. He did it "in view of the surpassing value of knowing Christ" (Phil. 3:8 NASB). Having seen the radiance of Christ's glory in the bright light of gospel truth, nothing else would ever again take first place in his heart.

May that be the testimony of our lives as well.

ACKNOWLEDGMENTS

Without the help of several key people it would be impossible to meet publishing deadlines while keeping up with all my other duties. Several people deserve special mention and my profound appreciation for their work on this book.

Thanks first of all to Phil Johnson, who helped assemble and shape the contours of the original manuscript. He then retyped and carefully polished every revision I scribbled in the margins, right up to the final draft. Phil is not only a skilled wordsmith with a special gift for clarity and precision, he is also a gifted preacher and teacher of God's Word. His literary skills, his passion, and his knowledge of biblical theology are obvious in every book he edits. Phil is also the executive director for the worldwide media ministry of Grace to You and an elder at Grace Community Church. But our mutual interest in publishing verse-by-verse exposition for serious Christian readers is what brought us together, and he has been my main editor for the past thirty-five years. It has been an extremely blessed and fruitful partnership.

Thanks also to Janene MacIvor, who did meticulous work editing the final draft, as well as Jenn McNeil, who offered excellent feedback. I'm especially grateful to Brian Hampton, Webster Younce, and the entire team at Thomas Nelson. They graciously accommodated our need for several deadline extensions and still managed to deliver the finished book on schedule.

Finally, I owe a great debt of gratitude to my son Matt, who managed the business side of the project, organized the scheduling and other details on our end, and acted as a conduit for communications between the publisher and my staff.

Appendix 1

IN DEFENSE OF SUBSTITUTIONARY ATONEMENT

This appendix offers a more thorough discussion of penal substitution and some of the alternative theories of the atonement. (We briefly considered the various theories in chapter 5.) This is an expanded and updated version of an essay I wrote at the start of the new millennium. The original version was first published as a chapter in a symposium on open theism: Doug Wilson, ed., *Bound Only Once: The Failure of Open Theism* (Moscow, ID: Canon, 2001), 95–107. For those unfamiliar with open theism, it is a deviant view whose best-known feature is a denial that God perfectly knows the future. It is usually paired with an emphatic denial that the principles of propitiation and penal substitution are necessary aspects of Christ's atoning work.

Jesus Christ the righteous . . . is the propitiation for our sins

—1 John 2:1–2

In February 1990, a highly controversial article in *Christianity Today* heralded several radical developments in the way many theologians were beginning to think and write about theology. The article was written by

Robert Brow, a prominent Canadian theologian. Brow announced that a radical change was looming on the evangelical horizon—a "megashift" toward "new-model" thinking, away from "old-model" theology (Brow's moniker for historic evangelical doctrines).[1] The article dispassionately described how the new theology was radically changing the evangelical concept of God by proposing new explanations for biblical concepts such as divine wrath, God's righteousness, judgment, the atonement—and just about every aspect of evangelical theology.

At the time, the "progressive" ideas described in the article were more or less confined to academic circles at the outer fringe of the evangelical movement. But the megashift the article foretold did gradually invade more mainstream theological discussions. Within ten years, evangelicals were debating *open theism* (the idea that the future is unknown even to God and thus open to practically any eventuality). Open theists denied virtually every major tenet of classic theism, including the sovereignty of God, His foreknowledge, His immutability, and (of course) His omniscience. To one degree or another, they all denied the inerrancy and authority of Scripture as well. Their movement was a rationalistic effort to make God manageable and politically correct.

By 2005, many in the evangelical community were fixated on the so-called Emerging Church movement, a grass-roots effort to alter and blur the evangelical perspective on God and His Word. Many of the leaders in that movement were enthralled with the claims of the open theists. Their influence resulted in a widespread, popular-level drift away from historic evangelical beliefs, in precisely the direction Robert Brow had predicted in his 1990 article.

The Emerging Church movement disintegrated and fell off the evangelical radar by 2011, and nowadays open theism doesn't seem to generate as much interest or controversy as it used to. But the liberalizing ideas those movements planted in the evangelical consciousness are still germinating, and their influence is still spreading. I'm convinced we still have not seen the last (or most destructive) wave of Robert Brow's megashift. New-model theology is alive and flourishing, even if the early movements it spawned look like they have lost steam.

Brow died in July 2008, but not before he saw most of his predictions fulfilled to the letter. Although his 1990 article purposely left unanswered the question of whether he personally would cheer or condemn the megashift, those who knew anything about him were well aware that he was deeply sympathetic to all the unorthodox opinions he described. By the mid-1990s he had emerged as one of open theism's most enthusiastic cheerleaders.

THE QUEST FOR A MANAGEABLE DEITY

Brow's article portrayed new-model theology in benign terms. He described the movement as a positive attempt to remodel some of the more difficult truths of Scripture by employing new, friendlier paradigms to explain God.

According to Brow, old-model theology casts God in a severe light. In old-model evangelicalism, God is a fearsome Magistrate whose judgment is a harsh and inflexible legal verdict; sin is an offense against His divine law; God's wrath is the anger of an indignant sovereign; hell is a relentless retribution for sin; and atonement may be purchased only if payment in full is made for sin's judicial penalty.

In new-model theology, however, the God-as-Magistrate model is set aside in favor of a more congenial model—that of God as a loving Father. New-model thinkers want to eliminate the negative connotations associated with difficult biblical truths such as divine wrath and God's righteous retribution against sin. So they simply redefine those concepts by employing models that evoke "the warmth of a family relationship."[2] For example, they suggest that divine wrath is really nothing more than a sort of fatherly displeasure that inevitably provokes God to give us loving encouragements. God is a "judge" only in the sense of the Old Testament judges ("such as Deborah or Gideon or Samuel")—meaning He is a defender of His people rather than an authority who sits at the bar of justice.[3] Sin is merely "bad behavior" that ruptures fellowship with God—and its remedy is always correction, never retribution. Even hell isn't really a punishment;

it is the ultimate expression of the sinner's freedom, because according to new-model thought, "assignment to hell is not by judicial sentence"—so if anyone goes there, it is purely by choice.[4]

Gone are all vestiges of divine severity. God has been toned down and tamed. According to new-model theology, God is not to be thought of as righteously indignant over His creatures' disobedience. In fact, Brow's article was subtitled "Why you may not have heard about wrath, sin, and hell recently." He characterized the God of new-model theology as a kinder, gentler, more user-friendly deity.

Indeed, one of the main goals of the megashift was apparently to eliminate the fear of the Lord completely. According to Brow, "No one would deny that it is easier to relate to a God perceived as kindly and loving."[5]

Of course, the God of old-model theology is also unceasingly gracious, merciful, and loving (a fact one would not be able to glean from the gross caricature new-model advocates like to paint when they describe "old-model orthodoxy"). But old-model theologians—with Scripture on their side—teach that there is more to the divine character than beneficence. God is also holy, righteous, and angry with the wicked every day (Ps. 7:11). He is fierce in His indignation against sin (cf. Ps. 78:49; Isa. 13:9–13; Zeph. 3:8). Fear of Him is the very essence of true wisdom (Job 28:28; Ps. 111:10; Prov. 1:7; 9:10; 15:33). And "the terror of the Lord" is even a motive for our evangelism (2 Cor. 5:11). "For our God is a consuming fire" (Heb. 12:29; cf. Deut. 4:24), and "It is a fearful thing to fall into the hands of the living God" (Heb. 10:31).

Nonetheless, open theists have shown a passionate determination to eliminate or explain away every feature of the divine character except those that are instantly "perceived as kindly and loving." They want nothing to do with a God who demands to be feared. Their theology aims to construct a manageable deity, a god who is "easier to relate to"—a quasi-divine being who has been divested of all the features of divine glory and majesty that might provoke any fear or dread in the creature. Instead, they made Him into a kindly, nonthreatening, heavenly valet.

REDEFINING THE ATONEMENT

Above all, the new-model god never demands any payment for sin as a condition of forgiveness. According to the new-model view, if Christ suffered for our sins, it was only in the sense that He "absorb[ed] our sin and its consequences"—certainly not that He received any divinely inflicted punishment on our behalf at the cross. He merely became a partaker with us in the human problem of pain and suffering. (After all, earthly "pain and suffering" are just about the worst consequences of sin new-model theologians can imagine.)

The most disturbing line in Robert Brow's article is an almost incidental, throwaway remark near the end, in which he states that according to new-model theology, "the cross was not a judicial payment," but merely a visible, space-time expression of how Christ has *always* suffered because of our sin.[6]

In other words, according to new-model theology, the atoning work of Christ was not truly substitutionary; He made no ransom-payment for sin; no guilt was imputed to Him; nor did God punish Him as a substitute for sinners. None of His sufferings on the cross were administered by God. Instead, according to the new model, *atonement* means that our sins are unceremoniously waived aside out of the bounty of God's loving tolerance; our relationship with God is normalized; and Christ "absorbed the consequences" of our forgiveness (which presumably means He suffered the indignity and shame that go with enduring an offense).

So what *does* the cross mean according to new-model theologians? Many of them say Christ's death was nothing more than a public display of the awful consequences of sin—so that rather than offering His blood to satisfy *God's* justice, Christ was merely demonstrating sin's effects in order to fulfill a *public* perception of justice.* Other new-model theologians

---

* This is a version of Grotius's governmental atonement theory discussed later in this appendix. See also appendix 1 ("How Are We to Understand the Atonement?") in John MacArthur, *The Freedom and Power of Forgiveness* (Wheaton: Crossway, 1998), 197–203, for a more thorough critique of Grotius's view of the atonement.

go even further, virtually denying the need for any kind of ransom for sin altogether.* Indeed, the entire concept of a payment to expiate sin's guilt is nonsense if the open theists are right.**

Thus new-model theologians have rather drastically remodeled the doctrine of Christ's atonement, and in the process they have fashioned a system that is in no sense truly evangelical—but is both a repudiation of core evangelical distinctives and a denial of the gospel. It is surely no overstatement to say that their emasculated doctrine of the atonement obliterates the true meaning of the cross. According to open theism, the cross is merely a demonstrative proof of Christ's "willingness to suffer"—and in this watered-down view of the atonement, He suffers *alongside* the sinner, rather than *in the sinner's stead.*

This error is the bitter root of a corrupt tree that can never bear good fruit (cf. Matt. 7:18–20; Luke 6:43). Church history is rife with examples of those who rejected the vicarious nature of Christ's atonement and thereby made shipwreck of the faith.

---

* John Sanders, a leading proponent of open theism, begins his discussion of the cross by writing, "I understand sin to primarily be alienation, or a broken relationship, rather than a state of being or guilt." With such a definition of sin, what need is there of any propitiation? Indeed, Sanders goes on to characterize the cross as a public display of God's willingness to "suffer the pain, foregoing revenge, in order to pursue the reconciliation of the broken relationship." In other words, the "cost of forgiveness" in Sanders's system is a sacrifice God makes pertaining to His personal honor and dignity, rather than a price He demands in accord with His perfect righteousness. So Sanders believes God ultimately *relinquishes* the rightful claims of His justice and holiness rather than *satisfying* them through the atoning blood of Christ. That is the typical view of open theism toward the atonement. *The God Who Risks* (Downers Grove: InterVarsity, 1998), 105.

** Open theist David Basinger suggests that the believer's own free-will choice—rather than Christ's atonement—is what "bridges" the "initial separation . . . between God and humans." Basinger moreover describes the gap "between God and humans" without any reference to sin whatsoever; it is merely "an initial inability for God and humans to interact to the extent possible." He depicts the gospel as "'good news'—the joy and excitement of being properly related to God." Utterly missing from his discussion of open theism's evangelistic ramifications is any reference to the cross of Christ or the meaning of atonement. No wonder—for if Basinger and other open theists are right, the cross is really superfluous as far as divine forgiveness is concerned. The crucifixion of Christ becomes little more than a melodramatic display of sentiment, not a ransom for anything. Clark Pinnock, et al., *The Openness of God* (Downers Grove: InterVarsity, 1994), 173–75.

SOCINIANISM REDUX

In fact, the "new-model" innovations described in Robert Brow's 1990 article—and the distinctive principles of open theism, including the open theist's view of the atonement—are by no means a "new model." They all smack of Socinianism, a heresy that flourished in the sixteenth century.

Like modern open theism, sixteenth-century Socinianism was an attempt to rid the divine attributes of all that seemed harsh or severe. According to Socinianism, love is God's governing attribute; His love essentially overwhelms and annuls His displeasure against sin; His goodness makes void His wrath. Therefore, the Socinians contended, God is perfectly free to forgive sin without demanding a payment of any kind.

Furthermore, the Socinians argued, the idea that God would demand a payment for sins is contradictory to the very notion of forgiveness. They said sins can be either remitted or paid for, but not both. If a price must be paid, then sins are not truly "forgiven." And if God is really willing to pardon sin, then no ransom price should be necessary. Moreover, according to the Socinian argument, if a price is demanded, then forgiveness is no more gracious than any legal transaction, like the payment of a traffic ticket.

That argument may seem subtly appealing to the human mind at first. But biblically it falls far short. In fact, it is completely contrary to what Scripture teaches about grace, atonement, and divine justice. It hinges on definitions of those terms that ignore what Scripture clearly teaches.

Grace is not incompatible with the payment of a ransom. It was purely by grace that God Himself (in the Person of Christ) made the payment we owed. In fact, according to 1 John 4:9–10, this is the consummate expression of divine grace and love: that God willingly sent His Son to bear a world of guilt and die for sin in order to propitiate His righteous indignation, fully satisfy His justice, and thereby redeem sinners: "In this the love of God was manifested toward us, that God has sent His only begotten Son into the world, that we might live through Him. In this is love, not that we loved God, but that He loved us and sent His Son *to be the propitiation for our sins.*" Christ came to be "the Lamb of God who takes away the sin of the world" (John 1:29). That language is a plain reference to the Old Testament sacrificial system, deliberately evoking the concept of expiation, which in the Jewish sacrificial system involved the payment of a blood-price, a penalty for sin.

Furthermore, anyone who studies what Scripture has to say about the forgiveness of sin will see very quickly that the shedding of Christ's blood is the only ground on which sins may ever be forgiven. There can be no forgiveness unless the ransom price is paid in blood. Remember, that is the very thing both Socinians and open theists deny. They say forgiveness is incompatible with the payment of a penalty—sins that must be paid for haven't truly been remitted. But Hebrews 9:22 clearly refutes their claim: "Without shedding of blood there is no remission."

THE BIBLICAL DOCTRINE OF SUBSTITUTIONARY ATONEMENT

On the cross, God made Christ a *propitiation*—a satisfaction of the divine wrath against sin (Rom. 3:25). The sacrifice Christ rendered was a payment of the penalty for sin assessed by God. Christ offered Himself on the cross *to God.* "Christ also has loved us and given Himself for us, an offering and a sacrifice *to God* for a sweet-smelling aroma" (Eph. 5:2). His death was a sacrifice offered to appease God's justice. It was the only way God could remain just while justifying sinners (Rom. 3:26). It was the only way He could forgive sin without compromising His own justice and holiness.

Scripture expressly teaches this. Christ died in our place and in our stead. He "was offered once to bear the sins of many" (Heb. 9:28). He "bore our sins in His own body on the tree" (1 Peter 2:24). And as He hung there on the cross, He suffered the full wrath of God on our behalf. "Surely He has borne our griefs and carried our sorrows; yet we esteemed Him stricken, smitten by God, and afflicted. But He was wounded for our transgressions, He was bruised for our iniquities; the chastisement for our peace was upon Him, and by His stripes we are healed" (Isa. 53:4–5). "Christ has redeemed us from the curse of the law, having become a curse for us" (Gal. 3:13). These are principles established in the Old Testament sacrificial system, not concepts borrowed from Greek and Roman legal paradigms, as open theists are so fond of claiming.

It was *God* who decreed and orchestrated the events of the crucifixion. Acts 2:23 says Christ was "delivered by the determined purpose and foreknowledge of God." God's hand and His counsel determined every facet of Christ's suffering (Acts 4:28). According to Isaiah 53:10, "It pleased the LORD to bruise Him; *He* has put Him to grief." That same verse says Jehovah made His Servant "an offering for sin." In other words, *God* punished Christ for sin on the cross and thereby made Him a sin offering. All the wrath and vengeance of the offended Almighty was poured on Him, and He became the sacrificial Lamb who bore His people's sin.

This is the whole gist of the book of Hebrews as well. "It is not possible that the blood of bulls and goats could take away sins" (10:4). Verse 10 says, "We have been sanctified through the offering of the body of Jesus Christ once for all." Verse 12 says His death was "one sacrifice for sins forever." Very clearly those verses are teaching that Christ was sacrificed as a blood atonement to meet the demands of God's righteousness. No wonder many find that a shocking truth. It *is* shocking. And it is profound. It ought to put us on our faces before God. Any "new model" that diminishes or denies the truth of Christ's vicarious suffering at God's own hand is a seriously flawed model.

What do you think of when you ponder Christ's death on the cross? Open theism reasserts the old liberal lie that He was basically a martyr, a victim of humanity—put to death at the hands of evil men. But Scripture says He is the Lamb of God, a victim of divine wrath.

What made Christ's miseries on the cross so difficult for Him to bear was not the taunting and torture and abuse of evil men. It was that He bore the full weight of divine fury against sin. Jesus' most painful sufferings were not merely those inflicted by the whips and nails and thorns. But by far the most excruciating agony Christ bore was the full penalty of sin on our behalf—God's wrath poured out on Him in infinite measure.

Remember that when He finally cried out in distress, it was because of the afflictions He received from *God's own hand*: "My God, My God, why have *You* forsaken Me?" (Mark 15:34). "We esteemed Him stricken, smitten *by God*, and afflicted" (Isa. 53:4). We cannot even begin to know what Christ suffered. It is a horrible reality to ponder. But we dare not follow open theism in rejecting the notion that He bore His Father's punishment for our sins, for in this truth lies the very nerve of genuine Christianity. It is the major reason the cross is such an offense (cf. 1 Cor. 1:18).

Scripture says, "[God] made [Christ] who knew no sin to be sin for us, that we might become the righteousness of God in Him" (2 Cor. 5:21). Our sins were imputed to Christ, and He bore the awful price as our substitute. Conversely, His righteousness is imputed to all who believe, and they stand before God fully justified, clothed in the pure white garment of His perfect righteousness. As we observed in chapter 5, this is the distilled meaning of what happened at the cross for every believer: *God treated Christ as if He had lived our wretched, sinful life, so that He could treat us as if we had lived Christ's spotless, perfect life.*

Deny the vicarious nature of the atonement—deny that our guilt was transferred to Christ and He bore its penalty—and you in effect have denied the ground of our justification. If our guilt wasn't transferred to Christ and paid for on the cross, how can His righteousness be imputed to us for our justification? Every deficient view of the atonement must deal with this same dilemma. And unfortunately, those who misconstrue the meaning of the atonement invariably end up proclaiming a different gospel, devoid of the principle of justification by faith.

THE BATTLE FOR THE ATONEMENT

The atonement has been a theological battleground ever since Anselm of Canterbury (1033–1109) first began to focus the clear light of Scripture on this long-neglected and often misunderstood aspect of redemption. The early church, consumed with controversies about the Person of Christ and the nature of the Godhead, more or less took for granted the doctrine of the atonement. It was rarely a subject for debate or systematic analysis in early church writings. But when church fathers wrote about the atonement, they employed biblical terminology about ransom and propitiation.

Few would argue that the church fathers had a well-formed understanding of the atonement as a penal substitution, but Augustus Hodge pointed out that the idea of vicarious atonement was more or less implicit in their understanding, even if it was "often left to a remarkable degree in the background, and mixed up confusedly with other elements of truth or superstition."[7] Specifically, some of the fathers seemed confused about the nature of the ransom Christ paid—especially on the question of to whom the ransom was due. Some of them seemed to think of it as a ransom paid to Satan, as if Christ paid a fee to the Devil to purchase release for sinners. That is the *ransom theory* of the atonement.

Nonetheless, according to Hodge, "With few exceptions, the whole church from the beginning has held the doctrine of Redemption in the sense of a literal propitiation of God by means of the expiation of sin."[8] Selected church fathers' comments about the ransom of Christ should not be taken as studied, conscientious doctrinal statements but rather as childlike expressions of an unformed and inadequate doctrine of the atonement. Philip Schaff, commenting on the lack of clarity about the atonement in early church writings, said, "The primitive church teachers lived more in the thankful enjoyment of redemption than in logical reflection upon it. We perceive in their exhibitions of this blessed mystery the language rather of enthusiastic feeling than of careful definition and acute analysis."[9] "Nevertheless," Schaff added, "all the essential elements of the later church doctrine of redemption may be found, either expressed or implied, before the close of the second century."[10]

Until Anselm, no leading theologian really focused much energy on systematizing the biblical doctrine of the atonement. Anselm's work on the subject, *Cur Deus Homo? (Why Did God Become Man?)*, offered compelling biblical evidence that the atonement was not a ransom paid *by* God to the Devil but rather a debt paid *to* God on behalf of sinners, a satisfaction of the divine honor. This is the *satisfaction theory* of the atonement. (It is sometimes called the *commercial theory.*)

Anselm's work on the atonement was a huge step forward, and it established a foundation for the Protestant Reformation. This understanding of the atonement was refined and further developed by the Reformers. Their view, that the atonement is a *penal substitution,* was the first full-orbed understanding of Christ's atonement that did full justice to all the texts that speak of Christ's death "for sins" on behalf of sinners. Penal substitution became the very heart of evangelical theology and has long been considered an essential tenet of historic evangelical conviction. All who have abandoned this view have led movements away from evangelicalism.

A close contemporary of Anselm's, Peter Abelard, responded to Anselm's theory with a view of the atonement that is virtually the same as the view held by some of the leading modern open theists. According to Abelard, God's justice is subjugated to His love. He demands no payment for sin. Instead, the redeeming value of Christ's death consisted in the power of the loving example He left for sinners to follow. This view is sometimes called the *moral influence theory* of the atonement. Abelard's view was later adopted and refined by the Socinians in the sixteenth century (as discussed earlier).

Of course, as is true with most heresies, there is a kernel of truth in the moral influence theory. The atoning work of Christ is the consummate expression of God's love (1 John 4:9–10). It is also a motive for love in the believer (vv. 7–8, 11). But the major problem with Abelard's approach is that he made the atonement nothing more than an example. If Abelard was correct, Christ's work on the cross accomplished nothing objective on the sinner's behalf—so there is no real propitiatory aspect to Christ's death. That essentially makes redemption from sin the believer's own responsibility. Sinners are "redeemed" by following the example of Christ. "Salvation" is reduced to moral reform motivated by love. It is a pure form of works salvation.

Abelard's castrated view of the atonement is the doctrine that lies at the core of liberal theology. Like every other form of works salvation, it is a different gospel from the good news set forth in Scripture.

Hugo Grotius (1583–1645) devised a completely different view of the atonement during the Arminian controversy in Holland. Known as the *governmental theory* of the atonement, this view is something of a middle road between Abelard and Anselm. According to Grotius, Christ's death was a public display of God's justice, but not an actual payment on behalf of sinners. In other words, the cross shows what punishment for sin would look like if God recompensed sin. But Christ made no actual vicarious payment of the sinner's debt.

Grotius, like Abelard and the Socinians, believed God could forgive sin without any payment. But Grotius said the dignity and authority of God's law still needed to be upheld. Sin is a challenge to God's right to rule. If God simply overlooked sin, He would in effect abrogate His moral government of the universe. So Christ's death was necessary to vindicate God's authority as ruler, because it proved His willingness and His right to punish, even though He ultimately relinquishes the claims of His justice against repentant sinners. Christ's death therefore was not a substitute for anyone else's punishment, but merely a public example of God's moral authority and His hatred of sin.

In other words, unlike Abelard, Grotius saw that the death of Christ displayed the wrath, as well as the love, of God. Like Abelard, however, Grotius believed the atonement was exemplary rather than substitutionary. Christ did not actually suffer in anyone's place. The atonement accomplished nothing objective on the sinner's behalf; it was merely a symbolic gesture. Christ's death was an example only. And redemption therefore hinges completely on something the sinner must do. So the governmental theory also results inevitably in works salvation.*

* Most governmentalists stress repentance as a human free-will decision. Charles Finney, a conscientious defender of Grotius's view of the atonement, preached a message titled "Making a New Heart," in which he argued that regeneration (and particularly the change of heart that involves removal of the stony heart and implantation of a heart of flesh—cf. Ezekiel 36:26), is something each sinner must accomplish for himself. Moreover, in his *Systematic Theology*, Finney wrote, "[Sinners] are under the necessity of first changing their hearts, or their choice of an end, before they can put forth any volitions to secure any other than a selfish end. And this is plainly the everywhere assumed philosophy of the Bible. That uniformly represents the unregenerate as totally depraved [a voluntary condition, not a constitutional depravity, according to Finney], and calls upon them to repent, *to make themselves a new heart*" (Minneapolis: Bethany House, 1994), 249 (emphasis added).

New-model open theists seem to halt between two wrong opinions—sometimes echoing Grotius's governmentalism, sometimes sounding suspiciously Abelardian.* But one thing all open theists would agree on is this: Anselm and the penal substitution view of the atonement are obsolete, part of an outdated model they can hardly wait for the evangelical movement to shed.

EVANGELICALISM? HARDLY

The leading advocates of new-model doctrine typically self-identify as evangelicals. Robert Brow foresaw that as well. Near the end of his article, he wonders aloud if new-model thinking has any place under the evangelical umbrella. Does it provide a more helpful picture of God's good news, or is it "another gospel"?[11]

Earlier generations of evangelicals would have answered that question without qualm or hesitation by declaring that the new-model message is "another gospel" (Gal. 1:8–9). Indeed, that is precisely how they have answered whenever Socinians, Unitarians, liberals, and various other peddlers of new theologies have raised these very same challenges to the "old model."

Unfortunately, the major segment of this generation of evangelicalism has lacked either the will or the conviction to regard open theists and liberal Emergents as wolves in sheep's clothing rather than true reformers. But let it be clearly stated: by any definition of evangelicalism with historical integrity, any new-model doctrine that abandons penal substitution stands in opposition to core truths that have always been deemed essential principles of evangelical theology.** And by any truly *biblical* definition,

---

* In his article "From Augustine to Arminius: A Pilgrimage in Theology," Clark Pinnock recounted his own retreat from the penal substitution view via a route that took him from Anselm to Grotius to Barth. Pinnock, ed. *The Grace of God, the Will of Man: A Case for Arminianism* (Grand Rapids: Zondervan, 1990).

** Quite simply, the label *evangelical* has historically been used to identify those who hold to both the formal and material principles of the Reformation—*sola Scriptura* (Scripture as the supreme authority) and *sola fide* (justification by faith alone). Although in recent years much broader and more complex definitions have been proposed, the history of the evangelical movement is inextricably linked with a resolute defense of those two vital principles. Absolutely essential to the doctrine of justification by faith is the truth of a vicarious atonement, where the guilt of the

they are heretics, purveyors of a different gospel. Both of these charges are substantiated by new-model theology's abandonment of substitutionary atonement alone.

In fact, the only significant difference between today's open theists and the Socinians of yesteryear is that the Socinians denied the deity of Christ, whereas most open theists ostensibly do not. But in effect, they have denied the deity of *God Himself* by humanizing Him and trying to reconcile Him with modern standards of political correctness.

In "Evangelical Megashift," Robert Brow claims that "the wind of [new-model theology's] influence blows in through every crack when we read C. S. Lewis's Chronicles of Narnia stories."[12] Lewis was no theologian, and there's no doubt that his views were squidgy on the question of eternal punishment. He held other views that make old-model evangelicals shudder. But one wonders if he really would have been in sympathy with open theists' quest for a tamed and toned-down deity.

In the Narnia Chronicles, Aslan, the fierce but loving lion, represents Christ. His paws are frighteningly terrible, sharp as knives with the claws extended, but soft and velvety when the claws are drawn in.[13] He is both good *and* fearsome. When the children in Lewis's tale looked at him, they "went all trembly."[14] Mr. Beaver says of him, "He's wild, you know. Not like a *tame* lion."[15] And Lewis as narrator observes, "People who have not been in Narnia sometimes think a thing cannot be good and terrible at the same time."[16]

That same basic false assumption was the starting point for the heresy of open theism. New-model theologians began with the assumption that God could not be good and terrible at the same time, so they set out to divest Him of whatever attributes they didn't like. Like the Socinians and liberals who preceded them, they set out on a misguided quest to make God "good" according to a humanistic, earthbound definition of "good." They ended up with a god of their own making.

---

sinner is imputed to Christ and paid for, while the merit of Christ is imputed to the believer as the sole ground of acceptance with God. All who have denied substitutionary atonement have either been far outside the historic evangelical mainstream, or they have led movements that quickly abandoned evangelical distinctives.

In the final book of the Narnia series, a wicked ape drapes a lion skin over a witless ass and pretends the ass is Aslan. It is a sinister and dangerous pretense, and in the end it leads countless Narnians astray. The god of new-model theology is like an ass in an ill-fitting lion's skin. And it is leading many away from the glorious God of Scripture.

God is both good *and* fearsome. His wrath is as real as His love. And though He has "mercy for thousands, forgiving iniquity and transgression and sin, [He will] by no means [clear] the guilty" without satisfying His own justice and wrath (Ex. 34:7).

True evangelicals can never relinquish those truths. And those who cannot stomach God the way He has revealed Himself have no right to the label "evangelical." These are issues worth fighting for, as both church history and Scripture plainly prove. The rise of open theism is a grave threat to the cause of the true gospel. May God raise up a new generation of evangelical warriors with the courage and conviction to contend for the truth of substitutionary atonement.

APPENDIX 2

CHRIST DIED FOR GOD

This appendix is a sermon transcript, abridged and edited for publication. It is adapted from a Sunday-morning message originally delivered at Grace Community Church in January 2006. I've included it here in response to the common notion that *propitiation* (both the word and the idea) is too technical or too troublesome for lay people. This message also demonstrates that the idea of Christ's death as a propitiation was not unique to the apostle Paul. It is a truth that was pervasive in all the apostles' teaching, and it was absolutely essential to their understanding of the gospel.

In this is love, not that we loved God, but that He loved us
and sent His Son to be the propitiation for our sins.

—1 JOHN 4:10

Paul is not the only apostle who used the word *propitiation* in an epistle to brethren in the church's early years. John likewise employed it. He was not a theologian with formal academic credentials but a career fisherman, drafted into discipleship while mending his nets and subsequently appointed as one of Christ's twelve apostles, tasked with introducing the gospel to the world. We can safely surmise that he did not consider the concept of propitiation either excessive or too obscure for the majority of his readers.

Indeed, when we consider the cross from a heavenly perspective, propitiation is an essential concept, and one that vastly expands our understanding of whom Christ died for.

Viewing the cross from the perspective of God is not the usual way of thinking about it. We almost exclusively think of the cross in regard to our own lives—focusing on what it means for those who believe. "Christ died for the ungodly," we say (Rom. 5:6). "Christ died for *us*" (v. 8). "Christ died for our sins" (1 Cor. 15:3). He died for our salvation. He died for our eternal benefit. He died to rescue us from judgment and hell. All of those statements are absolutely true, and certainly we should celebrate what the cross means for us.

But looking at the atonement from heaven's perspective, we also need to recognize and confess that *Christ died for God.* And all those other truisms hinge on this fact. "[Christ] gave Himself for our sins . . . *according to the will of our God and Father*" (Gal. 1:4). "What the law could not do in that it was weak through the flesh, *God did by sending His own Son* in the likeness of sinful flesh, on account of sin" (Rom. 8:3). The Father "did not spare His own Son, but delivered Him up for us all" (v. 32).

Jesus Himself said, "My food is to do the will of Him who sent Me, and to finish His work" (John 4:34). "I have come down from heaven, not to do My own will, but the will of Him who sent Me" (6:38). "My Father loves Me, because I lay down My life that I may take it again. No one takes it from Me, but I lay it down of Myself. I have power to lay it down, and I have power to take it again. *This command I have received from My Father*" (10:17–18). God sent Christ to earth to die.

Even Isaiah 53, that profound Old Testament prophecy about Christ's death on the cross, says, "It pleased the LORD to bruise Him; He has put Him to grief" (v. 10). Why? As the punishment for our sin. "Surely He has borne our griefs and carried our sorrows; yet we esteemed Him stricken, *smitten by God,* and afflicted" (v. 4). Christ gave His life at the behest of His own Father. Christ died for God.

Just to hear that statement may cause cognitive dissonance in some Christian's minds. That's only because they have not understood how the death of Christ satisfied the perfect justice of God, as well as how it glorifies Him.

Romans 11 ends with a great doxology:

> Oh, the depth of the riches both of the wisdom and knowledge of God!
> How unsearchable are His judgments and His ways past finding out!
>
> *"For who has known the mind of the LORD? Or who has become His counselor?"*
>
> *"Or who has first given to Him and it shall be repaid to him?"*
>
> For of Him and through Him and to Him are all things, to whom be glory forever. Amen."
>
> (vv. 33–36)

My mind is seized by that phrase, "Of Him and through Him and to Him are all things." What things does the apostle have in mind? "*All* things" is absolutely comprehensive, of course. Nothing is excluded. But Paul's specific emphasis here is on things related to salvation. He has had the gospel in focus throughout the previous eleven chapters. The "all things" he speaks of here are the same things he has already said repeatedly are *from* God and accomplished *through* God alone. These same realities have a purpose that ultimately looks *to* God. They are instruments through which His glory is manifest and magnified. God is the source, the means, and the object of all redemptive work. Everything is for Him.

Paul says in Romans 1:5 that we have been given the ministry of proclaiming the gospel so that people can obey it in faith for His name's sake. In verse 7 of 3 John, the apostle says of the brethren and pilgrims who spread the gospel across the Empire in the first century, "They went forth for His name's sake." Jude's epistle ends with this benediction: "Now to Him who is able to keep you from stumbling, and to present you faultless before the presence of His glory with exceeding joy, to God our Savior, who alone is wise, be glory and majesty, dominion and power, both now and forever. Amen" (vv. 24–25).

Everything points to God. Again, that was Jesus' clear perspective throughout His earthly life. On the last night before He died, He prayed to His Father, "I have glorified You on the earth. I have finished the work which You have given Me to do" (John 17:4). He never sought anything other than "the glory of the One who sent Him" (John 7:18). He said this about the Father's will: "I always do those things that please Him" (John 8:29). "I can of Myself do nothing. As I hear, I judge; and My judgment is righteous, because I do not seek My own will but the will of the Father who sent Me" (John 5:30). Everything Jesus ever did was for God. Including His death.

It was not without a struggle that He gave His life for the glory of God. In John 12:27–28, as Christ anticipated the cross, He said, "Now My soul is troubled, and what shall I say? 'Father, save Me from this hour'? But for this purpose I came to this hour. Father, glorify Your name." He looked at the cross as the consummate way in which He would glorify the Father. Jesus had devoted His whole life to glorifying God, and His death was likewise for the glory of God.

That is fitting. As Peter says, the goal of *everything* should be this: that "in all things God may be glorified through Jesus Christ, to whom belong the glory and dominion forever and ever. Amen" (1 Peter 4:11).*

We tend to think too much of what the cross means to *us* and too little of what it meant to God. In order for the cross to mean anything to us, it must mean everything to God. The better we understand this, the more clearly we understand the cross.

CHRIST'S DEATH WAS A SACRIFICE TO GOD

The Old Testament reminds us of a divinely ordered and carefully detailed system of sacrifice and offerings to God. No sacrifice was ever to be offered to any other being. God alone was the recipient of every legitimate sacrifice, every proper offering. They were all for Him. They were to rise, as it were, to His nostrils, as sweet-smelling savor, as incense to please Him. The

* See appendix 3, "The Reason for Everything."

offerer was guilty of sin before our holy God and was, therefore, subject to God's wrath. God had been offended and dishonored—as He is by every sin ever committed by any person who has ever lived.

In the Old Testament, God provided the way in which the sinner could come before Him and symbolically, temporarily have his sin dealt with. The offerer would bring an animal to the priest at the tabernacle or at the temple and the sinner himself (not the priest) would lay his hands upon the animal as a symbol of identification with that animal as a kind of proxy for his own guilt and punishment.

The punishment, of course, was death, because that is the wage every sinner deserves (Rom. 6:23). So the animal was killed through the shedding of its blood, vividly signifying that "the soul who sins shall die" (Ezek. 18:4, 20). The blood of the animal was collected and then poured out all over the altar, and the offerer was temporarily cleared by God. But that animal sacrifice was merely symbolic. It could offer no permanent or truly effectual sacrifice, "for it is not possible that the blood of bulls and goats could take away sins" (Heb. 10:4). So the practice had to be repeated again and again and again and again. The endless repetition of daily sacrifices—and especially the annual sin offering—was mandated by the law itself, as "a reminder of sins every year" (v. 3).

The people of God were learning that one essential aspect of God's eternal, unchanging righteousness is His holy hatred of sin. His righteous indignation and His perfect justice require an appropriate penalty for sin, because to forego punishment would be to allow His holiness to be trampled underfoot by agents of evil. For God to do that would be to abdicate His authority over His own universe. That is not even remotely possible.

But this point is the whole point of the gospel: Jesus was the ultimate sacrifice to God for sin. Those animal sacrifices merely symbolized and pointed toward Christ's full, final, once-for-all, perfect sacrifice. Jesus was the only offering to God that could really take away sin (Heb. 10:11–14).

He was not only the sacrifice but also the priest—the true High Priest whose offering of Himself, a sinless, perfect life, was the full and final and acceptable blood sacrifice to God.

So Jesus died as a sacrifice to God—a sweet-smelling savor. And "after He had offered one sacrifice for sins forever, [He] sat down at the right hand of God" (Heb. 10:12). The atonement never needs to be repeated. God was *satisfied*, or "propitiated."

Hold that thought. We'll come back to it.

CHRIST'S DEATH WAS A SUBMISSION TO GOD

As Christ speaks about the sacrifice that pleases God, He borrows language from the Old Testament: "Sacrifice and offering You did not desire, but a body You have prepared for Me. In burnt offerings and sacrifices for sin You had no pleasure. Then I said, 'Behold, I have come . . . *to do Your will*, O God'" (Heb. 10:5–7). Animal sacrifices and burnt offerings for sin are not what God desires, but after quoting again the prophetic words of Christ in Hebrews 10:9 ("Behold, I have come to do Your will, O God"), the writer adds in verse 10: "*By that will* we have been sanctified through the offering of the body of Jesus Christ once for all." The death of Christ was an act of obedience to His Father's will.

Christ's whole life was perfect. He did everything the Father wanted Him to do. He testified to that fact again and again, particularly in the gospel of John. Always, at all levels, even with the limited understanding of a child, He obeyed God to whatever degree He understood that. ("Did you not know that I must be about My Father's business?" [Luke 2:49].) His was a life of complete and perfect obedience. His delight was to *do* the will of God.

Of course, obeying God is something vastly different from receiving the wrath of God. In all of His life of obedience, never did obedience stir the kind of agony in His perfect soul that we see as He approached the judgment of the cross. That is because on the cross, He would be given to drink the full cup of His Father's wrath. Never had He received a hint of disapproval (much less a curse) from the Father. But in order to bear all the sins of His people, He would have to suffer that inconceivable, infinitely abhorrent chastisement for a world of sin. The level of submission Jesus offered to His Father on the cross is inconceivable.

Everything Christ did was in perfect compliance to the will of God, and His perfect, flawless righteousness in all its fullness is imputed to all who believe.

In other words, Christ's work on our behalf did not begin at the cross. All His life, He was fulfilling all righteousness in every way. At the very start of His public ministry, He insisted on being baptized because, as He told John the Baptist, "Thus it is fitting for us to fulfill all righteousness" (Matt. 3:15). He didn't need baptism. John's baptism was a symbol of repentance. But He did it to provide a perfect righteousness on behalf of those for whom He would die. It's a righteousness that encompasses even the symbol of our repentance.

He remained impeccably holy and obedient to God—subject to God's law and in perfect obedience to it throughout His entire life. That very righteousness is credited as justification to those who believe. It is the only *human* righteousness in the history of time and eternity that meets the standard of perfection God's law requires. That is why it was essential for the incarnate Son of God (and Him alone) to be the One who puts us into a right relationship with YHWH. Only when His perfect life is credited to our account are we fit to stand before God.

So in His living as well as in His dying, there was saving power for us. His perfect life is credited to our account as righteousness, just as His obedience in death is credited to our account as a payment for our sin. God had to be *satisfied* with both Christ's submission and His sacrifice before His wrath and righteousness could be propitiated.

CHRIST'S DEATH WAS A SUBSTITUTION OFFERED TO GOD

The New Testament is rich with the language of substitution. Christ was offered once to bear the sins of many. He didn't die for His own sins; He had none. He was offered as a substitute for us. "One died for all" (cf. 2 Cor. 5:14). God made Him sin for us (cf. 2 Cor. 5:21). "[He] Himself bore our sins in His own body on the tree, that we, having died to sins, might live for righteousness—by whose stripes you were healed" (1 Peter 2:24). That verse borrows language from Isaiah 53, which says that He was oppressed and afflicted. And for whom? He bore *our* griefs. He carried *our* sorrows. He was smitten of God and afflicted, pierced through for *our* transgressions, crushed for *our* iniquities. The chastening for *our* peace fell on Him. By His scourging, *we* are healed.

The Lord caused the iniquity of us all—everyone who would ever believe—to fall on Him. That's substitution. He takes our place. First Peter 3:18 says it this way: "Christ . . . suffered once for sins, the just for the unjust." He died as a *penal substitute.*

Remember God is absolutely holy, and sin is by definition not only a violation of God's law but also an assault on the very principle of holiness. One seemingly trivial sin—Adam's disobedience—spoiled the peaceful perfection of Eden and poisoned the whole human realm with every brand of evil, inconvenience, and sorrow that plagues our race. If one bite from a piece of forbidden fruit is rebellion enough to unleash so many bitter consequences, it should be clear why every violation of God's law must be dealt with. All sin must be punished. Justice demands that no sin ever committed by anybody who has ever lived in the history of this world will go unpunished. That includes every sin, great or small, in your life and in mine and every other transgression that ever has been or ever will be committed.

The obstacles to redeeming humanity from such a fall would seem to be insurmountable. Except for the cross.

In the death of Christ, God acts in the role of a just Lawgiver, giving a proper punishment for violation of His law. God determined that the penalty for sin, the just and right penalty for sin, is death. That's what is required. Christ is the Substitute who bears that penalty on behalf of His people.

Lamentably, we live in a culture that has conditioned us to think differently about sin and justice. Our tendency is to think the remedy for sin ought to be therapy rather than punishment. We even tend to look at prison as an environment where criminals can get better, as a place to rehabilitate people. Society as a whole has begun to regard the idea of a penalty for wrongdoing as outmoded, overly harsh, and even *un*just. We've lost the concepts of law, justice, and virtue, and we have crippled our own moral sensibility in the process.

The exception, of course, is when we are personally victimized by wrongdoing. Then we tend to want justice. We don't object to the idea of punishment so much when the strong arm of justice is brought against someone who has wronged us. In fact, some of the most liberal-minded progressives are the first ones to cry aloud for vengeance when they feel they have suffered wrong.

And the gravity of any offense is never measured merely by its immediate consequences, or by asking who was hurt by it. The real gauge of a sin's seriousness is the question of whom the sin was against. If you are angry with your neighbor and you yell and insult him, you're not going to prison for that offense. But curse a judge in his courtroom, and you will be sent to jail. Or send a letter to the White House threatening the president of the United States, and you will be charged with a federal crime. Again, the true enormity of any misdeed or insult is determined by whom the offense is committed against.

For that reason, sin against almighty God is never a trivial matter. True justice demands a penalty for sin, and the penalty is commensurate with the offense. Since all sin is a violation of God's infinite holiness and a challenge to His eternal authority, every sin is a capital crime (Rom. 6:23).

Jesus died on the cross because a just penalty was required. God, the Lawgiver, also determined that the penalty for sin is death. And He executed that penalty on His Son. A death was owed to divine justice. What is staggering is that Christ only suffered on the cross for about three hours, then He died. How is it possible that He could bear the full penalty for sin for all who will ever believe when, if we had to bear it, we would all spend eternity in hell and it would never be enough?

Because He is an infinite Person, He offered a *perfect* sacrifice. He is God incarnate. "The death of the Son of God is the only and most perfect sacrifice and satisfaction for sin; is of infinite worth and value, abundantly sufficient to expiate the sins of the whole world."[1]

But the brevity of time does not diminish the intense severity of what Christ suffered on our behalf. He drank the full cup of His Father's wrath. He took all the guilt of all the sins of all who would ever believe, and He bore the full fury of God's wrath as their penal substitute. All the horrors of eternal hell that all the redeemed should have collectively suffered were endured instead by Christ in three hours. The fury of God spent itself against Him in three hours. It is a staggering thought that He bore so much for us. And He did it willingly.

CHRIST'S DEATH WAS A SATISFACTION TO GOD

Romans 3:25, 1 John 4:10, and 1 John 2:2 all say that Christ made ***propitiation*** for our sins, meaning that His sacrifice on the cross satisfied God. The offering of Christ was sufficient to placate God's wrath against sin and fulfill all the holy demands of His perfect justice. God could not be satisfied with us until His own Son's sacrifice fully paid the price of our sin. He could not take us into His family until His Son bought our forgiveness.

How do we know God was satisfied? Because He raised Christ from the dead, took Him into glory, and seated Him at His own right hand (Heb. 1:3).

When we talk about being saved, when we talk about being delivered, it's important to know what we are being saved from. We are delivered from our own sin, of course. We are saved from an eternity in hell. But those things are possible only because God Himself safeguards us from His judgment, through the sacrifice of His only begotten Son. That's what John 3:16 is saying: "God so loved the world that He gave His only begotten Son, that whoever believes in Him should not perish but have everlasting life." Christ was sent from God to satisfy divine judgment by bearing the punishment for our sin. "He who believes in Him is not condemned; but he who does not believe is condemned already" (v. 18).

CHRIST'S DEATH WAS OUR SALVATION TO GOD

When we were rescued from condemnation, when we were delivered from sin's bondage, God "delivered us from the power of darkness and conveyed us into the kingdom of the Son of His love" (Col. 1:13). This salvation can best be understood by understanding two words. We were *redeemed*, and we were *ransomed*.

To redeem someone is to purchase his or her freedom from slavery, captivity, or punishment. A ransom is the price paid for redemption. Matthew 20:28 says Jesus came "to give His life a ransom for many." To whom is that ransom paid? Some people mistakenly imagine that He paid a ransom to the Devil. The ransom was not paid to the Devil, but to God.

God is the One who "is able to destroy both soul and body in hell" (Matt. 10:28). He is the "the Judge of all" (Heb. 12:23)—"from whose face the earth and the heaven [will flee] away" (Rev. 20:11). He is the One before whom the whole world has been found guilty (Rom. 3:19). Therefore He is the One to whom the ransom price for souls must be paid—and it is a costly price (Ps. 49:7–8). Yet it is God Himself, in the Person of Christ, who purchases us with His own blood (Acts 20:28). "You were not redeemed with corruptible things, like silver or gold, from your aimless conduct received by tradition from your fathers, but with the precious blood of Christ, as of a lamb without blemish and without spot" (1 Peter 1:18–19).

Through death Christ paid the ransom to redeem His people from the curse of the law. He *became* a curse for us to *remove* the curse from us (Gal. 3:13). And God was well pleased.

CHRIST'S DEATH WAS THE MEANS OF OUR SONSHIP WITH GOD

By reconciling us to God, Christ provides all that is necessary for us to become children of God. God takes us into His most intimate relationship and fellowship as family. "When we were enemies we were reconciled to God through the death of His Son" (Rom. 5:10).

A lot of preaching today puts all the stress on the sinner's hostility to God, and I fear it tends to give sinners the impression that all that is needed for salvation is their own free-will decision to stop being at odds with God. The idea of a sacrificial atonement that propitiates God has all but disappeared from the message Christians proclaim to the world. I think a lot of people picture God as a harmless, passive deity sitting in heaven just wishing people would stop hating Him, hoping they'll stop being indifferent to Him, and yearning for people to start loving Him.

That is not the gospel. The gospel message is not that God is really a lot nicer than you think, and He would really, really like it if you'd like Him. What Christ did on the cross was not designed to remove our hostility toward God, but to remove God's hostility toward us. Thus the good news is that God's dreadful wrath against sin has been placated by the death of His own Son.

All who believe are now welcome to come to Christ for forgiveness. The only reason we can even come to Him by faith is because—in a decisive act on the cross—God's hostility was ended toward all who believe.

The cross can't be anything to us until it's everything to God.

Appendix 3

THE REASON FOR EVERYTHING

A thorough *biblical* discussion of the gospel will inevitably raise a number of hard questions for which the Bible gives no in-depth answers. Paul acknowledges a couple of them in Romans 9:19. Since God is sovereign, either showing mercy or hardening whomever He wills, "Why does He still find fault? For who has resisted His will?" Paul's reply to that query may at first seem merely dismissive: "Who are you to reply against God? Will the thing formed say to him who formed it, 'Why have you made me like this?'" (v. 20). But that's not merely a glib brush-off. Paul's point is that the sovereign Creator of the universe has every right to do what He wishes with His own creation. God does not have to answer to us. That's a vital point to remember.

The apostle then goes on to explain that God deals with the wicked in a manner designed "to show His wrath and to make His power known" (Rom. 9:22), and He shows mercy to His elect so that He can "make known the riches of His glory" (v. 23). Both reasons amount to the same thing: *God does what He does in order to put His glory on display.* As a matter of fact, *everything* is made to serve that same end. It is God's ultimate purpose. And that is the biblical answer to virtually all the questions the gospel message raises about God's hidden purposes. It's a fine answer too—not in any sense an evasion. This appendix is an essay I wrote in order to explore that truth.

Praise the name of the LORD, for His name alone is exalted; His glory is above the earth and heaven.

—PSALM 148:13 (NASB)

In the entire universe there is nothing loftier or more important than the glory of the Lord. God's glory constitutes the whole purpose for which we were created. Indeed, this is the ultimate reason for everything that has ever happened—from the dawn of creation until now. "The heavens declare the glory of God" (Ps. 19:1). The sun, the moon, and the stars of light all praise Him (148:3). "His glory is above the earth and heaven" (v. 13). And "the whole earth is full of His glory!" (Isa. 6:3). Even the beasts of the field bring Him glory (43:20).

This is what gives meaning to our existence: God is putting His glory on display, and it is our unspeakable privilege to participate in that demonstration and to savor the joy of it without ceasing.

That, of course, is the very first lesson taught in both the Westminster Larger and Shorter Catechisms:

Q1: What is the chief and highest end of man?
A: Man's chief and highest end is to glorify God, and fully to enjoy Him forever.

That is also a succinct summary of everything Scripture teaches about why God made us in the first place. He did not create us because He was bored or lonely. He made us so He could glorify Himself through us.

Despite all the talk among contemporary evangelicals about "purpose-driven" life and ministry, the most important point of all is too often obscured or omitted. *Our one ultimate purpose is to glorify God*—to celebrate and reflect His glory; to magnify Him; and to "declare His glory among the nations, His wonders among all peoples" (Ps. 96:3).

That is God's eternal plan, and it was not thwarted or changed when the entire human race fell because of Adam's rebellion. In fact, it is the whole reason for the gospel. The redeemed are "predestined according to the purpose of Him who works all things according to the counsel of His will, *that we who first trusted in Christ should be to the praise of His glory*" (Eph. 1:11–12).

God is doing all this *for His own name's sake* (Ps. 25:11; 31:3; 79:9; 109:21; Jer. 14:21; Rom. 1:5; 1 John 2:12). His mercy and our salvation are not granted in our honor, as if to exalt us. We're not raised from our fallen condition for our own sake, to give us an elevated sense of self-esteem. All glory belongs to the Lord, and to Him alone. As David prayed, "Yours, O LORD, is the greatness, the power and the glory, the victory and the majesty; for all that is in heaven and in earth is Yours; Yours is the kingdom, O LORD, and You are exalted as head over all" (1 Chron. 29:11).

God is very jealous of His glory. He says emphatically, "I am the LORD, that is My name; and My glory I will not give to another" (Isa. 42:8).

Too often we speak of "God's glory" without really contemplating what the expression means. It is not an easy concept to define. We are dealing with something that is infinite, unfathomable, inconceivable, and utterly foreign to fallen human minds—something so pure and powerful that an unobstructed, unmediated view of it would be fatal to our sinful flesh (Ex. 33:20; Isa. 6:5; 1 Tim. 6:16).

The *Oxford English Dictionary* defines *glory* as "resplendent majesty, beauty, or magnificence." But the glory of God entails much more than that. It includes His holiness, His absolute perfection, and the stunning radiance of unapproachable light. God's glory is the very essence of beauty, majesty, and splendor. It likewise includes His justice, power, and wrath. It is at once captivating and terrifying. It is a reality so sublime that if you were permitted one glimpse of it and it weren't so overwhelming that you would die, you would never want to look away.

God's glory embodies everything praiseworthy and everything we ought to desire. It is the centerpiece of heaven's joys, so radiant and all-pervasive that it totally eliminates the need for any other source of illumination in the realm where God dwells (Rev. 21:23). Heaven will never be boring or monotonous, precisely because God's glory will be on full display throughout every detail of the new heavens and new earth. In short, no other charm or pleasure could conceivably provoke more wonder, interest, or delight. Best of all, God's glory will never lose its appeal or its luster.

John Gill (London's leading Baptist preacher a century before Spurgeon's time) pointed out that if God's glory occupies so lofty a place in the plan of God, it ought therefore to have first place in every Christian's priorities. He wrote,

> God's glory is the end [the goal and purpose] of all his works and actions; in creation, providence, and grace; in election, in the covenant, in the blessings and promises of it, in redemption, in effectual vocation, and in bringing many sons to glory. The same is the end of all Christ's actions, as man and Mediator, of his doctrines and miracles, of his obedience, sufferings, and death in this world, and of his interceding life in the other; who, as he lives to make intercession for us, lives unto God, to the glory of God; and therefore the glory of God should be the end of all our actions; besides, without this no action can be truly called a good one; if a man seeks himself, his own glory, and popular applause, or has any sinister and selfish end in view in what he does, it cannot be said, nor will it be accounted by God to be a good action.[1]

Gill's observation applies in particular to preachers. To paraphrase him: if a preacher exalts himself, seeks to exhibit his own glory, craves admiration or applause, or has any greedy or self-serving design in his sermon, it cannot be said (nor will it be accounted by God) to be legitimate preaching.

The preacher's one job is to proclaim the whole counsel of God in a way that makes the gospel clear and magnifies the glory of God. "We do not preach ourselves, but Christ Jesus the Lord. . . . For it is the God who commanded light to shine out of darkness, who has shone in our hearts *to give the light of the knowledge of the glory of God in the face of Jesus Christ*" (2 Cor. 4:5–6). The Word of God is our text; the gospel message is the crux of it; Christ is its main theme and central character; and the glory of God is the ultimate purpose. All of that is implied in the apostle's instruction to Timothy: "Preach the word! . . . in season and out of season" (2 Tim. 4:2).

Notice: *"We do not preach ourselves"* (2 Cor. 4:5). That statement is contrary to every dominant style of contemporary ministry. Pulpits today are full of narcissists, show-offs, and self-promoters. But no preacher who is thinking properly about the glory of God would ever want to uplift himself or make himself the focus of a sermon. Humility is the natural expression of a God-glorifying attitude. The person who is egotistical or self-absorbed has never really understood the grandeur of God's glory.

At the same time, our knowledge of God's glory ought to make us bold for the truth. You can tell a preacher is focused on God's glory when he fearlessly proclaims the hard or unpopular truths regardless of whatever opposition, criticism, or persecution he receives as a result.

The preacher who keeps God's glory in proper focus will likewise be indifferent to praise and flattery. To see the glory of God is to understand that nothing else really matters in the ultimate sense.

Obviously, the supreme renown of God's glory is a priority no minister should ever lose sight of. But remember, the same principle governs every activity in every believer's life: "Therefore, whether you eat or drink, or whatever you do, do all to the glory of God" (1 Cor. 10:31). Everything we do—mundane things as well as Christian ministry—must be done for the glory of God. That is the top priority and the bottom line in all our lives. It is the most important thing in the universe.

Consider this: a universe full of galaxies was made to glorify God, and for the most part all of His vast creation cooperates. The animal kingdom never rebelled against God. The earth is still full of His glory. The stars continually bear mute but powerful testimony to His glory, just as they have done from the dawn of creation. "The heavens declare His righteousness, and all the peoples see His glory" (Ps. 97:6). "What may be known of God is manifest in them, for God has shown it to them. For since the creation of the world His invisible attributes are clearly seen, being understood by the things that are made, even His eternal power and Godhead" (Rom. 1:19–20).

Out of all creation, only the two highest of God's creatures ever rebelled against Him. A third of the angelic host (Rev. 12:4) and all of humanity sinned. They tried to refuse the singular purpose for which they were made. They disclaimed the glory of God and wished instead to exalt themselves. "Although they knew God, they did not glorify Him as God, nor were thankful, but became futile in their thoughts, and their foolish hearts were darkened" (Rom. 1:21).

Their rebellion will ultimately only amplify the glory of God, because He will glorify Himself in the defeat of evil and the triumph of divine justice. Even the wrath of men will praise Him (Ps. 76:10).

Meanwhile, glorifying God is the ultimate goal of every duty God has ever given us. It remains the supreme purpose for which He created and then redeemed us. So the fundamental issue and the basic consideration that should govern everything we do is summed up in this simple question: *Will it glorify God?*

Alongside that simple query are a host of related factors to consider. *Can this thing that I am doing (and the way that I am doing it) truly honor God? Does it reflect His character or exemplify His goodness or otherwise pay homage to Him? Can I sincerely praise and thank Him while doing it? Does it make me more fit to serve Him, or otherwise enhance my labor in the Lord? Is it Christlike—consistent with the righteous character of our glorious God?*

Now, this seems like a simple principle, and it is. It's *simple*, but it's not *easy*. We all know from bitter experience what a struggle it is to maintain a proper focus on the glory of God in this fallen world. In Paul's words, "I know that in me (that is, in my flesh) nothing good dwells; for to will is present with me, but how to perform what is good I do not find" (Rom. 7:18). Evil and temptation continually assault us, and it is much too easy to become preoccupied with the cares and crises of our mundane lives. Our priorities continually need to be reordered to keep the first thing first.

Scripture is full of encouragement and instruction that addresses this very problem. For example, the apostle Paul reminds us that we belong to the Lord and His Spirit indwells us. Sins of the flesh dishonor His dwelling place. "Do you not know that your body is the temple of the Holy Spirit who is in you, whom you have from God, and you are not your own? For you were bought at a price; therefore *glorify God* in your body and in your spirit, which are God's" (1 Cor. 6:19–20).

Furthermore, because the Holy Spirit now permanently indwells believers, we have a lasting connection with God's glory such as no Old Testament saint ever enjoyed. In fact, Scripture highlights the stark difference between the experience of Moses and the way Christians in this era relate to the glory of God.

Moses' face shone temporarily with a brilliant reflection of God's glory. The Israelites were so frightened by the phenomenon that Moses had to hide the glow behind a veil. But over time the reflected glory faded away (2 Cor. 3:7).

In sharp contrast to that, Scripture says, God's glory actually indwells today's believers in the person of the Holy Spirit. He is transforming us from the inside out—conforming us to the image of Christ—"from glory to glory" (2 Cor. 3:18). In other words, God's glory shines from within us; it is not merely a reflection. And it shines with ever-increasing brilliance rather than diminishing with time.

Meanwhile, "we all, with unveiled face, beholding as in a mirror the glory of the Lord, are being transformed into the same image from glory to glory, just as by the Spirit of the Lord" (2 Cor. 3:18). Moses saw only a shielded view of God's back as He passed by. We are invited to gaze intently and face-to-face at God's glory from an up-close perspective ("as in a mirror"), without a veil of any kind. Through the Spirit who indwells us we have an unbreakable union with Christ. ("By this we know that we abide in Him, and He in us, because He has given us of His Spirit" [1 John 4:13].) God's glory is perfectly revealed in Christ (John 1:14). So we have unfettered access to the divine glory.

Dear reader, bear these truths in mind. The glory of God is the singular goal and the all-important thread that ties every aspect of our lives together and keeps our hearts properly focused. It is the reason for everything.

Appendix 4

PAUL'S GLORIOUS GOSPEL

Adapted from Sermons by C. H. Spurgeon

The material in this appendix is adapted and abridged from two sermons by Charles Haddon Spurgeon, "The Glorious Gospel,"[1] and "Coming Judgment of the Secrets of Men."[2] The former message dates from March 21, 1858, and was delivered to an audience of more than ten thousand people. Within three years of Spurgeon's arrival in London as a twenty-year-old preacher, his congregation had outgrown their historic meeting place, the New Park Street Chapel on the south bank of the Thames. They moved their Sunday services to a venue less than two miles to the southwest, the Music Hall at Surrey Gardens. It was a vast, three-tiered auditorium with seating for twelve thousand, and it was full every week. Spurgeon had been preaching at the Music Hall for two years when he gave this sermon.

In 1861, the church moved to their permanent home at the Metropolitan Tabernacle. With fifty-five hundred seats and standing room for five hundred more, the Tabernacle was a more modest site than the Music Hall, but it was located at the hub of London's busiest intersection, a junction of roads fanning out in six directions. On Sunday morning, July 12, 1885 (in the last decade of his life and ministry), Spurgeon preached the second of these two sermons to a capacity crowd at the Tabernacle.

The majority of this appendix is drawn from the earlier sermon, which is an exposition of 1 Timothy 1:15. But I have blended a good bit of material from the later sermon into the introduction, because in that message Spurgeon had much more to say about Paul's use of the expression "my gospel." Like Spurgeon, I find my heart resonates with the way the apostle employed that phrase to signify how personal and precious the gospel was to him. About that, Spurgeon said, "As for myself, looking at the matter afresh, amidst all the filthiness which I see in the world at this day, I lay hold upon the pure and blessed Word of God, and call it all the more earnestly, *my* gospel—mine in life, and mine in death; mine against all comers; mine forever, God helping me. With emphasis: '*my* gospel.' "

The text from 1 Timothy is another of Paul's pithy statements of gospel truth. Spurgeon does a superb job expressing the meaning and the passion of Paul's words. His preaching on this subject makes a fine addendum to our study.

This is a faithful saying and worthy of all acceptance, that Christ Jesus came into the world to save sinners, of whom I am chief.

—1 TIMOTHY 1:15

Paul's exposition of the gospel in Romans starts with that long, terrible exposé on human depravity. Paul knew that it must be written to put to shame the abominations of an age that was almost past shame. Monsters that revel in darkness must be dragged into the open, that they may be withered up by the light. After he had thus written in anguish, Paul's mind was drawn to his chief comfort. While his pen was black with the words he had written in the first chapter, he was driven to write of his great delight. He clings to the gospel with a greater tenacity than ever. Indeed, he did not speak of it as *the* gospel, but as *my* gospel. "God will judge the secrets of men by Jesus Christ, according to my gospel" (Rom. 2:16).

Paul felt he could not live in the midst of so depraved a people without holding the gospel with both hands, and grasping it as his very own. *"My gospel,"* says he. Not that Paul was the author of it, not that Paul had an exclusive monopoly on its blessings, but that he had received the message from Christ Himself, and Paul regarded himself as so responsibly put in trust with it, that he could not disown it even for an instant. So fully had he taken it into himself that he could not do less than call it "*my* gospel." He had a gospel, a definite form of truth, and he believed in it beyond all doubt. Therefore he spoke of it as "my gospel."

In 2 Corinthians 4:3, 1 Thessalonians 1:5, and 2 Thessalonians 2:14 he speaks of "our gospel," using a plural possessive pronoun, to show how believers identify themselves with the truth that they preach. Herein we hear the voice of faith, which seems to say, "Though others reject it, I am sure of it, and I will allow no shade of mistrust to darken my mind. To me it is glad tidings of great joy: I hail it as 'my gospel.' If I be called a fool for holding it, I am content to be a fool, and to find all my wisdom in my Lord."

Should all the forms that men devise
Assault my faith with treacherous art,
I'd call them vanity and lies,
And bind the gospel to my heart.

Is not this expression "my gospel" the voice of love? Does he not by this term embrace the gospel as the only love of his soul—for the sake of which he had "suffered the loss of all things, and count them as rubbish" (Phil. 3:8)—for the sake of which he was willing to stand before Nero, and proclaim, even in Caesar's palace, the message from heaven? Although each word might cost him a life, he was willing to die a thousand deaths for the holy cause.

"My gospel," says he, with a rapture of delight, as he presses to his heart the sacred deposit of truth. "My gospel." Does this not show his courage? As much as to say, "I am not ashamed of the gospel of Christ, for it is the power of God to salvation for everyone who believes." He says, "my gospel," as a soldier speaks of "my colors," or of "my king." He resolves to bear this banner to victory, and to serve this royal truth even to the death.

"*My* gospel." There is a touch of discrimination about the expression. Paul perceives that there are other gospels, and he makes short work with them, for he says, "But even if we, or an angel from heaven, preach any other gospel to you than what we have preached to you, let him be accursed" (Gal. 1:8). The apostle was of a gentle spirit; he prayed heartily for the Jews who persecuted him, and yielded his life for the conversion of the Gentiles who maltreated him. But he had no tolerance for false gospellers. He exhibited great breadth of mind, and to save souls he became all things to all men. But when he contemplated any alteration or adulteration of the gospel of Christ, he thundered and lightninged without measure. When he feared that something else might spring up among the philosophers, or among the Judaizers, that should hide a single beam of the glorious Sun of Righteousness, he used no measured language. He cried concerning the author of such a darkening influence, "Let him be accursed. . . . Let him be accursed" (Gal. 1:8–9).

Every heart that would see men blessed whispers an "Amen" to the apostolic malediction. No greater curse can come upon mankind than the obscuration of the gospel of Jesus Christ. Paul says of himself and his true brethren, "We are not as many, which corrupt the word of God" (2 Cor. 2:17 KJV); and he cries to those who turned aside from the one and only gospel, "O foolish Galatians! Who has bewitched you?" (Gal. 3:1). Of all new doctrines he speaks as of "a different gospel, which is not another; but there are some who trouble you and want to pervert the gospel of Christ" (Gal. 1:6–7).

In 1 Timothy 1:15, Paul makes a formal affirmation of the gospel's good news, and in doing so he clearly explains why this message is so dear to him: *"This is a faithful saying and worthy of all acceptance, that Christ Jesus came into the world to save sinners, of whom I am chief."*

That text is one pride would never prompt a preacher to select. It is quite impossible to flourish about it, it is so simple. Human nature is apt to cry, "Well, I cannot preach upon that text. It is too plain. There is no mystery in it. I cannot show my learning. It is just a stark, commonsense announcement. I scarcely would wish to take it, for it lowers the man, however much it may exalt the Master."

So expect nothing but the text, and the simplest possible explanation of it from me.

THE SAVIOR

In explaining Paul's gospel, we must begin with Christ. The Person of our Savior is the foundation-stone of our hope. Upon His Person depends the usefulness of our gospel. Should someone arise and preach a Savior who was a mere man, he would be unworthy of our hopes, and the salvation preached would be inadequate to what we need. Should another preach salvation by an angel, our sins are so heavy that an angelic atonement would have been insufficient; and therefore his gospel totters to the ground.

I repeat: upon the Person of the Savior rests the whole of our salvation. If He be not able—if He be not commissioned to perform the work—then indeed, the work itself is worthless to us and falls short of its design. But when we preach the gospel, we need not stop and stammer. We proclaim to the world such a Savior that earth and heaven could not produce His equal. He is one so loving, so great, so mighty, and so well adapted to all our needs that it is evident enough that He was prepared of old to meet our deepest wants.

We know that Jesus Christ who came into the world to save sinners is God; and that long before His descent to this lower world, He was adored by angels as the Son of the Highest. When we preach the Savior to you, we tell you that although Jesus Christ was the Son of man, bone of our bone, and flesh of our flesh, yet He is eternally the Son of God, and He has in Himself all the attributes that constitute the perfect Godhead. What more of a Savior can any man want than God? Is not He who made the heavens able to purge the soul? If He of old stretched the curtains of the skies and made the earth, that man should dwell upon it, is He not able to rescue a sinner from the destruction that is to come?

When we tell you He is God, we have at once declared His omnipotence and His infinity; and when these two things work together, what can be impossible? Let God undertake a work and it cannot meet with failure. Let Him enter into an enterprise, and it is sure of its accomplishment. Since Christ Jesus the man was also Christ Jesus the God, we have the fullest confidence that we are offering you Someone who is worthy of all acceptance.

The name given to Christ suggests something concerning His Person. Our text calls Him "Christ Jesus." The two words mean "Anointed Savior." He was anointed to come "into the world to save sinners."

Pause here, my soul, and read this again: *He is the anointed Savior.* God the Father from before all worlds anointed Christ to the office of a Savior of sinners. Therefore, when I behold my Redeemer coming from heaven to redeem people from sin, I note that He does not come unsent or uncommissioned. He has His Father's authority to back Him in His work.

Hence there are two immutable things whereon our souls may rest: there is *the Person of Christ,* divine in Himself. And there is the *anointing from on high,* giving to Him the stamp of a commission received from Jehovah His Father.

O sinner, what greater Savior do you want than He whom God anointed? What more can you require than the eternal Son of God to be your ransom, and the anointing of the Father to be the ratification of the treaty?

Yet we have not fully described the Person of the Redeemer until we have noted that He was human. We read that He came into the world; by which coming into the world we do not understand His usual way of coming, for He often came into the world before. We read in Scripture that the Lord said of Sodom and Gomorrah, "I will go down now and see whether they have done altogether according to the outcry against it that has come to Me; and if not, I will know" (Gen. 18:21).

In fact, He is always here. The goings of God are to be seen in the sanctuary; both in providence and in nature they are to be seen most visibly. Does not God visit the earth when He "makes the clouds His chariot, [and] walks on the wings of the wind" (Ps. 104:3)?

But this visitation was different from all those. Christ came into the world in the sense of the fullest and most complete union with human nature. Oh, sinner, when we preach a Divine Savior, perhaps the name of God is so terrible, that you can scarcely think the Savior is adapted to you.

But hear again the old story. Although Christ was the Son of God, He left His highest throne in glory and stooped to the manger. There He is, an infant whose length is measured in inches. See, He grows from boyhood up to manhood, and He comes forth into the world to preach and suffer! See Him as He groans under the yoke of oppression. He is mocked and despised; "His visage was marred more than any man, and His form more than the sons of men" (Isa. 52:14)! See Him in the garden, as He sweats drops of blood! See Him in Pilate's chamber, in which He is scourged and His shoulders run with gore! On the bloody tree behold Him! See Him dying with agony too exquisite to be imagined, much less to be described! Behold Him in the silent tomb! See Him at last bursting the bonds of death, and rising the third day, and afterward ascending up on high, leading captivity captive!

Sinner, you now have the Savior before you, plainly manifested. He who was called Jesus of Nazareth, who died upon the cross, who had His superscription written, "JESUS OF NAZARETH, THE KING OF THE JEWS" (John 19:19). This man was the Son of God, the brightness of His Father's glory, and the express image of His Father, "begotten of the Father before all worlds . . . begotten not made, being of one substance with the Father."* He "did not count equality with God a thing to be grasped, but made himself nothing, taking the form of a servant, being born in the likeness of men. And being found in human form, he humbled himself by becoming obedient to the point of death, even death on a cross" (Phil. 2:6–8 ESV).

Oh, if I could bring Him before you; if I could now bring Him here to show you His hands and His side; if you could now, like Thomas, put your fingers in the holes of the nails and thrust your hand into His side,

* This is a quotation from the Nicene Creed, as formally adopted by the First Council of Constantinople (381). Spurgeon is quoting from the version used in the Anglican Book of Common Prayer. Other versions say "eternally begotten" rather than "begotten before all worlds." The sense is the same. The words omitted in Spurgeon's ellipsis are "God of God, Light of Light, very God of very God," the Creed's way of affirming that Father and Son are one in substance. There's no significance to the omission, except that the point Spurgeon is making in this context is about the eternal generation of the Son.

I'm certain you would not be faithless, but believing. This much I know: if there is anything that can make men believe under the hand of God's most Holy Spirit, it is a true picture of the Person of Christ. Seeing is believing in His case. A true view of Christ, a right-looking at Him, will most assuredly beget faith in the soul.

Oh, I doubt not if those who doubt, fear, and tremble could know Him, they would say, "Oh, I can trust Him; a Person so divine, and yet so human, ordained and anointed of God, must be worthy of my faith! I can trust Him. Nay, more: If I had a hundred souls I could trust Him with them all. Indeed, if I stood accountable for all the sins of all mankind and were myself the very reservoir and sink of this world's infamy, I could trust Him even then—for such a Savior must be 'able to save to the uttermost those who come to God through Him'" (Heb. 7:25).

THE SINNER

If a large gathering of listeners had never heard this passage before, or any other text of similar import, I like to think that the most breathless silence would reign over them if for the first time someone should commence to read to them: "This is a faithful saying and worthy of all acceptance, that Christ Jesus came into the world to save—" If they could but grasp this truth, people would thrust forward their heads to listen. They would cup their hands behind their ears and watch closely as if they could hear with the eye as well as with the ear, wanting to know for whom the Savior died.

Every listening heart would say, *whom* did He come to save? And if we had never heard the message before, how would our hearts palpitate with fear lest the character described should be one unto which it would be impossible for us to attain!

Oh, how pleasant it is to hear again that one word that describes the character of those whom Christ came to save: He "came into the world to save *sinners*."

Monarch, there is no distinction here. Princes, He has not singled you out to be the objects of His love. But beggars and the poor shall taste His grace. Learned men and masters of Israel, Christ does not say He came specially to save you alone. The unlearned and illiterate peasant is equally welcome to His grace. Jewish person, with your pedigree of honor, you are no more justified than the believing Gentile. People of modern sophistication, with your advanced civilization and your civic freedom, Christ does not say He came to save you. You are not named as the distinguishing class who are the objects of His love. No, and those who are devoted to religion, philanthropy, or other good works—you who reckon yourselves saints among men—He does not designate you either.

The one simple title, large and broad as humanity itself, is simply this: "Christ Jesus came into the world to save *sinners.*" Now, mark: We are to understand this in a general sense when we read it—namely, that all whom Jesus came to save are sinners. But if any man asks, "May I infer from this that I am saved?" we must then put another question to him.

Those whom Christ came to save were by nature sinners, nothing less and nothing more than sinners. I have often said that Christ came into the world to save *awakened* sinners. It is quite true; so He did. But those whom He saves were not awakened sinners when He came to save them—they were nothing but sinners "dead in trespasses and sins" (Eph. 2:1) until He made them alive.

It is a common notion that we should preach that Christ died to save *sensible* sinners—sinners who are aware of and convicted about their lost condition. Now it is true that "those who are well have no need of a physician, but those who are sick" (Luke 5:31). No one will be saved who does not sense his need of a savior. But not one of us was under conviction of sin when Christ died to save sinners. Our sensibility to our own sin is one of the fruits of His atoning death. It is the work of the Holy Spirit through the gospel, to convict us "of sin, and of righteousness, and of judgment" (John 16:8).

Those whom Christ died for are described, without any adjective to diminish the breadth of it, as "*sinners*"—without any badge of merit or mark of goodness that might distinguish them above their fellows. *Sinners!*

Now, the term includes some of all kinds of sinners. There are some whose sins appear but little. Trained up religiously, and educated in a moral way. They are content to coast along the shores of vice; they do not launch out into the depths. Christ has died for such as these, for many of these have been brought to know and love Him. Let no man think because he is less of a sinner than others, there is therefore less hope for him. Strange it is that some have often thought that.

"If I had been a blasphemer," says one, "or injurious, I could have had more hope! Although *I* know I have sinned greatly in my own eyes, yet so little have I erred in the judgment of the world, that I can scarcely think myself included."

Oh, say not so. It says, "*sinners.*" If you can put yourself in that category whether it be at the top or at the bottom, you are still within it, and the truth still holds good that those Jesus came to save were originally sinners. You being such, you have no reason to believe that you are shut out.

Again, Christ died to save sinners at both ends of that spectrum. I have known people to be saved whose former character I dare not describe. It would be a shame to speak of the things that were done by them in secret. There have been men who have invented vices of which the Devil himself was ignorant until they invented them. There have been men so bestial that their dogs were a more honorable creatures than they. I have heard of beings whose crimes have been more diabolical, more detestable, than any action ascribed even to the Devil himself.

Yet this text does not shut them out.

Have we not met with blasphemers so profane that they could not speak without an oath? Blasphemy, which at first was something terrible to them, has now become so common that they would curse themselves before they said their prayers, or swear when they were singing God's praises. It has come to be part of their meat and drink, a thing so natural to them that the very sinfulness of it does not shock them, they do it so continually. As for God's laws, they delight to know them for the mere sake of breaking them. Tell them of a new vice and you will please them. They have become like that Roman emperor whose parasites could never please him better than by inventing some new crime. They have gone head over ears in the Stygian gulf of hellish sin—men, who not content with fouling their feet while walking through the mire have lifted up the trapdoor with which we seal down depravity and have dived into the very kennel. They revel in the very filth of human iniquity.

But there is nothing in my text that can exclude even them. *Many* of these shall yet be washed in the Savior's blood, and be made partakers of the Savior's love.

Nor does this text make a distinction as to the age of sinners. There are elderly people whose hairs if they were the color of their character would be the very reverse of what they are. They have added layer to layer of crime; and, now, if one were to dig down through the various deposits of numerous years, he would discover stony relics of youthful sins, hidden down in the depths of stone-cold hearts. Where once all was tender, everything has become sere and hardened. Many have gone far into sin over a lifetime of rebellion against God. If they were to be converted now, would it not, indeed, be a wonder of grace? For the old oak to be bent, oh, how hard!

Can the Great Husbandman train it? Can He graft on so old and so rough a stem something that shall bring forth heavenly fruit? Ah, *He can*, for age is not mentioned in the text, and many of the most ancient of men have proved the love of Jesus in their latest years.

"But," says one, "my sin has had peculiar aggravations connected with it. I have sinned against light and against knowledge. I have trampled on a mother's prayers; I have despised a father's tears. Warnings given to me have been neglected. On my sick bed God Himself has rebuked me. My resolves have been frequent and as frequently forgotten. As for my guilt, it is not to be measured by any ordinary standard. My little crimes are greater than other men's deepest iniquities, for I have sinned against the light, against the prickings of conscience, and against everything that should have taught me better."

Well, my friend, I do not see that you are shut out here. The text makes no distinction but just this: "*Sinners!*" And as far as the text is concerned, there is no limit whatever. We must deal with the text as it stands; and it says, "Christ Jesus came into the world to save sinners." There have been many of your sort saved. Why, then, should you not be saved? There have been the grossest blackguards, and the vilest thieves, and the most debauched harlots saved. Why not you?

Sinners a hundred years old have been saved. We have instance on record of such cases. Why not you? If from one of God's instances we may generally infer a rule, and moreover, we have His own Word to back us, where lives the man who is so wickedly arrogant as to shut himself out and close the door of mercy in his own face?

No, the text says "sinners," and why should it not include you and me within its list? "Christ Jesus came into the world to save sinners."

That does not mean Christ will save *all* sinners. There are some sinners who undoubtedly will be lost, because they reject Christ. They despise Him. They will not repent. They choose their own self-righteousness. They do not turn to Christ. They will have none of His ways and none of His love. For such sinners, there is no promise of mercy, for there remains no other way of salvation. Despise Christ, and you despise your own mercy. Turn away from Him, and you have proved that in His blood there is no efficacy for you. Despise Him, die without giving your soul into His hands, and you have given a most awful proof that although the blood of Christ was mighty, yet it was never applied to you, never sprinkled on your heart to the taking away of your sins.

Therefore I said (and I must return to this point) you cannot necessarily infer from this text that Christ came to save *you*. Before you can make a particular application of this text to your own case, there is another question that must be answered: *Do you confess that you are a sinner?* The question is not merely whether you will *say* so. But do you feel the weight of your guilt? In your inmost soul is that a truth printed in great capitals of burning fire? Are you a sinner?

If it be so, renounce your sin and turn to Christ alone for salvation. Now knowing and humbly acknowledging yourself to be a sinner, if you cast yourself upon that simple truth, believing it and trusting in it to be your anchor in every time of trouble Christ died for you, then you are included in His special purpose. The covenant of grace includes your name in the ancient roll of eternal election. There your person is recorded, and you shall, without a doubt, be saved.

Are you not prepared to trust in Christ? I beseech you, dear reader, believe this great truth, which is worthy of all acceptation—Christ Jesus came to save. I know your doubts. I know your fears, for I have suffered them myself. And the only way whereby I can keep my hopes alive is just this: I am brought every day to the cross; I believe that to my dying hour I shall never have any hope but this:

Nothing in my hands I bring;
Simply to thy cross I cling.

My only reason for believing Jesus Christ is my Redeemer is just this: I know that I am a *sinner.* This I feel, and over this I mourn. And though I mourn it much, when Satan tells me that I cannot be the Lord's, I draw from my very mourning the comfortable inference, that inasmuch as He has made me feel I am lost, He would not have done this if He had not intended to save me.

And inasmuch as He has given me to see that I belong to that great class of characters whom He came to save, I infer from that, beyond a doubt, He *will* save me. You can do the same—even if you are a sin-stricken, weary, sad, and disappointed soul to whom the world has become an empty thing. If you are a weary spirit who has gone your round of pleasure, now exhausted with sin's bondage and longing to be rid of it; if you are looking for something better than this mad world can ever give you—here is the blessed truth Paul called "my gospel": Jesus Christ, the Son of God, born of the Virgin Mary, suffered under Pontius Pilate, was crucified, dead and buried, and raised again the third day *to save sinners.* That is why He came into the world.

THE SALVATION

What is meant by *saving* sinners? "Christ Jesus came into the world to *save* sinners." If you want a picture to show you what is meant by being saved, let me give it to you. There is a poor wretch who has lived many a year in the grossest sin; so inured to sin has he become that the Ethiopian might sooner change his skin than he could learn to do well. Drunkenness, vice, and folly have cast their iron net about him. He has become loathsome and is unable to escape from his loathsomeness.

Do you see him? He is tottering onward to his ruin. From childhood to youth, from youth to manhood, he has sinned right on, and now he is going toward his last days. The pit of hell is flaring across his path, flinging its frightful rays immediately before his face—yet he sees it not. He still goes on in his wickedness, despising God and hating his own salvation. Leave him there.

A few years have passed. Now hear another story. Do you see that spirit yonder—foremost among the ranks most sweetly singing the praises of God? Do you mark it robed in white, an emblem of its purity? Do you see it as it casts its crown before the feet of Jesus and acknowledges Him the Lord of all? Hark! Do you hear it as it sings the sweetest song that ever charmed Paradise itself? Listen to it, its song is this:

I, the chief of sinners am,
But Jesus died for me.

"To Him who loved us and washed us from our sins in His own blood, and has made us kings and priests to His God and Father, to Him be glory and dominion forever and ever. Amen" (Rev. 1:5–6).

Who is that whose song thus emulates the seraph's strains? It is the same person who a little while ago was so frightfully depraved, the selfsame man! But he has been washed; he has been sanctified; he has been justified.

If you ask me, then, what is meant by salvation, I tell you that it reaches all the way from that poor, desperately fallen piece of humanity to that high-soaring spirit up yonder, praising God. That is what it means to be saved—to have our old thoughts made into new ones; to have our old habits broken off and new habits given; to have our old sins pardoned and righteousness imputed; to have peace in the conscience, peace to man, and peace with God; to have the spotless robe of imputed righteousness cast about our loins; and to have ourselves healed and cleansed.

To be saved is to be rescued from the gulf of perdition; raised to the throne of heaven; delivered from the wrath to come and the thunders of an angry God; liberated from the curse of sin; and made to feel and taste the love, the approval, and applause of Jehovah, our Father and our Friend.

All of this Christ gives to sinners. This simple gospel has nothing to do with those who will not confess themselves to be sinners. If you must be canonized, if you claim a saintly perfection of your own, the good news has nothing to do with you. Paul's gospel is a message for sinners, and sinners alone. The whole of this salvation—so broad, so brilliant, so unspeakably precious, and so everlastingly secure—is addressed this day to the outcast, to the offscouring. In a word, it is addressed to *sinners.*

THE SAYING

Five times in the pastoral epistles, Paul writes, "This is a faithful saying. . . ." (1 Tim. 1:15; 3:1; 4:9; 2 Tim. 2:11; Titus 3:8). These appear to be common sayings—mostly practical aphorisms and words of encouragement that were probably familiar truisms exchanged among believers in the early church. "Christ Jesus came into the world to save sinners" echoes several statements made by Christ Himself: "The Son of Man has come to save that which was lost" (Matt. 18:11). "The Son of Man did not come to destroy men's lives but to save them" (Luke 9:56). "God did not send His Son into the world to condemn the world, but that the world through Him might be saved" (John 3:17). Paul adds several words of affirmation to the saying in our text.

First, "This is a faithful saying." That is a commendation to the *doubter.* Oh, the Devil, as soon as he finds men under the sound of the word of God, slips along through the crowd, and he whispers in one heart, "Don't believe it!" and in another, "Laugh at it!" and in another, "Away with it!" And when he finds a person for whom the message was intended—one who feels himself a sinner, he is generally doubly in earnest, that he may not believe it at all: "Don't believe it—it's too good to be true."

Let me answer the Devil by God's own words: "This is a faithful saying." It is good, and it is as true as it is good. It *would be* too good to be true if God Himself had not said it. But inasmuch as He said it, it is not too good to be true. I will tell you why you think it too good to be true: because you measure God's corn by your own bushel. Please remember, God Himself tells us, "My thoughts are not your thoughts, nor are your ways My ways. . . . For as the heavens are higher than the earth, so are My ways higher than your ways, and My thoughts than your thoughts" (Isa. 55:8–9). You might think that if someone had offended you as badly as you have sinned against God, you could not forgive him. But God is not a man. He will forgive where we would not; and where you might take your own brother by the throat, God would forgive him seventy times seven. You do not know Jesus, or else you would believe Him.

We think we are honoring God when we think great thoughts of our sin. Let us recollect, that while we ought to think very greatly of our own sin, we dishonor God if we think our sin is greater than His grace. God's grace is infinitely greater than the greatest of our crimes. There is but one exception that He has ever made, and a penitent cannot be included in that. I beseech you, therefore, get better thoughts of Him. Think how good He is, and how great He is; and when you know this to be a true saying, I hope you will thrust Satan away from you, and not think it too good to be true.

I know what the Devil will say to you next: "Well, if it is true, it is not true to you. It is true to all the world, but not to you. Christ died to save sinners. It's true you are a sinner, but you are not included in it."

Tell the Devil he is a liar to his face. There is no way of answering him except by straightforward language. Tell him on the authority of Christ Himself that he is a liar. Christ says, "I did not come to call the righteous, but sinners" (Mark 2:17 NASB). The Devil says you don't qualify. Tell him he is a liar, and send him about his business. At any rate, never put his testimony in comparison with that of Christ.

I must endeavor to reassure you by repeating again this text: "Christ Jesus came into the world to save sinners." It is a true saying. I cannot have you reject it.

You say you cannot believe it.

Let me ask you: "Do you not believe the Bible?"

"Yes," you say, "every word of it."

Then this is one word of it: "Christ Jesus came into the world to save sinners." There it stands. Do you believe Jesus Christ? Come, answer me. Do you think He lies? Would a God of truth stoop to deceit?

"No," you say. "Whatever God says, I believe."

It is God who says, "Christ Jesus came into the world to save sinners." That is His Word. Didn't Christ rise from the dead? Doesn't that prove the gospel to be authentic? Will you deny the testimony of all the saints in heaven and of all the saints on earth? Ask any one of them, and they will tell you this is true: "Christ Jesus came into the world to save *sinners*." All the people of God say the same.

But, you say, you are too great a sinner.

You are not a greater sinner than some who are in heaven already.

You say you are the greatest sinner who ever lived.

I say you are mistaken. The greatest sinner died some years ago and went to heaven. The text says so: "Christ Jesus came into the world to save sinners, *of whom I am chief*." Paul was not using hyperbole when he wrote that. He genuinely saw himself as the lowest sinner, worse than the most depraved derelict—and he enumerated the reasons why: "I was formerly a blasphemer, a persecutor, and an insolent man" (1 Tim. 1:13). He had just listed every conceivable class of atrocious sinners, including "the lawless and insubordinate . . . the ungodly . . . the unholy and profane . . . murderers of fathers and murderers of mothers . . . manslayers . . . fornicators . . . sodomites . . . kidnappers . . . liars . . . perjurers, and . . . any other thing that is contrary to sound doctrine" (vv. 9–10). But Paul still portrayed himself as the lowest of the low.

No wonder he called the gospel "my gospel." Imagine there are sinners standing in a line, and one starts out from the ranks. He says, "Make way; make way! I stand at the head of you. I am the chief of sinners. Give me the lowest place; let me take the lowest room."

"No," cries another. "Not you; I am a greater sinner than you."

Then the apostle Paul says, "I challenge you all. Manasseh and Magdalene, I challenge you. I will have the lowest place. I was a blasphemer, a persecutor, and an insolent man toward God Himself; but I obtained mercy."

Now, if Christ has saved the greatest sinner that ever lived, oh, sinner, great as you may be, you cannot be greater than the greatest, and He is able to save you. I beseech you by the myriads of witnesses around the throne; by the thousands of witnesses on earth; by Jesus Christ, the witness on Calvary; by the blood of sprinkling that is a witness even now; by God Himself; and by His Word, which is faithful—I beseech you, believe this faithful saying: "Christ Jesus came into the world to save sinners."

Finally, one more word to the *careless.* This text is "worthy of all acceptance." Do not scorn it. Do not curl your lip in derision. You may have heard the story badly told, and therefore you ridiculed it. Or you said in your heart, "What is that to me? If this is the gospel it is nothing; I care not to hear it." It is worthy of your acceptance. No matter how poorly it may be communicated, there is no greater subject. Neither Demosthenes himself nor Cicero could ever have a weightier subject. Though a child might tell you of it, the gospel is of eternal importance.

It is not your house that is in danger. It is not your body only. It is your soul that is at stake. "What will it profit a man if he gains the whole world, and loses his own soul?" (Mark 8:36).

Are you wise? This is more worthy than your wisdom. Are you rich? This is worthier than all your wealth. Are you famous? This is worthier than all your honor. Are you princely? This is worthier than your ancestry or your goodly heritage. The gospel is the worthiest thing under heaven, because it will last when all other things fade away. It will stand by you when you have to stand alone. In the hour of death it will plead for you when you have to answer the summons of justice at God's bar. And it shall be your eternal consolation through never-ending ages. It is "worthy of all acceptance."

The Lord bless you for Jesus' sake. Amen.

GLOSSARY

Alien righteousness: A righteousness that is not the sinner's own, but is imputed—the merit legally transferred—to the sinner's account.

Antinomianism: The belief that Christians are not bound by any moral law, or the notion that behavior and belief are unrelated.

Christology: The doctrines of the Person and work of Christ.

Christus victor: A theory of the atonement that sees Christ's death and resurrection as a triumph over sin, death, the Devil, and the law—the enemies of fallen humanity. Triumph, not propitiation, is the central feature of this theory. It is seen as an alternative to penal substitution.

Commercial theory: See *satisfaction theory.*

Deeds of the law: Any thought, action, or attitude that aims to gain God's approval through a show of obedience to the standard of righteousness set by the Old Testament's 613 commandments.

Eschatology: The doctrine of things to come.

Evangelical: Of or pertaining to the gospel.

Forensic: Pertaining to a law court; having to do with the legalities of a judiciary system.

Gospel: Glad tidings, or good news. Specifically, the good news that Jesus Christ (the incarnate Son of God) gave His life on the cross as a payment for His people's sins, and then rose from the dead to demonstrate that the sacrifice was accepted; and therefore sinners can receive full forgiveness and all the blessings of heaven solely and simply through repentant faith in Christ.

Governmental theory: The idea that the cross was chiefly a symbolic display of God's wrath against sin—not a true ransom or expiation, but a demonstration of what justice *should* require. This view suggests that the atonement is really little more than a public vindication of God as the rightful moral governor of the universe.

Grace: Divine favor freely and sovereignly bestowed on unworthy sinners.

Hamartiology: The doctrine of sin.

Imputation: A legal reckoning whereby guilt or credit is transferred from the account of one person to another.

Justification by faith: The truth that God graciously declares believing sinners perfectly righteous for Christ's sake. He not only forgives their sins, but He also imputes to them the full merit of Christ's unblemished righteousness. They therefore gain a right standing with God, not because of any good thing they have done (or will do), but solely because of Christ's work on their behalf.

Legalism: The false belief that people can earn merit with God by what they do or don't do.

Moral influence theory: The belief that Christ's death on the cross is an example of loving self-sacrifice, but not a payment of any kind.

Open theism: The belief that the future is unknown even to God and thus open to practically any eventuality.

Original sin: Adam's disobedience, in which he partook of the forbidden fruit. Because he was acting as the representative head of the entire human race, his misdeed plunged all his offspring into sin. All humanity fell in Adam, and guilt and corruption were passed down from him to all his progeny.

Penal substitution: The belief that through Christ's death on the cross, He made full atonement, purchasing His Father's gracious forgiveness, by suffering the full penalty of sin as a substitute for those whom He redeems.

Pentateuch: The portion of the Old Testament written by Moses, consisting of the first five books in our canon. (See: *Torah.*)

Phylacteries: Leather boxes containing Scripture that Orthodox Jews and Pharisees would bind to their foreheads and arms. (See Deuteronomy 6:8.)

Propitiation: A sacrifice or offering meant to appease an offended deity.

Ransom: The price paid to redeem someone.

Ransom theory: The idea that Christ's death was a payment rendered to Satan for the souls of the faithful.

Redemption: The act purchasing someone's freedom from slavery, captivity, or punishment—or recovering something of value—through the payment of a price or the fulfillment of an obligation.

Regeneration: A miracle wrought by the Holy Spirit, whereby He gives life to a spiritually dead soul. This life-giving act of God is described variously as a resurrection or a rebirth, always unto eternal life.

Sanhedrin: A council of men who served as judges and religious authorities in Israel. Every major city had such a council, but when the term is used without modification, it normally refers to the Jerusalem Sanhedrin (known as the Great Sanhedrin). In Scripture, the Great Sanhedrin was always called "the council" (cf. Acts 23:1), or "the elders of Israel" (Ezek. 14:1; Acts 4:8). That council consisted of seventy-one elite priests and scholars. They oversaw the temple, and they served as Judaism's highest court of religious affairs. The majority in the Great Sanhedrin were Pharisees, but the line of the high priests were Sadducees, so an aristocratic line of Sadducees held the reins of political power within the Sanhedrin.

Satisfaction theory: Anselm's view of the atonement (sometimes called the *commercial theory*) namely, that the death of Christ was a satisfaction of God's honor.

Sola fide: Latin for "faith alone."

Soteriology: The doctrine of salvation.

Torah: A transliteration of the Hebrew word for "instruction" or "law." In English the term commonly refers to the first five books of the biblical canon, all written by Moses, containing the law handed down at Sinai. This portion of Scripture is often referred to collectively as "the Law." (See: *Pentateuch.*)

NOTES

Introduction

1. Herbert Danby, trans., *The Mishnah: Translated from the Hebrew with Introduction and Brief Explanatory Notes* (Oxford: University Press, 1933), 306.
2. John MacArthur, *The Gospel According to Jesus* (Grand Rapids: Zondervan, 1988); *The Gospel According to the Apostles* (Nashville: Thomas Nelson, 1993).
3. John MacArthur, *Ashamed of the Gospel* (Wheaton: Crossway, 1993).
4. Together for the Gospel: http://t4g.org/about/affirmations-and-denials-2/.

Chapter 2: First, the Bad News

1. See John MacArthur, "The Sinner Neither Willing Nor Able" in *Proclaiming a Cross-centered Theology*, ed. Mark Dever (Wheaton: Crossway, 2009), 81–98.
2. Jean Lawrence, "Learning to Forgive Yourself," WebMd.com, accessed July 25, 2016, http://www.webmd.com/balance/features/learning-to-forgive-yourself?page=2.
3. Robert Haldane, *Exposition of the Epistle to the Romans*, 3 vols. (Edinburgh: William Whyte, 1842), 1:240.

Chapter 4: Sola Fide

1. Cited in Oswald Bayer, *Martin Luther's Theology: A Contemporary Interpretation*, trans. Thomas H. Trapp (Grand Rapids: Eerdmans, 2008), 98.
2. *Institutes*, 3.11.1. This version is from John Calvin, *Institutes of the Christian Religion*, trans. Henry Beveridge (Edinburgh: T&T Clark, 1863), 37.
3. Westminster Confession of Faith 11:1.
4. John MacArthur, *The Gospel According to the Apostles* (Nashville: Nelson, 1993), 260.

Chapter 5: The Great Exchange

1. Westminster Confession of Faith 3:1.
2. Charles Spurgeon, "A Defense of Calvinism" in *The Autobiography of Charles H. Spurgeon*, eds. Susannah Spurgeon and Joseph Harrald, 4 vols. (London: Passmore & Alabaster, 1899), 1:177.

Chapter 6: Alive Together with Christ

1. John Eadie, *A Commentary on the Greek Text of the Epistle of Paul to the Ephesians* (Edinburgh: T. & T. Clark, 1883), 121.
2. On the doctrine of original sin, see John MacArthur, "A Sin of Historic Proportions," chapter 13 in *What Happened in the Garden? The Reality and Ramifications of the Creation and Fall of Man*, ed. Abner Chou (Grand Rapids: Kregel, 2016), 287–98.
3. G. K. Chesterton, *Orthodoxy* (London: John Lane, 1908), 24.
4. Ibid.
5. This sermon, edited for publication by Lloyd-Jones himself, is found in *The Christ-Centered Preaching of Martyn Lloyd-Jones* , eds. Elizabeth Catherwood and Christopher Catherwood, (Wheaton: Crossway, 2014), 117–30.
6. Ibid., 119.
7. Charles Haddon Spurgeon, "Faith: What Is It? How Can It Be Obtained?" Sermon #1609 in *The Metropolitan Tabernacle Pulpit*, vol. 27 (London: Passmore & Alabaster, 1881), 401.
8. William Paxton, "Salvation as a Work," in *Princeton Sermons* (New York: Revell, 1893), 83.

Chapter 7: The Lessons of Grace

1. Steve Brown, *A Scandalous Freedom: The Radical Nature of the Gospel* (New York: Howard, 2004), 82.

Appendix 1: In Defense of Substitutionary Atonement

1. Robert Brow, "Evangelical Megashift," *Christianity Today*, February 19, 1990, 12–14.
2. Ibid., 12.
3. Ibid., 13.
4. Ibid.
5. Ibid., 14.
6. Ibid.

7. A. A. Hodge, *The Atonement* (Philadelphia: Presbyterian Board of Publication, 1867), 267.
8. Ibid., 269.
9. Philip Schaff, *History of the Christian Church* (New York: Scribners, 1910), 2:584.
10. Ibid., 585.
11. Brow, "Evangelical Megashift," 14.
12. Ibid., 12.
13. C. S. Lewis, *The Lion, the Witch, and the Wardrobe* (New York: MacMillan, 1950), 125.
14. Ibid., 123.
15. Ibid., 180.
16. Ibid., 123.

Appendix 2: Christ Died for God

1. The Canons of the Synod of Dort, 2:3.

Appendix 3: The Reason for Everything

1. John Gill, *Gill's Commentary* (Grand Rapids: Baker, 1980), 6:219.

Appendix 4: Paul's Glorious Gospel

1. Charles H. Spurgeon, "The Glorious Gospel," *The New Park Street Pulpit* (London: Passmore & Alabaster, 1858), 4:153–60.
2. Charles H. Spurgeon, "Coming Judgment of the Secrets of Men," *The Metropolitan Tabernacle Pulpit* (London: Passmore & Alabaster, 1885), 31:373–84.

INDEX

SCRIPTURE INDEX

ABOUT THE AUTHOR

John MacArthur has served as the pastor-teacher of Grace Community Church in Sun Valley, California, since 1969. His ministry of expository preaching is unparalleled in its breadth and influence; in more than four decades of ministry from the same pulpit, he has preached verse by verse through the entire New Testament (and several key sections of the Old Testament). He is president of the Master's University and Seminary and can be heard daily on the *Grace to You* radio broadcast (carried on hundreds of radio stations worldwide). He has authored a number of bestselling books, including *The MacArthur Study Bible*, *The Gospel According to Jesus*, *Twelve Ordinary Men*, and *One Perfect Life*.

For more details about John MacArthur and his Bible-teaching resources, contact Grace to You at 800-55-GRACE or gty.org.

CPSIA information can be obtained
at www.ICGtesting.com
Printed in the USA
LVHW031612261221
707082LV00007B/83

9 780718 096243